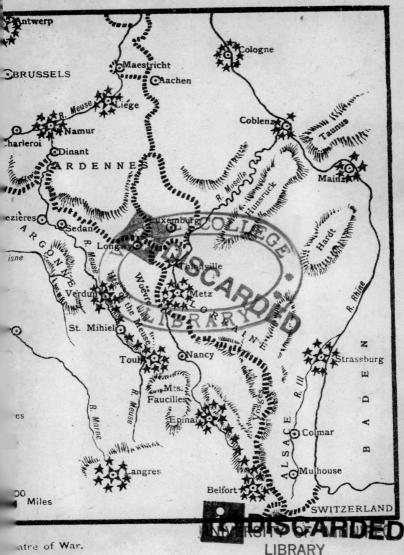

Theatre of War.

NELSON'S HISTORY OF THE WAR. By John Buchan.

Volume XXIII. The Dawn.

THOMAS NELSON AND SONS, Ltd.
LONDON, EDINBURGH, AND NEW YORK

CONTENTS.

APPENDICES.

LIST OF MAPS.

NELSON'S
HISTORY OF THE WAR.

—◆◆—

CHAPTER CLVIII.

THE TURN OF THE TIDE.

The Mind of Foch—The Secret of his Battle Plan—The German Retreat across the Marne—The Attack of Degoutte—Fall of Château-Thierry—The Allies cross the Marne—Von Boehn's Defence of the Northern Bank—Débeney attacks North of Montdidier—Fall of Oulchy-le-Château—Von Boehn retires to the Ourcq and Vesle—Fall of Fère-en-Tardenois—German Resistance stiffens—Mangin carries Hill 205—French re-enter Soissons—Von Boehn falls back on the Vesle—Ludendorff's Plans for the Future—Sir Douglas Haig attacks on 8th August.

THE final battle had been joined, but it was bound to develop slowly. Let us attempt to discover what was in Foch's mind.

All former Allied offensives had, after a shorter or longer time, come to a halt for the same reason —wearied troops were met by fresh enemy reserves. The battle became, as it were, stereotyped ; the enemy was able to perfect his defence ; and the action ended in stalemate. Even after further success was impossible, there was a tendency in the attacker to continue hammering at an unbreakable front, because he had set the stage for action in that one area and could not easily shift his batteries and communications elsewhere. In a word, the offensive lacked mobility, and was apt to end in a needless waste of men. This trait was as notable in the Allied attacks on the Somme, at Arras, and at Passchendaele, as in the futile German attempts at Verdun.

The first problem was, therefore, to get a superior mobility in the attack, and to bring in the element of surprise. This the Germans achieved at St. Quentin by the use of storm battalions and the method of " infiltration." Their plan was bettered by Foch by the use of his light tanks. There was now no need for a prolonged artillery bombardment; the tanks were sufficient to sweep a path for the infantry. There was less need also for elaborate preparations before the battle, and consequently an attack could be rapidly designed for any area where the prospects seemed favourable. It was precisely this consequence of the new system of war which the German Staff did not grasp. They allowed an action which was based essentially on surprise to drift into a stationary battle. They permitted their army to become *accroché*, alike on the Somme, on the Lys, and on the Marne ; and, therefore, sooner or later they were faced by Allied reserves and brought to a standstill. Their method could only have succeeded had there been no such reserves—a point on which Ludendorff was in singular error.

Foch drew the logical deduction from the tactics of surprise. He resolved to make the battle highly mobile. After striking a blow he would stay his hand as soon as serious resistance developed, and attack instantly in another place. The enemy would be subjected to a constant series of surprises. Before his reserves could be got up he would have lost heavily in ground and men ; his mass of manœuvre would be needed to fill up the gaps in his front ; and by swift stages that mass of manœuvre would diminish. This was obviously the right strategy to fit the new tactics, and it was Foch's supreme merit that he grasped this truth from the early days of the German offensive. He had to wait long for his chance ; but when the opportunity came he seized it with the precision of genius. He broke down the whole system of trench warfare and restored the open battle ; and he was able to do this because he had found a method to obviate the clumsiness of the modern military machine. His secret lay in the combination of three things—the weapon of the tank, the tactics of surprise, and the strategy of complete mobility.

At first it would appear that von Boehn did not realize the meaning of Mangin's success. He had eight divisions beyond the Marne, and the loss of the main highway from Soissons meant that they depended for supply upon the parish roads thread-ing the wooded hills of the Tardenois. Every hour, too, that his 80,000 men remained south of the river increased the peril of the thirty divisions inside the salient. But for the moment confusion seems to have reigned at German Headquarters, and nothing was done to protect the apex on Thursday, nor yet on Friday, the 19th, when Man- *July* 19. gin and Degoutte were establishing their ground and beating off counter-attacks. For thirty-six hours von Boehn hesitated ; then on the after-noon of the Friday he gave orders for the retreat.

It began at 9 p.m. that evening. The plan seems to have been to crowd up all available reserves against Mangin, who was regarded as the chief danger. Two divisions were borrowed at once from Prince Rupprecht, and before the end of the month the enemy's strength against the Tenth French Army had risen to twenty-five divisions.

Mangin, according to Foch's orders, held his hand. He had done all he had set out to do, and had cut the Soissons road ; it was now for Degoutte and de Mitry and Berthelot to take up the running.

July 20. On Saturday, the 20th, the eight German divisions staggered back across the river under the concentrated fire of the French batteries from the high ground on their flanks. Degoutte advanced to the line Bouresches-Latilly-Plessier Huleu, where he linked up with Mangin, whose right had now reached the villages of Parcy-Tigny and Villemontoire. De Mitry and Berthelot between them that evening had the whole southern bank of the Marne, and their outposts had begun to cross the river, while Berthelot had also made an advance between the Marne and Rheims. On the 19th he had received part of the British 22nd Corps, under Sir Alexander Godley, which took the place of the Italian 2nd Corps, and its 51st and 62nd Divisions made progress in the region of Marfaux and the Bois de Courton, thereby endangering the highroad along the Ardre which joined Fismes on the Vesle with Chatillon on the Marne.

On Sunday, the 21st, the Sixth and Fifth Armies *July* 21. struck in earnest. Degoutte's object was to outflank von Boehn on the north bank of the Marne and drive him from the river.

His French and American troops * in a magnificent movement swept eastward to a front from Breny, on the Ourcq, to the west of Rocourt and Epieds ; while de Mitry, who had also American divisions in his command, forced the river passage between Gland and Chartèves. Château-Thierry was no longer tenable, and that evening the Sixth Army were in its streets. The Allies were now close on the vital road junction of Oulchy-le-Château. Von Boehn had substantially narrowed his salient, and left only some six miles of river front as the mouth of the pocket. As his flank was turned on the west, it seemed reasonable to assume that he was in process of evacuating the whole area, and falling back on the Ourcq and the Vesle.

On the contrary, he attempted a stand. On Monday, the 22nd, de Mitry crossed the river between Passy and Dormans, and at *July 22.* Port-à-Binson, south of Chatillon, occupying in the former area all the ground in the loop of the stream. His left also made a slight advance north of the Ourcq, and Berthelot took the village of Bouilly at the northern end of the Montagne de Rheims. But on the 23rd there was a sudden stiffening of resistance in the south of *July 23.* the salient. Degoutte alone had some twenty German divisions against him, four of them from the fresh reserves of Prince Rupprecht. Von Boehn held out stoutly on his few miles of river front, the very place where his supply problem was

* The Americans were the 1st Corps, under Major-General Liggett, including the 3rd, 25th, and 26th Divisions, the two first of which had greatly distinguished themselves in this area during the Third Battle of the Aisne.

at its worst. It is hard to see how this defence, which involved the crowding of large reinforcements into a narrow area, was necessary for a safe withdrawal. It was his flanks on which he should normally have concentrated, and the point of the salient should have retired with the utmost possible speed. The explanation would seem to be that Ludendorff still hoped at all costs to make the main Château-Thierry-Epernay-Châlons railway unusable by the Allies, and while he could stay on the Dormans-Chatillon front it would remain under his fire. If so, it was an error in judgment for which Germany paid high in the loss of guns and men.

On the 23rd, under the pressure of the counterattack, the French were driven out of Vincelles ; but de Mitry managed to press northwards at Jaulgonne, and between Passy and Dormans. That day Degoutte's left wing was in the outskirts of Oulchy, and had gone east of Plessier Huleu, while his left centre south of the Ourcq entered Rocourt. Berthelot was heavily engaged, the British 51st and 62nd Divisions taking Marfaux, and Mangin began his attack against the slopes of Buzancy, east of the Soissons-Château-Thierry road, where two British divisions, the 34th and the Scottish 15th, were in action.* On the 23rd, too, with the object of preventing Prince Rupprecht from sending further troops to the aid of the Crown Prince, the French First Army, under Débeney, attacked north of Montdidier, with the assistance of British tanks. It advanced 3,000 yards on a front of 7,000, capturing the villages of Mailly-Raineval, Sauvillers, and Aubvillers, and won the heights overlooking the Avre

* The 15th relieved the 1st United States.

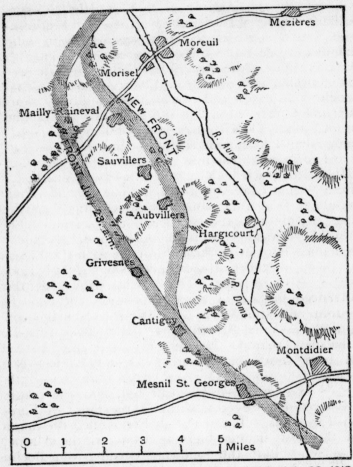

The Allied Advance on the left bank of the Avre, July 23, 1918.

valley. By the evening of that day the Soissons-Château-Thierry road, save for the small section on the plateau south of Soissons, was wholly in Allied hands ; three more miles had been gained up the Ourcq valley ; the Americans with Degoutte were pressing along the Château-Thierry-Fère road ; von Boehn's front on the Marne was crumbling ; and Berthelot was within two miles of the Fismes-Chatillon road. Twenty-five thousand prisoners and more than 400 guns had fallen to Foch.

The main threat now was against Fère-en-Tardenois, to which Oulchy was an advance guard. If Fère were to fall, the southern end of the salient would be gone, and von Boehn accordingly put his chief weight into the defence of this section. The next move was now with Degoutte, though Berthelot remained hard at work ; and on the 24th the British

July 24. 22nd Corps captured Vrigny, with 1,000 prisoners. The Sixth Army that day advanced in face of fierce opposition between the Ourcq and the Marne, and finished on the line Oulchy-la-Ville-Armentières-Coincy-Beuvardes-Le Charmel-Treloup. Degoutte's alignment, instead of being north and south, was now almost east

July 25. and west. Next day, Thursday, 25th, Oulchy-le-Château fell, and the centre advanced to Bruyères, within three miles of Fère-en-Tardenois. The threat to Fère sealed the doom of the now slender German front on the Marne.

July 26. Late the following evening von Boehn began a comprehensive retirement between the Ourcq and the Ardre.

Von Boehn had suffered the penalty of his tardiness. His Marne front was in desperate case, for the roads, from Fère in the west and from Fismes in the east, were alike threatened. There was no time to be lost if he wished to straighten his line. Nor had Degoutte a lesser need for haste, for he must carry Fère-en-Tardenois before the enemy could establish his front from the Upper Ourcq to the Upper Vesle. Even if von Boehn secured such a front, it would be little better than his front on the Marne, for Mangin lay waiting with an army rested and refitted to strike at its flank as Degoutte had struck at Château-Thierry. Such is the difficulty of a piece-meal withdrawal from a salient in face of a strong and watchful enemy ; a fresh position finds itself already turned. With the facts of each new situation as it revealed itself Foch played as a master plays on an instrument of music.

Nevertheless, the German retreat from the Marne, by encumbered roads through a broken country, was a fine performance. Costly in life, hugely costly in *matériel*, it was much to von Boehn's credit that he achieved it at all. On the 27th Degoutte and de Mitry pressed hard in pursuit, *July 27.* and Berthelot advanced to conform. East of Rheims Gouraud's Fourth Army made progress in the Moronvilliers region south of Mont San Nom, and took nearly 2,000 prisoners. The whole day was a good example of skilful pressure exercised upon an embarrassed and retreating enemy. By the evening Berthelot was on the line Bligny-Chaumuzy, south of Ville-en-Tardenois, to just south of St. Gemme. On his left de Mitry's line ran north-west through the forests of Ris and Fère. Degoutte was astride the Ourcq from Nanteuil Notre Dame to

Cugny. Mangin was slowly working up the slopes east of the Soissons-Château-Thierry road, but was in difficulties at the château and village of Buzancy, while the advance of his right wing north of Plessier Huleu was being strongly resisted in the wood of Plessier.

Next day, the 28th, Degoutte swung his right wing across the Ourcq and entered Fère-en-Tarde-

July 28.   nois, while de Mitry pushed out of the Forest of Ris and took Ronchères. Berthelot was less fortunate, and had a hard struggle between St. Gemme and Chambrecy, but the British division with him succeeded in retaking the Montagne de Bligny. Signs were appearing of a comprehensive German retreat, and the villages in rear of the enemy's line from Soissons to Bazoches were in flames. That day, too, Mangin had carried the strong point of Buzancy, where the 15th Scottish Division so distinguished themselves that by the orders of the French Command a memorial was erected on the battlefield to commemorate their valour. For the moment it seemed as if the German retreat was to be turned into a rout.

But the enemy was as yet far from beaten. On the morning of the 29th his whole front stiffened.

July 29.   Reinforcements had been huddled into his front lines, and all day vigorous counter-attacks took place in the battle area. At Sergy the 4th Guards Division attacked part of an American division, and were repulsed after many hours of desperate fighting. It was the same on

July 30.   the 30th, when, on the eastern side of the salient, Berthelot had to face a series of heavy counter-attacks in the neighbourhood of

St. Euphraise. The enemy won back the station of Fère-en-Tardenois, and the Americans * between Seringes and the Meunière Wood found every yard disputed. Seringes was lost and won several times, but by the evening remained in their hands. On the last day of July they swept forward and captured Cierges and the slopes *July* 31. beyond, while the French on their right were at last able to debouch from the Meunière Wood.

Von Boehn had found a line which he believed he could hold, and it was now the turn of Mangin to turn the flank of the defence as Degoutte had turned it on the Marne. We have seen that the ridge culminating in the heights of Grand Rozoy gave him an avenue into the heart of the German position. His right wing east of Plessier Huleu and the Soissons road was now ready for its final attack on the key-point, the hill called 205. Von Boehn lay along the edge of the plateau east of the lower Crise and its western tributary, and thence along the watershed between the Ourcq and the Vesle. As the Allies now stood, they had no direct observation over this plateau and the roads from Braisne, Bazoches, and Fismes, which were the arteries of the German supply. But if they could carry Hill 205, they would enfilade the Crise valley, look over the five or six miles of down to the Vesle, and even beyond to the roofs of Fismes. The hill was the key of the whole countryside, and its capture would force von Boehn back upon the line of the Vesle heights.

Mangin struck at dawn on Thursday, 1st August, with his whole army, but especially with his right

* The 32nd and 42nd Divisions.

wing; and by nine in the morning he had the crest of Hill 205. Then followed two hours of

Aug. 1. furious counter-attacks, which achieved nothing. Late in the afternoon a new division of shock troops, borrowed from Prince Rupprecht, advanced to an attack which dwindled away into isolated rushes. Von Boehn admitted defeat, for not only was his front turned between the Ourcq and the Vesle, but his hold on Soissons was fatally loosened. There was nothing for it but retirement, and the Americans on Degoutte's right, fighting north of Sergy, found the enemy's resistance suddenly beginning to falter. On the 2nd the

Aug. 2. whole Allied line swept forward. Mangin entered Soissons and Billy-sur-Aisne; Degoutte was in Branges; de Mitry was at Dravegny and Cohan; while Berthelot's left was in Brouillet and his centre beyond the Ardre. Already, since 15th July, the Allies had taken some 40,000 prisoners.

There could be no resting-place short of the Vesle. During the first days of August the whole countryside between Ourcq and Aisne was murky with the smoke of burning villages, while the four armies of France pressed in the contracting arc of the German front. On the 4th they had reached

Aug. 4–5. the line of the Aisne and the Vesle. Next day they forced the passage of the latter river at many places on both sides of Braisne, and crossed the Aisne just east of Soissons. That

Aug. 6. day American troops entered Fismes, and on the 6th gained ground on the northern bank of the Vesle.* Then once again came

* On this day Foch was made a Marshal of France. "The dignity of Marshal," said the decree of the President,

a halt. Von Boehn had reached a line on which he could stand.

It was not a position to be altogether desired. The Chemin des Dames and the heights of the Vesle do not form a continuous ridge, for there is the valley of the Aisne between ; and on the east the hills die away into levels, with Rheims as an Allied outpost to menace that flank. The Germans, however, mindful of the strength of the Aisne defences in 1914, turned to it as a natural refuge. But 1914 was not 1918. Then Germany had had a great superiority in men and guns ; now the superiority had gone beyond recall. The Crown Prince had thrown in seventy-four divisions since 15th July, and had wholly used up his reserves, besides drawing largely from the neighbouring group commanders. Ludendorff at the best had no more than twenty-six reserve divisions at his disposal. Foch had now a greater mass of manœuvre than his antagonist. Moreover, the disastrous Second Battle of the Marne had played havoc with the German first-line troops. Every division was under strength, and some, even of the picked troops, were short by more than 30 per cent. The establishment of battalions had been reduced from 850 to 750, or less. Indeed, so bad was the case that Ludendorff was compelled to appeal to Austria for men, and now for the first time an Austrian division was identified on the front in France.

The dream of an attack on Amiens was gone

" will not be merely a recompense for past services ; it will consecrate for the future the authority of the great soldier who is called to lead the armies of the Entente to final victory."

for ever ; the initiative had definitely passed to the Allies, and Ludendorff's one aim was to find security for the coming winter. He must build up as soon as possible a new reserve, and to do this he must shorten his front at certain useless salients, such as those on the Lys and at Montdidier. He had now stabilized the position on the Aisne, and he hoped that the French would break their teeth on his new front, and that the battle would decline into one of those fruitless struggles for a few miles of trench in which the old actions had been wont to die away.

He hoped in vain. Foch had no mind to waste one hour in operations which were not vital. At a conference held on 23rd July he had expounded his plan to his colleagues. He had won in the salient by carrying an attack no further than the limit placed by the advantage of surprise, and then striking swiftly elsewhere. It was his supreme merit that he saw the battle as a whole, and he was now preparing his deadly *arpeggio* on a far broader front. On Thursday, 8th August, Sir Douglas Haig, *Aug.* 8. south of the Somme, flung his Fourth Army against Prince Rupprecht.

But before we can consider the further progress of the Western campaign it is necessary to survey the whole area of conflict, and trace some of the influences in far distant lands which were to hinder or assist the Allies' advance to victory.

CHAPTER CLIX.

THE FOURTH YEAR OF WAR : THE OUTLOOK.

IF we make the anniversary of the outbreak of war the day of the Serajevo murder, as has been done in former volumes, we have to look back upon a year of nearly continuous Allied misfortunes. If we take it as 4th August, the date of the actual start of hostilities, we can discern the first flush of the dawn of victory. It had been a twelvemonth of supreme tension and grave searching of heart. The Allies had seen Eastern Europe fall wholly into the grasp of the Central Powers. They had seen a German domination established over a nerveless Russia which it might well take a century to unloose. They had found their whole scheme of battle ineffective in the West. Costly partial victories had succeeded each other until the pendulum swung backwards, and in a week those partial successes had been turned into something not far from disaster. There was a time in April when those who were honest with themselves were compelled to admit that what seemed a little before to be the last stage of the war, had been but the prelude to an indefinable campaign which stretched darkly into the future—unless, indeed, the Allies were to acknowledge defeat.

The crisis called out the noblest qualities of the civilized Powers, and that in itself was a guarantee of victory. But the foundations of popular thought had been shaken, and till the turn of the tide in July there were few willing to prophesy and none to dogmatize. An air of expectation was abroad, for though reason seemed to point to a protracted campaign, the instinct of mankind argued otherwise. This was true of all the belligerents alike. The German people spoke of peace in the autumn— peace on their own terms ; the Allied peoples, while preparing for years of further campaigning, had a sense that these preparations would not be called for. All wars are fought under a time limit determined by human endurance, and there was an instinct abroad that that limit was not far off. There was a feeling in the air of a climax approaching. The skies were dim and tenebrous, but behind the clouds men felt that there was light—either apocalyptic lightnings or the glow of a beneficent dawn.

Our object in the present chapter is first to assess the mood in which the nations, while the end seemed yet afar off, yet waited instinctively for its speedy event. Only after some understanding of this can we realize the atmosphere of the last phase. In the second place, we must pick up the tangled threads in the East. Towards the end of a long struggle destiny seems to select one area in which the ultimate battle is waged. This in truth had always been the West. From 21st March onward the wildest of military dreamers, whose fancies had hitherto ranged throughout the globe, admitted that here the final lists had been set. But the confusion in the East could not be without its effect on the Western campaign, for it must attract to itself not only the troops and guns of the Allies, but much of the time and thought of the Allied leaders. Again, Germany had so mortgaged her assets in the East that what did not help her to victory there would beyond doubt hasten her progress to defeat. If Russia proved a handicap instead of an aid, if Bulgaria and Turkey fell out of the contest, it would go far worse with her than if she never sent a man beyond the Vistula and the Danube. Finally, there could be no universal peace until the Eastern tangle was un-ravelled, and on the situation left there at the close of war depended the ease or the difficulty of the reconstructive task laid upon the civilized world.

In analyzing the popular mood it will be well to select two types of the belligerents—Britain and Germany. France and Italy were invaded, and were, so to speak, in the battle-line. Their intimate peril subordinated all other questions to the urgent one of defence, and, though they had their malcontents and doctrinaires, the strong discipline of self-protection held them quiescent. America was like a young man girding on his armour for battle. Her spirit was that of Europe in 1914 ; she had not yet felt the sad satiety of war ; she was absorbed in earnest preparation ; and President Wilson, after the crisis of March, had abandoned his exploration of the fundamentals of policy for the more urgent task of stimulating and directing the effort of his countrymen. Among the Central Powers, Bulgaria was tired and apathetic ; Turkey broken by suffering out of the semblance of a nation ; and Austria flaccid with hunger and internal dissolution. Germany had always been the centre of the ill-assorted confederacy, and now she was more than ever its sole support. If we understand her mood we shall understand the policy of the Central Powers. Britain, too, was a mirror for the Allies. Her freedom from invasion gave her a certain detachment ; yet she was not less deeply concerned in the war than Italy or France, for her safety, nay, her existence, depended upon victory. We can see in the free expression of her popular opinion the exact reflection not only of the Allies' moods, but of their many and varied ideals and policies.

The catastrophe of March had, as we have seen, roused to a high pitch the courage and resolution of every class of the British people. It was like the case of a runner who, when far advanced in a race, gets his " second wind." But a second wind does not mean that fatigue has gone, or that the limbs are as vigorous as at the start. Below the splendid renascence of the early spring in Britain there lay a great weariness. Behind her stout front there were strained nerves and tired minds. Effort had ceased to be joy, and had become a grim duty—a dangerous phase for the enemy, had he understood it, for Britain has never been so formidable as when she has been heart-sick of a business. She wore down Philip of Spain and Louis XIV. and Napoleon because she continued to fight when she would have given anything for peace—except her soul. The strain was shown in gusty minor strifes which blew up like sandstorms in the desert. An instance was the Maurice affair in May. Sir Frederick Maurice, the Director of Military Operations at the War Office, published on 7th May a letter in the newspapers, in which he flatly contra- *May 7.* dicted certain statements made by the Prime Min- ister as to the strength of the British front before the attack of 21st March. The letter was intended to provoke a parliamentary inquiry ; but Mr. Lloyd George had no difficulty in providing in the House of Commons a kind of answer to its statements, and, after a somewhat clumsy defence of General Maurice by Mr. Asquith, made the matter a question of con- fidence in the Government, and secured a large majority. The vote given in the Maurice debate became a test of loyalty to the Prime Minister. The whole controversy was a jumble of half-truths. Many soldiers were justifiably irritated with the Government ; the Government, on the other hand, had a right to claim a tolerant judgment in their supreme difficulties ; but the affair showed how thin had worn the sheathing on the nerves of large classes in Britain.

It was the same with Labour. The unselfish co-operation of March and April began to show rifts

so soon as the worst danger was past. It would
have been a miracle if it had not, for the working-
man was as weary as other people. In July things
came to a head in a serious dispute among munition
workers and a threat of a general strike, which was
averted by the prompt action of the Government.
More serious still was the strike of the London
police at the beginning of August, when men serving under discipline extorted from the Government
concessions which, whether right or wrong on the
merits, should never have been granted to what was
in effect a mutiny. British Labour has one enduring
characteristic : it is patriotically united in the face
of grave peril, as happened in March ; it is united,
as after August, when victory is dawning ; but in
periods of stagnation it grows restless and self-con-
scious—a pathological state and not a reasoned policy,
and a condition which it shared with classes who had
not its excuse.

Of pacificism in the common sense of the word
there was little. Britain does not talk of peace when
things are going badly with her. A certain type of
shallow intellectual hankered after negotiation with
the enemy ; read miracles of moderation into every
evasive sentence of Czernin or Kuhlmann ; and
denied the possibility of a decision in the field.
But he found only a scanty audience. The ordinary
man, with a truer wisdom, saw that the Allies must
win decisively in battle or acknowledge an un-
qualified defeat. He was not distracted by the
enthusiasts who preached a League of Nations while
they refused to lay its foundations, or dreamed of
an *Internationale* when the foes of internationalism
were still at large, or who in their folly conceived

that the canker of civilization could be cured by
laying the axe of Bolshevism to the tree. *Aug.* 15.
The common sense of the country was
excellently expressed in a letter which Lord Hugh
Cecil wrote on 15th August :—

" The war must be fought till it end in the submission of
Germany. By submission I do not in the least mean destruction. Indeed it is not, I believe, possible to destroy a strong
and united nation by military defeat. Jena did not destroy
Prussia ; Sedan did not destroy France ; and a greater victory
than these cannot be won. We do not seek to destroy Germany, but we seek to force Germans to recognize that they
have been defeated, and to submit to the authority of a
world stronger than they. In familiar language we seek to
' abate their pride, assuage their malice, and confound their
devices ; ' for their pride made them strive to dominate the
world, their malice has defiled both land and sea with murder,
and their devices, untiring if also unskilful, have been traced
in every land, stirring up discord and violence and revolt. It
is the end of these crimes and of the spirit that prompts them
that I hope to see realized by the submission of Germany.
And submission cannot be attained by negotiations such as
are now suggested to us. Negotiation at the present time
might lead to an agreement as between equals, but not to
the submission of a defeated nation to superior power. And
until that submission is made it is idle to hope that the German Government will turn from the false gods it worships.
I dare say there are wise and good Germans who hate the
system of blood and iron. But they have no power, and will
have none so long as that system maintains its repute. Our
business is not to suffer it to save its credit, but to make its
failure plain according to its own standards. Moloch must
be humiliated in the sight of all his votaries if they are to
accept a purer faith."

On one matter during the spring and summer
the mind of the British people was becoming assured.
The submarine had been Germany's most trusted

weapon, and it was directed mainly against Britain
—not only against her belligerent effort, but against
the very foundations of her life. While its violence
continued a profound uneasiness filled the land,
which no success of our armies could allay. It was
fortunate that the darkest hour in France should
synchronize with a real mitigation of the submarine
pest. In the early months of 1918 there were many
naval losses. The liner *Tuscania*, carrying American
troops, was torpedoed off the Irish coast on the
night of 5th February ; the hospital ship *Glenart
Castle* was sunk in the Bristol Channel on the
morning of 26th February ; in June U-boats were
raiding small craft off the New Jersey and Delaware
coasts ; on 20th July the large White Star liner
Justicia was lost after a stout fight in Irish waters.
It was clear, too, that British shipbuilding was not
keeping pace with our losses. On 20th March the
March 20. First Lord of the Admiralty told the
House of Commons that the first twelve
months of unrestricted submarine warfare had cost
the world six million tons of shipping, and that the
output of British yards must be nearly doubled
before the monthly rate of loss was made good.
From January 1, 1918, to the end of May enemy
submarines sank 1,146,325 tons of British shipping,
and in the same period we completed only 629,087
tons—an adverse balance of more than half a million
tons. Yet our output during these months was
steadily growing and our losses were steadily shrinking, while the progress of the United States in production was advancing by leaps and bounds. It
was almost our most urgent problem, for on its solu-
tion depended the effectiveness of the great American

levies in the field. Meantime, by a thousand devices, we were hunting down the German submarines—by the new Channel barrage, by " mystery " ships and " dazzle " ships, by destroyers and patrol boats and seaplanes. The British Navy by devious ways was at length coming to its own. On 7th August the Prime Minister told the House of Commons that our Navy was, at the outbreak of war, the largest in the world, with a *Aug. 7.* tonnage of two and a half million, that now it was eight millions, and that, as a proof of its activity, in June it had steamed eight million miles. He added that 150 German submarines had already been destroyed, more than half in the course of the past year, and on 6th September the Admiralty, in proof, published the names of their commanding officers.

Another element should be noted as making for optimism in the British temper. This was the growing understanding with America. The contact with her soldiers in France, the contact with the many thousand Americans who came to these islands on war duties, the appreciation of America's superb activity, and, among thoughtful people, the gratitude to President Wilson for clarifying the issues of the war, combined to create a real warmth of feeling towards the other great branch of the English-speaking people. The Fourth of July, America's Independence Day, was celebrated *July 4.* this year throughout Britain as a popular festival ; for it is our illogical and generous fashion, after a deserved defeat, to join with the victors in acclaiming the justice of their triumph.

Yet, when all has been said, the months between March and August 1918 were for Britain the most critical in the war, and made extreme demands on her fortitude and stability. That she emerged from them with credit, and was able to summon all her strength for the final effort, and envisage with clearness and justice the new world of victory and peace, was due in large measure to the Prime Minister. He was the most fallible of mortals, without precision and continuity in his mental processes, too prone to trust to *finesse* when candour was required, ill-judging often in his methods and his manner, and apt to sow broadcast a needless distrust. Yet beyond doubt he was the foremost political figure of the campaign, and beyond doubt he was as great a War Minister as Britain had ever known. His fierce vitality, his amazing power of inspiration, his unfailing instinct for the heart of a situation, his robustness of soul, which was more than personal courage, and was like a strong wind which fanned the embers of fortitude in every heart—if these do not spell genius, then the word is without meaning.

Before we turn to Germany it is desirable to review the situation in the East during the spring and summer of 1918. It is, indeed, obligatory, for thither Germany looked for the material gains of which her victory in the West would give her quiet possession; and as difficulties thickened in that quarter the loss of this hope was to play a major part in that breakdown of her " home front " which attended her breakdown in the field.

By the end of March the Eastern front, which a year before had been continuous from the Baltic to the Persian Gulf, had largely disappeared. In such a history as this it is impossible to record in detail the mutations of each section—from the Baltic to the Bukovina, from the Bukovina to the Danube mouths, from the Black Sea to the Tigris. Suffice it to say that the Russian wing had been destroyed, the Rumanian left centre put out of action, the Caucasian right centre reduced to chaos, and General Marshall in Mesopotamia left to fight his battles without the support of allies, and no longer a partner in a continuous front. The result was that Finland had become an independent state and an ally of Germany's; Germany was advancing between the Baltic and the Black Sea exactly as she pleased; the Caucasus was torn with internal dissensions, and the Turks were pushing eastward towards the Caspian and southward into Persia; while throughout Transcaspia and Siberia combinations of Bolsheviks and Austro-German prisoners were following their own sweet will; and the British in Mesopotamia had not only the enemy to the north of them, but had on their right flank a distracted Persia, which at any moment might become an enemy Power under Turkish and German officers. It was a situation which none of the Allies, least of all Britain, could afford to neglect. A German Finland would give the Central Powers control of the bridge between the Baltic and the Arctic seas. Unless help came, Russian nationalism would be crushed under the twin weights of Bolshevism and Teutonism. The gap of the Caspian offered the enemy a highway into Central Asia, where already he had his outposts. The turning of the Persian flank not only placed Marshall in a position of great danger, but threatened to put a spark to the inflammable stuff around the Indian border.

To be sure, there were encouraging elements in the problem. The Murman coast and Archangel were open to our ships, and there we might form a bridgehead on which the Russian nationalist forces in the north could be based. The Czecho-Slovaks lay along the line of the Middle Volga, though cut off from the north by a solid wedge of Bolshevism. In the Don and Kuban provinces east of the Sea of Azov the Cossacks and the Nationalists were strong. In the Caucasus the Allies had many potential friends who might, with a little help from outside, prevent the Turks from making their way to the Caspian. The Czecho-Slovaks were at Vladivostok and also in Western Siberia, though the country between was in Bolshevik hands. In Mesopotamia Marshall had little to fear from an attack down the Tigris, and might be able to detach troops to keep Persia quiet, hold the south shore of the Caspian, and even defend Baku from the Turks. Allenby in Palestine was secure, and at any moment might begin to exercise a pressure which would distract the Turk from his Caucasian adventure. There were elements of hope, too, in connection with the internal politics of Turkey and Bulgaria, which we shall consider in other chapters. For the present let us fix our attention only on the military aspect of the situation.

The plain task of the Allies was to reconstitute the Eastern front. To do this it was necessary to occupy the Murman coast to keep guard on Finland ; to land troops at Archangel and push south from that bridgehead to join hands with the Czecho-Slovaks on the Volga ; to assist by some means or other Alexeiev and Denikin to continue the Czecho-

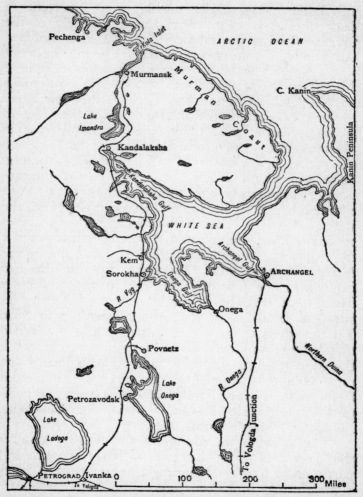

The White Sea, the Archangel region, and the Murman Railway.

Slovak left wing to the Caspian ; to intervene in
East Siberia, so as to control with the help of the
Czecho-Slovaks the whole Trans-Siberian railway,
and provide communications for supplying the front
on the Volga ; to send troops to Transcaspia to hold
the enemy there in check ; to assist the Armenians
and Georgians to resist the Turk in the Caucasus ;
and to continue the line of defence from the Caspian
through North Persia till it met Marshall's front in
Mesopotamia. Such was the ideal towards which
the Allied Staffs laboured. All of it was common
sense and sound policy ; much of it was impracticable, considering the limited numbers at their
command and their intense preoccupation in the
West. A more difficult problem, perhaps, never
confronted an Alliance, and it was not made simpler
by a certain divergence of political views among the
Allied Governments. To build up the Eastern
front with the few divisions spared with difficulty
from other battlefields might well have seemed as
hopeless as to stem the Atlantic with a broom.
Yet the attempt was gallantly made ; and if it failed
to achieve complete success, it yet served to check
the enemy's main ambition, and to strip him of his
most confident hope. Let us take the long front
from north to south, and consider in turn the position in European Russia, Siberia, the Caucasus,
Persia, and Mesopotamia.

The story of the doings of the Bolsheviks after
the Treaty of Brest Litovsk is partly tragedy and
partly *opéra bouffe*. It is tragic because of the hide-
ous sufferings of Russia, and comic from the failure
alike of the Bolshevik tyranny and its German ex-
ploiters. During April and May Trotski sulked

and raved in his tent, threatened vengeance against Germany, half-persuaded the Allies that he and his friends represented an undying hostility to German aims, and made abortive efforts to raise a Red Army to defy the invaders. But presently came the menace of the Czecho-Slovaks, which Germany was forced to treat with respect. She made a bargain with Lenin, undertaking not to advance farther east than a certain line from the Gulf of Finland to the Black Sea, so that the Red Forces would be able to give undivided attention to the danger on the Volga.

But she found that she had stumbled on a hornet's nest. In no part of her new sphere of activity did things go well during the summer. In Finland, which she regarded as now her own preserve, and proposed to endow with a German kinglet, Red Guards and White Guards continued their struggle; and when the former were beaten, there came the threat of the British from Murman. In Russia itself there seemed no substance hard enough for her steel to bite upon. Trotski was now sufficiently tame; but his writ ran in narrow bounds, and he was faced everywhere with hatred, conspiracy, and anarchy. The honest elements in Russia were struggling to draw together, struggling for the most part in vain, for they were widely scattered, and had no leaders; but their efforts gravely impeded the German machine. For the stiff German soldiers and the supple German diplomats it was like building on sand; the foundations were sucked in before the first stones could be laid of the superstructure. A Bolshevik ambassador was sent to Berlin; a German ambassador, Count Mirbach, was dispatched to

Moscow; but on 7th July Count Mirbach was assassinated, and his successor, Helfferich, paid a *July 7.* hurried visit and then departed from so insalubrious a habitation. The most that Germany could do was to lend troops to stiffen the Red Army now disputing with the Czecho-Slovaks on the Volga.

In the Ukraine she made a disastrous blunder. She showed too openly her hand, and methodically set about plundering the place of supplies. She got little, for the peasants rose in revolt, and everywhere there were murders and guerilla war, culminating in the assassination of Field-Marshal von Eichhorn, formerly of the X. Army, on 30th *July 30.* July, in the streets of Kiev. The Ukraine had become a German province under an ataman, General Skoropadski, who was nominated by Berlin; conscription had been decreed; the peasants had been forced to return property taken from the landlords the previous autumn, and compelled to cultivate their land for the benefit of Germany. The result was a *jacquerie* and universal resistance, and the effect was felt over the whole of Russia. Had Germany handled the matter with discretion she might have won a great triumph. Russia had lost most of her ideals, and sought only peace; even men like Miliukov inclined to favour the German faction because it promised a relief from anarchy. But Germany's treatment of the Ukraine had been too barefaced to leave any doubt as to her policy. She had entered Russia to bring not peace but fetters, and the spectacle convinced the bulk of the people that the German cure for Bolshevism was no better than the disease.

As for Lenin and Trotski, they had now sold
themselves to their masters, and provided proof of
what Kerenski in June told the British Labour
Conference, that " the actions of the Bolsheviks
made them the vanguard of triumphant German
militarism." About this time Trotski seems to
have lost his nerve, and the actual leadership passed
wholly into the hands of Lenin. He had far
greater nerve and courage than the other, and knew
precisely what he wanted. He cared nothing for the
dismemberment of Russia ; he did not want peace ;
he welcomed anarchy, for only by the road of
universal anarchy could the world reach that com-
munism of which he dreamed. The advent of
the Czecho-Slovaks and the imminence of Allied
intervention brought the wildest spirits to the front,
and what had formerly been a class tyranny now
became a class vendetta and an orgy of brigandage
and murder. On 16th July the ex-Tsar *July* 16.
was shot at Ekaterinburg, in the Urals,
after a mock trial ; and somewhere in that region,
about the same time, the other members of the
Imperial household perished miserably. The tragedy of the Romanovs had not even the dignity of
the fall of the Bourbons. Secretly, squalidly, they
were murdered in the wilds by madmen, and the
world heard only by accident of their fate.

From that date the " Government " of the Bolsheviks lost all semblance of decency. A handful
of armed bandits, backed up by Lettish and Chinese
mercenaries, did what they pleased with the
relics of the State and the lives of the people. The
cities of Russia fell into the state which Dr. Johnson
described—" the streets full of soldiers accustomed

to plunder, and the garrets of scribblers accustomed to lie." During August, in Moscow and Petrograd, Allied officials and residents were arrested wholesale, and suffered every indignity and privation. But their sufferings were nothing to what was endured by unfortunate Russians who incurred the suspicion of the Soviets. Armed bands of miscreants paraded the streets " smelling out " suspects like African witch-doctors. On 31st August Captain Cromie, *Aug.* 31. the British naval attaché, who as submarine commander had won the Cross of St. George, was murdered in the British Embassy at Petrograd. After that, terror was unloosed, mainly in Petrograd, where Zinoviev, the president of the Soviet, desired to rival the fame of Hébert. Priests, officers, officials, merchants, and employers perished in scores daily. A certain Uritski, appointed a special commissioner to " combat the counter-revolution," called upon his men to shoot down any suspected of bourgeois sentiments. He won the name of the " new Marat," and, like Marat, perished at the hand of a Charlotte Corday. Lenin, too, was seriously wounded, and such attempts at retribution fanned the fury of the tyrants. At Uritski's funeral Zinoviev declared that a thousand bourgeois lives must pay for any such attempt. On 1st September the official organ of the Red Army announced : " We will make our hearts cruel, hard, and immovable, so that no mercy will enter them, and so that they will not grieve at the sight of a sea of enemy blood. We will let loose the floodgates of that sea. Without mercy, without sparing, we will kill our enemies. For the blood of Lenin and Uritski, Zinoviev and Volodarski, let there be floods of the blood of the bourgeois—more blood, and ever more blood."

Amid this carnival of devilry Lenin found time, on 6th September, to sign three further treaties with Germany, giving every kind of security for the satisfaction of her claims. The Baltic Provinces, whose liberty had once been dear to Trotski's heart, were to have their frontiers defined as Germany pleased. Baku and its oil region were made a German preserve. And for her gracious permission to the Bolsheviks to remain in a truncated Russia an immediate payment was to be made of £50,000,000 in goods and £300,000,000 in gold. This from a bankrupt land throughout which industry was at a standstill and famine was stalking! In all this madness there was a strain of despair, as of men who knew that their time was short and had forgotten all else in their lust for destruction. It recalled the amazing debate of the Committee of Public Safety early on the morning of September 3, 1793, when the death of Marie Antoinette was decreed, and Hébert opened his heart. " I cannot see clearly when it is night. I cannot see roses where there are only daggers. I know not whether there remains to you any hope of the Republic or the Constitution, or of the safety of your persons; but I know this, that if you have any you are greatly deceived. We shall all perish. It cannot be otherwise. . . . We live for nothing but vengeance, and that may be immense. In perishing let us leave to our enemies the germs of their own death, and in France so great a destruction that the memory of it will never die."

From June onward the Bolsheviks were recog-

nized as the declared foes of the Allies. But to bring
help to the Russian nationalists and the Czecho-
Slovaks seemed a wellnigh impossible task, for all
inlets to Russia were closed save by way of the
Arctic and the Pacific. The Allied policy of intervention was based on two irrefutable facts—that the
Bolsheviks were open partisans of Germany, and
that the Allies were bound in honour to assist the
Czecho-Slovaks and those Russian elements who were
maintaining the front against the common enemy.
They desired scrupulously to avoid any interference
with Russia's internal policy—even with Bolshevism,
except in so far as it acted as Germany's agent.
Especially they did not wish to antagonize the Soviets,
where these represented the will of the people.

But it was obviously a most delicate task, since
many Russians who were honestly anti-German held
also fiercely partisan views on domestic policy, and
opposition to Germany was scarcely a link sufficiently strong in itself to keep monarchist, bourgeois,
and all the varieties of socialist working in harmony. The Allies were certain to be drawn into
situations where they might seem to be taking sides
in Russia's private disputes. The position was not
made easier by the fact that many among the Allied
peoples were strongly opposed to armed intervention : some holding that it was the same kind of
blunder as Britain had made in the early wars of
the French Revolution, and would only strengthen
Bolshevism ; others that it was a military blunder
to dissipate resources when every man was wanted
in the West ; others, who had the support of the
American Government, that the only wise kind of
intervention was economic and philanthropic, for-

getting that a trade circular and even baskets of food are poor comfort to a man if the knife of the enemy be at his throat.

These difficulties made it likely that, though the case for armed assistance was unanswerable, that assistance would be given slowly and feebly. This was in effect what happened. The Allies escaped no one of the disadvantages of intervention, and, because their forces were too few, they did not reap the fruits. Let us recount briefly the main stages.

In February and March 1918 the British effected a naval landing at Murman, at the head of the Kola inlet, the terminus of the new railway to Petrograd, and at Pechenga, a hundred miles farther west, the nearest Russian port to the Finnish frontier. There was no serious opposition, and soon the arrival of French and American cruisers made the occupation international. The local Soviet worked harmoniously with the Allies, and the landing was, in fact, approved of by Trotski. Then came the German alliance with Finland, who was promised all the Russian territory lying between her eastern borders and the White Sea. To meet this threat Allied reinforcements arrived in June, under General Poole. Presently the Bolsheviks changed their policy, and demanded the departure of all Allied forces from Russia—a demand refused by the Murman Provisional Government, who thereupon threw in their lot with the Allies. Then followed for three months attacks from the Finnish borders, which were beaten off by Allied troops and local levies, till Finland's enthusiasm for conquest waned and Germany's preoccupation elsewhere made her assistance impossible. The problem at

Murman was always simple. There was little trouble with the local population, and the enemy was too remote and the country too difficult to make invasion easy. The occupation served the useful purpose of checking German intrigue in Finland and giving the Allies a bridgehead on Russian soil, but the isolation of that bit of coast deprived it of strategic importance.

It was different with Archangel, which General Poole occupied on 2nd August by a surprise attack. *Aug. 2.* There lay vast quantities of war material sent by the Allies to Russia, which Lenin's Government was busy commandeering and selling to the Germans ; and there, too, the local Bolsheviks had imposed their crazy type of misgovernment over a starving province. The Allies' business was to feed the people, to prevent the disposal of war stores to Germany, to establish a free Russian Government in the area, and to push southward to join hands with the right wing of the Czecho-Slovaks west of the Urals. But the troops sent were wholly inadequate for the purpose, and the military operations up the river Dvina and the Vologda railway, conducted by British, French, American, and Russian detachments, failed completely to effect the desired junction. Moreover, there was endless trouble with the Russian troops and with the temporary Government—consisting of the members originally elected to the Constituent Assembly—which it was the first business of the Allies to establish. The whole Archangel affair was an example of how a wise policy can be wrecked by half-heartedness. The gallant efforts of General Poole in no way assisted the Czecho-Slovaks, and they brought little succour to the unfortunate provincials. By establishing a front astride the Dvina we cut off Archangel from her natural source of food supply, the Russian interior, and so saddled ourselves with the task of feeding the population by supplies carried over some thousands of miles of sea to a port which was ice-bound in winter. On the whole this duty was fulfilled, but a task which had been entered upon for high strategic reasons ended by becoming a mere business of commissariat.

The Siberian situation was the most hopeful, and at the same time the most perplexing. Its elements were the Czecho-Slovak forces, about 120,000 strong, some at Vladivostok, and some on the western borders of Siberia, while between them lay the railway, held in large patches by Bolsheviks and Austro-German prisoners ; a number of sporadic Russian nationalist troops, some in the Far East, some at points along the line, and a considerable number, under Alexeiev, in the Don and Kuban provinces, but separated by a wedge of Bolsheviks from the left wing of the Czecho-Slovaks in the west ; various Russian Governments, springing up throughout Siberia, and often dissolving a day or two after their creation ; the sympathy of the mass of the Siberian people, who desired order, and had few leanings towards the Lenin *régime ;* and the Allies, toying for long with the notion of sending help through Vladivostok, and finally dispatching troops, who, as at Archangel, were too few to meet the need, and were further embarrassed by a lack of a central command. Japan was willing enough to intervene in Eastern Siberia, but professed no interest in the Western battle-ground ; while America was never

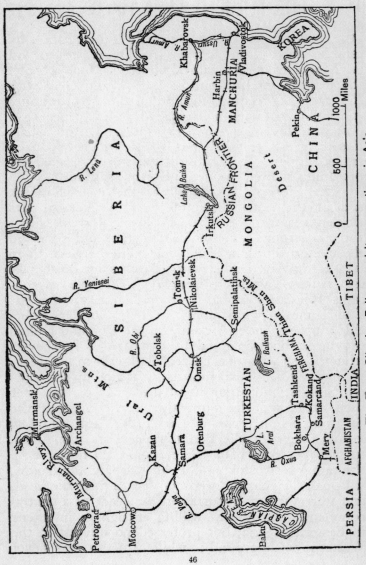

The Trans-Siberian Railway and its connections in Asia.

fully convinced of the wisdom of the step, and encumbered such aid as she gave with rigid conditions. Out of such a tangle it would have been a miracle if there had emerged either a clear policy or vigorous action. The Czecho-Slovaks from first to last had to bear the brunt of the contest themselves. The diplomatic *pourparlers* which went on all summer revealed the weakness of an alliance in any far-flung scheme of strategy.

On 3rd August the British contingent reached Vladivostok to find the Czecho-Slovaks hard pressed, various local Governments which had to be conciliated, and various Russian leaders *Aug. 3.* of *condottieri* who needed delicate handling. Two days later they had joined the Czechs on the river Ussuri, north of Vladivostok. Meantime the Czechs, under General Dite- *Aug. 5.* richs, had taken Irkutsk, and controlled most of the railway from the Volga to Lake Baikal, but without immediate Allied help they could not hope to maintain their ground. On 12th August the first part of the Japanese contingent, *Aug. 12.* under General Otani, landed at Vladivostok, where French troops had preceded them; and the first Americans appeared on the 16th. The situation in Eastern Siberia now began *Aug. 16.* to improve. The Japanese reinforced the Ussuri front, and by the 30th the enemy was in full retreat towards Khabarovsk, while the Czechs at Lake Baikal were holding their own, *Aug. 30.* and controlled all the railway east of the lake. By this time they had been formally recognized by all the Allies as a belligerent nation, and since the Czech control now extended to the Pacific, Bohemia,

as in Shakespeare, had now a sea coast. On 2nd
September the Czechs, moving east from Baikal,

Sept. 2.   joined hands with Semenov's Cossacks
moving westward, while the Japanese had
routed the Bolsheviks on the Amur railway. Communication was now open between Vladivostok and

Sept. 5.   the Volga. On the 5th Khabarovsk fell
to Otani. The enemy in Siberia had
virtually collapsed, and the way was clear for the
Allies to push west to the vital Volga front.

But the smallness of their numbers, their lack
of unity, and their endless civil difficulties about
railway control and the recognition of new-born
Russian Governments, made any swift action impossible. Much had been gained, for Siberia had
been won back from both Bolshevik and German ;
but the Czechs in the west were still in desperate
straits. At the beginning of September they held
a line along the Volga, running from Volsk, north of
Saratov, by Samara and Simbirsk, to Kazan, with
a detachment on the northern line between Ekaterinburg and Perm. But their ammunition was running low, and presently they lost Volsk and Simbirsk and Kazan. They were at the most, with
their Russian contingents, some 60,000 strong, and
with German aid the Bolsheviks had against them
a force of well over 100,000. The enemy had
18,000 troops between General Poole and the
Czechs in the Ekaterinburg area, and a large army
around Kharkov and Bielgorod to advance to the
Volga and prevent a junction with Alexeiev on the
Don. Moreover, out of their scanty reserves, the
Czechs had to maintain garrisons in Western Siberia.
For tenacity and courage they had no superiors in

any nation ; but they were fighting a hopeless battle, and must inevitably retire towards the Urals. Yet they had saved Siberia from anarchy, and so long as they remained an army they provided a rallying point for those elements in Russia with which lay the hope of the future.

The story of Transcaucasia at this period is one of the most confused in the war, and it cannot be dissociated from the obscure happenings in Transcaspia and Central Asia, for it was to the Caucasus that Germany looked for an alley to a new Asian dominion. The Russian Revolution of March 1917 had produced a national self-consciousness throughout the country, and, under the influence of Georgia, politically the most mature of the peoples, the independence of Transcaucasia was proclaimed in November, and a general Transcaucasian Government was formed in a republic to include Georgians, Armenians, and Tatars. Meantime there was anarchy among the Russian troops of the Caucasus, and Prjevalsky, who had succeeded Yudenitch, was compelled to ask Turkey for an armistice. The advance of the Turks began to weaken the allegiance of the Tatars to the new Government, and in March 1918 came the Brest Litovsk treaty, making over Batum, Kars, and Ardahan to Turkey. These cessions were a serious blow to the Georgians, but they had no alternative except to submit. Presently Turkey increased her demands beyond the Brest clauses, and at a conference held in Batum in May the Georgian delegates refused to accept them. The Transcaucasian Government had now ceased to exist ; an independent Armenian republic of Erivan was

4

proclaimed under Turkish protection; a Tatar republic on the same terms, which included Baku, was established in Azerbaijan; and Georgia was compelled to appeal to Germany.

Turkey, it was clear, intended to deal highhandedly with Transcaucasia, and this Germany had no mind to permit. She cared little what happened to the Armenians, but she was determined to control Baku and its oil-fields, and she had selected the Georgians to be her special allies and to play the part she had cast for the Finns in the north and the Bulgarians in the Balkans. General Kress von Kressenstein was recalled from Syria—where he was soon to be sorely needed—and sent to the Caucasus; and German troops were marched into Georgia, while German trading houses endeavoured to secure every possible contract for the development of the region. An attempt was made in July to settle affairs with Turkey by a Conference at Constantinople, and the Turks were categorically informed that they must abide by the Brest treaty. They paid no attention, continued their intrigues throughout the whole Caucasus, and advanced steadily to Baku. Their aim was to control the region by means of the Moslem inhabitants, and all Germany could effect was to withdraw Georgia from their influence, and to make a contract for oil with the Armenians and Bolsheviks of Baku, which would be worthless when the Turks took the town. The rift between Germany and her Moslem ally was widening.

Such is a rough sketch of the main events of six months of plot and counterplot. It was a matter in which Britain was acutely interested, for not only did it directly affect her Mesopotamian campaign, but it prejudiced the whole future of Persia and the immediate hinterland of India. Events east of the Caspian were equally disquieting. After nearly a year of contest, the Soviet of Tashkend had beaten the Provincial Government at Kokand, and over-powered all resistance between Baku and Ferghana. In May Russian Turkestan had been declared a Soviet republic. These events thrust the moderates into the background, and inclined the Central Asian Moslems towards Germany and Turkey as possible deliverers from this thralldom, while Pan-Islamic and Pan-Turanian propaganda took on a new lease of life.

The nearest British troops were the small contingents in Persia and Marshall's army in Mesopotamia, and their problem was sufficiently complex. In the first place, the road from Bagdad to the Caspian must be kept open against the Turkish assaults from the west. In the second place, the advance of the Transcaspian Bolsheviks must be checked. They had taken Merv, and if they had further successes, they might be joined by the Turcomans, and the whole region be set ablaze. Again, if the Eastern front was to be restored, the Caspian and its shipping must be mastered, and this meant that Baku must be held against the Turk. A British force was sent to Transcaspia, and after many vicissitudes succeeded in beating the Bolsheviks so soundly that they exchanged military operations for local atrocities. This remote side-show had in reality immense political importance for Britain, since the line from Merv to Kushk ended within two days' ride of Herat, the key of Afghanistan.

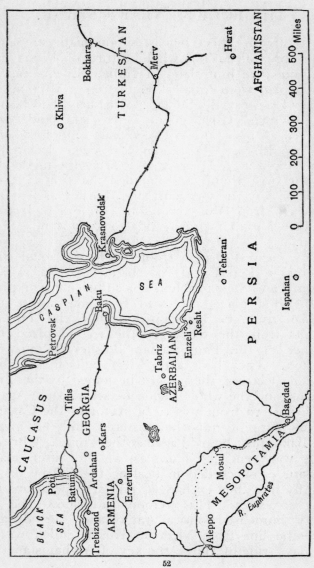

Sketch Map to illustrate the events in Transcaucasia and on the shores of the Caspian.

The defence of the Bagdad-Caspian route was maintained, in spite of the forays of Turkish cavalry from Tabriz and the ceaseless raids of the hill tribes, notably the Jangalis around Resht. But the main interest centred in Baku, where, on the night of 25th July, the Bolsheviks were over-thrown and a new Government set up, *July 25.* which at once begged for British assistance. They had control at the moment of the shipping on the Caspian, and sent transports to Enzeli to fetch the small British force under Major-General Dunsterville,* which was now more than 1,000 miles from its base. The main difficulty was the shipping, for the Caspian Fleet was not to be relied on. The second was the quality of the local levies—7,500 Armenians and 3,000 Russians—who proved wholly useless in action. On 17th August the former re-fused to fight, and presently went home ; *Aug. 17.* and a strong Turkish assault on 26th August was repulsed only by two British battalions, the North Staffords and the Worcesters. *Aug. 26.* At the close of the month Dunsterville was in seri-ous straits. The Turks were round the town, and on the 31st the local troops *Aug. 31.* failed once again, and the Warwicks had to cover their retirement.

Help came suddenly out of the void. The Russian partisan leader, Bicharakov, who had done good work with Marshall in Mesopotamia, took Petrovsk, on the Caspian, 200 miles to the north, and sent reinforcements to Baku. These

---

* Dunsterville was head of the Mission in Northern Persia, which was largely engaged in famine relief. His headquarters at the time were at Kasvin.

arrived on 9th September ; and after further trouble
with the Russian Fleet, and a serious rearguard

Sept. 9.

action on the 14th, the British evacuated Baku and reached Enzeli in safety

Sept. 14.

—a result which must be considered fortunate in
view of the immense risks run by the
expedition. It had never been our intention to garrison Baku ourselves, but merely to
assist the local Government to establish their hold
on the oil-fields, and to secure the Caspian shipping. Since the local Government proved incompetent to organize resistance, there was nothing for
Dunsterville to do but to leave the place to the
Turks. It was a possession which they were not
destined to enjoy for long.

The situation around the Caspian condemned
General Marshall to inactivity on his main battle
ground. He found himself involved in adventures
many hundred miles from his front, and, while this
duty continued, he must remain inactive on the
Tigris, though much could be done to restore order
and prosperity to the ancient land which his predecessor had redeemed. Sir Stanley Maude died on
November 18, 1917. In December an attack was
delivered against the Turkish 13th Corps, holding

Dec. 5–9,
1917.

the Diala and the Jebel Hamrin passes,
and on the 5th it was driven towards
Kifri with heavy casualties. On the 9th
Khanikin was occupied. Early in the New Year

Mar. 8,
1918.

General Marshall resolved to advance
his front on the Euphrates, and to break
up the new Turkish concentration two
miles north of Hit. On 8th March it was discovered that the enemy had retired fifteen miles

upstream to Salahiya, and next day Hit was occupied. The Turks were still retiring, and *Mar.* 10.
on the 10th Marshall was in Salahiya.
It was resolved to try an encircling operation

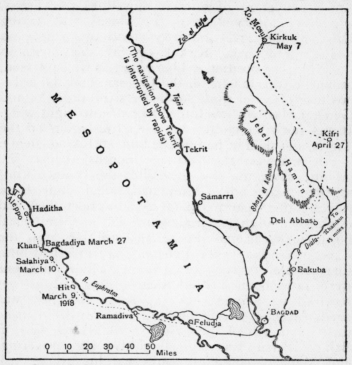

General Marshall's Operations in the Spring of 1918.

against the position at Khan Baghdad, where the
enemy proposed to stand. By 11.30 on *Mar.* 26.
the night of 26th March our cavalry had
got round his flanks and cut off his retreat; and
our infantry, attacking next morning at dawn, com-

pleted his discomfiture. Major-General Sir H. T.
Brooking occupied Haditha without trouble, and
pursued the Turks for seventy-three miles along
the Aleppo road, taking over 5,000 prisoners. In
April the centre of interest moved to the Tigris,
where we advanced along the Mosul road, taking
Kifri on the 27th and over 1,000 prisoners, and
May 7. entering Kirkuk on 7th May without
opposition. Thereafter, as we have seen,
came the distractions on the Caspian, and the ardu-
ous task of relief work on the Persian border * ; and
General Marshall was forced to retire his right wing.
It was not till October that he struck again on the
Tigris, and then he had before him a breaking enemy.

In reviewing these strange months we may say
on the whole that for the Allies the balance leant
to the credit side. They had failed, indeed, to
recreate the Eastern front. At the most they had
established it in patches, which left the strategical
position precarious. Poole was still far from the
Czecho-Slovaks on the Volga. The latter had both
their flanks turned, and, though communications
were now open behind them, they had as yet
received no supports or supplies ; Kornilov was
dead, Alexeiev was dying, and Denikin could make
little way north of the Caspian ; the Turks were in
Baku ; Persia was still disruptive and wavering,
and Marshall could not carry out his proper task
for attending to her vagaries.

Yet, if we compare the situation in September
with that after the signature of the Brest Litovsk
treaty in March, we shall see how far astray had gone
Germany's forecast. She had by her conduct in the

* See Appendix II.

Ukraine involved herself in a mesh of troubles; hopelessly antagonized the orderly elements in Russia; and got little in the way of supplies for herself. She had lost Siberia, and seen the Czecho-Slovaks spring up like a new seed of Cadmus, to dispute with her the way to the East. She was at variance with Turkey over the Caucasus, as she was at variance with Bulgaria over the Dobrudja. She was rapidly losing Finland, the northern pillar of her Eastern ambitions. Above all, the two Prussianisms—one of which was called Bolshevism—had proved incompatible, in spite of their formal alliance. A belief in force and the tyranny of a class is insufficient as a bond of union, if the two parties differ as to the class; and a common ruthlessness is more likely to lead to quarrels than to co-operation.

Germany had played with fire, and it was about to scorch her hands. To her statesmen it was plain long before September that the policy which seemed so hopeful at Brest Litovsk had utterly failed. There was no make-weight to be found in the East against a draw in the West; and if disaster befell in the West, from the East assuredly could come no succour. Nay, her oriental acquisitions would be like a millstone round the neck of a sinking man. When Prince Leopold of Bavaria and his glittering staff crossed the Vistula by the Warsaw bridge on that July day in 1915, they saw the sky reddened with the fires of great burnings, which marked the retreat of Russia into her wild spaces. It was the sight which Napoleon had seen, and it carried the same omen. Russia had retired into the wastes both of the earth and of the spirit, and the invader had followed to his destruction.

These things, as we have said, were beginning to be perceived by Germany's rulers. Their people had followed them blindly, and taken from them a confidence ready-made, for they had little reasoned assurance of their own. If the nerve of the leaders failed, there would be no popular endurance. We pass now to consider the mutations of German opinion between March and September.

In April Burian, who in December 1916 had been displaced by Czernin, succeeded him as Foreign Minister of the Dual Monarchy. It was one of those aimless changes of *personnel* which proved nothing except the rudderless character of Austrian statecraft. She was drifting now in an archipelago of reefs—the nationalism of her subject peoples, the truculence of Hungary, a cracking army, a starving population. Without affection or hope she continued to follow the will of her stronger partner, and, though passionately desirous of peace, she had not the energy left to initiate any independent policy. It was very clear that Austria could not secede from the war of her own will, for she had no strength in her limbs ; but it was clear, too, that some day soon her limbs might collapse beneath her.

In Germany the people had been moved to a sudden hope by the promises of February and the achievements of March and April. After that the hope waned, but a conviction endured—that there must be peace before the winter. The confidence of most of her statesmen had a longer life—till well into September. There were exceptions, and the most notable was the Foreign Minister, von Kuhlmann. He had never favoured the spring offensive, and by May he had convinced himself of its futility. Accordingly, on 24th June, in the Budget debate in the Reichstag, he warned his hearers that *June 24.* it was idle to look for a decision in the field. It was a remarkable speech, which revealed the perturbation of German civilian statesmen. He admitted the failure of the Eastern policy by granting that the Brest Litovsk treaty needed revising, and by candidly stating the difficulties with Turkey. He repeated the old tale of Germany's innocence of any thought of world dominion. She sought, he said, only the boundaries drawn for her by history, sufficient overseas possessions to correspond to her greatness, and freedom of trade with all continents over a free ocean. She was willing to listen to any honest offer of peace, and trusted that her opponents would approach her with a proposal ; but she would make no statement about Belgium which would bind her without binding her enemies. If one looked only to the battlefield no decision could be said to be in sight, and he quoted Moltke very much to the purpose. Germany could not be conquered, but " in view of the enormous magnitude of this coalition war, in view of the number of Powers, including those from overseas, involved in it, an absolute end can hardly be expected through military decisions alone."

The speech was the swan-song of Kuhlmann's diplomacy, of the whole policy of the German *politiques.* It was an attempt to break to the German people the news that the promises of February could not be met, and that the boasting of the early summer had been idle. Did Kuhlmann speak for himself alone ? It is highly improbable. Luden-

dorff's own confidence was waning, and it is likely
that he used Kuhlmann to prepare the popular
mind for worse tidings; for the great stroke on the
Aisne had not brought victory, and he was far too
good a soldier not to see the dangers ahead of him.
The result proved that both he and Kuhlmann had
miscalculated the popular mood. The drop was
too sudden, and the outcry was violent. The Pan-
Germans assailed the Foreign Minister as a partisan
of Britain; he was made to explain away his speech
by an admission of the necessity of victory in the
field, and the Imperial Chancellor made a further
and most unflattering apology for the "accidental"
indiscretions of his colleague. He found he had
no supporters, for truculence had become the
fashion again, and even Scheidemann bowed to it.
He was made the scapegoat, too, of all the blunders
of the Government, for, as von Holstein once
observed to Prince Buelow : "When the sun shines
the Chancellor suns himself; when it rains, it is
the Foreign Secretary who gets wet."

On 10th July he resigned, and was succeeded
by Admiral von Hintze. He had been the exponent
July 10. of the practicable, or what seemed to him
the practicable, as against the megalo-
maniacs, and there was no place for him in a world
where calculations were becoming as futile as
July 12. dreams. Two days later Hertling, with
the support of the Majority Socialists,
declared the policy of Germany on confident lines,
announcing, among other things, that she held
Belgium as "a pawn for future negotiations," and
thereby refusing what the Allies had always maintained to be a pre-condition of any discussion of

peace terms. The last German offensive was due in three days, and it was necessary to stiffen the spirit of the country.

July came to a close, and with it any confidence that remained to the High Command. During August there were signs that it was the leaders in the field rather than the *politiques* who wished to mitigate the arrogance which they had afore-time fostered. Hindenburg, now somewhat a lay figure, found himself compelled early in September to issue a manifesto against the growing movement towards compromise. He chose to ex-plain it by the success of Allied propaganda inside Germany—propaganda which it was the fashion to decry in the countries of origin, but which the Germans had come to regard with uneasy respect. On 12th September the Vice-Chancellor, von Payer, made a curious speech in *Sept. 12.* which, while declaring that he did not believe in a peace of conquest, he expounded Germany's terms in the fashion of a conqueror. There could be no handing back of Poland or Finland or the Baltic states to Russia, or any paring down of Germany's acquisitions in the East. " We can never permit any one to meddle with us in this matter from the standpoint of the present European balance of power, or rather British predominance. Just as little will we submit to the Entente, for its gracious approval or alteration, our peace treaties with the Ukraine, Russia, or Rumania. In the East we have peace, and it remains for us peace, whether it pleases our Western neighbours or not."

These were brave words, but they were inoppor-tune. The unhappy Government at Berlin might speak boldly one day, but the compulsion of events compelled it to change its tone on the morrow. *Sept.* 14. On 14th September Germany made an offer of a separate peace to Belgium, who at once rejected it. She offered also to refrain from attacking Eastern Karelia if the Allied troops would withdraw from the Murman coast, having found it impossible to induce Finland to make any effort to fight for the territory she had claimed. More significant still, Austro-Hungary addressed a Note to all belligerents and neutral states proposing a conference for a " non-binding confidential discussion " as to the possibility of peace. This offer, though Germany officially denied any connection with it, was undoubtedly made with her knowledge. The truth is, that Austria was desperate, and was approaching that condition when she must sue for peace on any terms. Germany was willing to permit the Note as a *ballon d'essai*. If it failed, she could save her dignity by repudiating any part in it ; if it succeeded, it would give her the conference for which she had always intrigued.

The reply of the Allies was instant and unequivocal ; and it was that of Lucio's comrade in *Measure for Measure*—" Heaven grant us its peace, but not the King of Hungary's ! " Mr. Balfour, on *Sept.* 16. 16th September, asked pertinently what use would such a conference be, if the policy of the Central Powers was the policy of von Payer's speech of 12th September. That same day came America's answer : " The Government of the United States feels that there is only one reply which it can make to the suggestion of the Imperial Austro-Hungarian Government. It has repeatedly and with entire candour stated the terms on which the United States would consider peace, and can and will entertain no proposal for a conference upon a matter concerning which it has made its position and purpose so plain."

This, then, was the position in the third week of September. The German people were in a mood of deep depression, careless of the arguments booming above their heads, but clinging blindly to the certainty of a peace of some kind before the winter. Their rulers were not less disconsolate. They saw their front in the West cracking, and the whole fabric of their power in the East beginning to crumble about their ears. They knew the terms upon which alone the Allies would think of peace, and these terms meant the downfall of all they had builded, and the reversal of Germany's policy since the days of Bismarck. They could not bring themselves as yet to bow to them, and they hoped against hope for some diversion, some gift from the gods at the eleventh hour. On 24th September both *Sept. 24.* the Imperial Chancellor and the Vice-Chancellor spoke in the Reichstag, clinging to their old dogmas, but striving so to phrase them that, while maintaining their substance, they might fall more soothingly on Allied ears. It was clear that Germany would not admit defeat till her armies were decisively beaten in the field.

That decision was very near. Two days later Foch launched his final battle. We *Sept. 26.* must turn to that epic campaign of August and September which had prepared the stage for this, the last act of the play.

CHAPTER CLX.

THE LAST BATTLES OF THE SOMME, ARRAS, AND THE AISNE.

The Meaning of the "Initiative"—*Final* Superiority in Effective Strength—Foch's Strategy—Ludendorff's First Plan—The British Advance previous to 8th August—Haig's Attack of 8th August — The Advance of the British Centre — The Fight at Chipilly — The Attack of the French Third Army —Recapture of Montdidier—The Results of the Battle— Humbert attacks Lassigny Hills—Von Boehn's New Army Group—Change in Ludendorff's Plan—Mangin attacks between the Oise and the Aisne—Byng's Attack of 21st August —Rawlinson's Attack of 22nd August—The German Retreat —British Advance on the Scarpe—Fall of Bapaume—Fall of Noyon—Fall of Péronne—Plumer retakes Kemmel Hill— British break through the Drocourt-Quéant Switch—Rawlinson and Débeney cross the Upper Somme—Mangin attacks the St. Gobain *massif*—General Allied Advance—German Losses—Byng breaks into Main Siegfried Front—The American Attack at St. Mihiel—St. Mihiel Salient wiped out— Northern Armies advance to Edge of Siegfried Zone—Foch's Preparations for the Final Battle—The News from the East.

THE Second Battle of the Marne restored to the Allies the initiative. That is to say, they had now power to impose their will upon the enemy to the extent of deciding the form and the time of an action. The enemy might attack, but his attack would be the result of Allied compulsion, and so foreseen and prepared for, whereas the Allied offensives would come of their own free will. During most of the campaign in the West the Allies had kept the initiative, for they won it at the First Battle of the Marne, and did not lose it till Ludendorff's advance of March 21, 1918. But the initiative of itself could not give victory, or Germany would have been victor after the latter date. For that it must be combined with a *final* superiority in effective strength ; that is, one side must have increased and be able to go on increasing, while the other must have passed the summit of its power and be on the decline. To this position the Allies had never as yet attained. They had come very near to it before the close of the First Battle of the Somme, and they would have achieved it during 1917 had the Russian front held. But the defection of the East turned the tables on them, and gave Germany the initiative, and a temporary, though not a *final*, superiority in effective strength. For three months the Allies stood precariously on the defensive, while that temporary supremacy slowly vanished. Then came the hour when the balance inclined towards them, and the blunder of his opponents gave Foch the chance of a *coup* which restored to him the initiative. He had now in addition a *final* superiority in men and material, and, moreover, had— what is not necessarily the same thing—this superiority translated into a greater number of reserve divisions. He had, therefore, the means to his hand of using to the full the advantage of the initiative, and nothing but an incredible blunder could have lost him this crowning asset.

He made no blunder, for the wisdom which had patiently stood the shock for nearly four months and bided its time was not likely to fumble when

the chance for which it had striven appeared at last.
As has been well said, he had opposed to the blud-
geon of Ludendorff the lithe blade of the swords-
man. He had avoided his enemy's shattering
blows ; he had pinked him again and again, and
had drawn much blood ; he had baffled and confused and wearied him till the brute force of his
opponent was less than his own trained and elastic
strength. But the time for the *coup de grâce* was
not yet. In 1813 the Prussian Staff, studying the
methods of Napoleon, laid down as the first prin-
ciple of that great master of war the rule : " Econo-
mize forces, while keeping the battle nourished,
right up to the moment when the transition is made
from the preparation to the main attack." Germany
had forgotten this maxim, but Foch had remembered
it, and had made it the text of a homily in his famous
work, *Les Principes de la Guerre*. It was now, as
ever, the basis of his policy.

He was not yet ready for the grand climax, the
decisive blow. It was his business to wear down the
enemy continuously and methodically by attacks on
limited fronts, aiming at strictly limited objectives.
The tactical freedom which was now his enabled
him to ring the changes over the whole battle-ground.
He would use his reserves discreetly and economically
to " nourish the battle " and inflict the maximum
damage on his opponents. But he would not press
in any section for an ambitious advance, or endeavour to force a decision. The action must develop organically like a process of nature. From
21st March to 18th July he had stood patiently on
the defensive ; from July 18th to 8th August he
had won back the initiative, freed his main com-

munications, and hopelessly dislocated Ludendorff's plan. From 8th August to 26th September it was his task to crumble the enemy's front, destroy the last remnants of his reserves, force him beyond all his prepared defences, and make ready for the final battle which should give victory.

Ludendorff, shaken to his foundations by the events on the Marne, had the intention, as we have seen, of withdrawing his front to a safe line and of building up a new reserve. He was prepared to retire at his leisure from the Lys and Montdidier salients, and form a front for the winter running along the Ypres and Wytschaete heights, continuing on the low ridges between the Lys and La Bassée, and from Arras to the Oise holding the crest of the Bapaume and Lassigny uplands. During July the British and French armies had been slowly improving their position, and preparing a starting-place for attack. For example, on the 28th of June Plumer, with the 5th and 31st Divi- *June 28.* sions, advanced to the eastern edge of the Forest of Nieppe and improved his position at Merris ; on the night of 30th June Byng took ground *June 30.* north-west of Albert ; on the morning of 4th July the Australians with Rawlinson, south of the Somme, advanced for more than a mile, and captured the village of Hamel. *July 4–7.* On the nights of 5th and 7th July the same commander gained ground on both sides of the Somme, and secured the whole ridge which runs east of Hamel and the Bois de Vaire. On 12th July the French First Army advanced *July 12.* more than a mile between Castel and Mailly-Reneval, capturing the former village. On the 19th

the 9th Division retook the village of Meteren, while
on the 23rd, as we have already seen,
July 19–23. the French advanced two miles north of
Montdidier ; on the night of the 28th
the Australians with Rawlinson went forward north
of the Somme, and next day the village of
July 28–29. Merris, south-west of Bailleul, was taken
by the 1st Australian Division with Plumer.
Early in August Ludendorff began his first withdrawal. On the 2nd von der Marwitz
Aug. 2. fell back across the Ancre between Dernancourt and Hamel, and there was a slight retirement north of the La Bassée Canal. Between the
5th and the 9th, east of Robecq, our line
Aug. 5–9. was advanced more than a mile on a
front of six. Ludendorff's intention was clear, and
the moment had come for Sir Douglas Haig to speed
and confuse his departure.

The British Commander-in-Chief had two alter-
natives—to advance on the Lys or on the Somme,
and he decided that the latter should take precedence. The area chosen for the new attack was the
front of fourteen miles astride the Avre, the Luce,
and the Somme from just south of the Amiens-
Roye road to Morlancourt. The British Army for
the past three months, save for the divisions engaged
on the Aisne and the Marne, had had a time of
comparative quiet, and the arrival of the Americans
had given it opportunities of training new drafts
out of the line. In this area were disposed the
British Fourth Army under Rawlinson, and the
left wing of the French First Army under Débeney
—both forces temporarily under the British Commander-in-Chief. Infinite pains had been taken to

make the surprise complete. By an elaborate piece of *camouflage* the enemy was induced to believe that an attack in Flanders was imminent. The Canadians, who, along with the Australians, were the principal British attacking troops, had been secretly brought down from the north a few days before, and only went into line just before the battle. The German front—the left of von der Marwitz's II. Army and the right of von Hutier's XVIII. Army—was at the moment held by seven divisions, and there was no great depth of reserves behind. For the attack Sir Douglas Haig had accumulated not less than 400 tanks, mostly of the "whippet" type. It was an occasion for the use of Foch's tactics in their purest form. There was to be no artillery bombardment except just at the moment of advance ; the ground had been perfectly reconnoitred from the air ; the objectives were ambitious but strictly defined ; and the troops to be used were among the *corps d'élite* of assault in the British Army.

The British commander had seven divisions in line of battle. On the right the Canadian Corps had the 3rd, 1st, and 2nd Canadian Divisions in line, with the 4th in support. In the centre the Australian Corps had the 2nd and 3rd Australian Divisions in line, with the 5th and 4th in support. The left wing, north of the Somme, was held by the 3rd Corps, with the 58th and 18th Divisions in line, and the 12th in support. The three divisions of the Cavalry Corps under Kavanagh were waiting east of Amiens, and a special force of motor machine-gun brigades and Canadian cyclists, under Briga-dier-General Brutinel, had orders to operate along the Amiens-Roye road.

Strategically the area was of high importance. Haig's ultimate purpose was that of Foch, which has been already described ; his immediate aim was to free his communications, as the French had freed theirs on the Marne.   To this end the enemy must be driven out of range of Amiens and the Paris railway, Montdidier must be retaken, and the enemy's own communications must be broken by the domination of the important road and rail centre of Chaulnes. The battle-ground was of the familiar type of the Santerre plateau.   North of the Somme the downs ran southward into an awkward spur in the bend of the river at Chipilly.   In the south, in the valley of the Avre, long bare slopes gave a similar advantage to the German defence.   The centre between the Somme and the Avre was open upland, sprinkled with coppices, which presented no natural obstacle. From Amiens ran straight as an arrow the two great Roman highways to St. Quentin and to Roye, and there were dozens of good parish roads to link them up.   The whole countryside was an ideal area for tanks, being dry and unenclosed, while the Roman highways provided avenues to direct the assault. An immediate success in the centre was a practical certainty, but it looked as if the two flanks might have severe fighting.

In the first week of August much rain fell, and on the night of the 7th a heavy mist soaked out of the ground.   When day dawned on
Aug. 8.
Thursday, the 8th, it was such another morning as 21st March.   Just before daybreak an intense bombardment was opened between the Ancre and the Avre, so intense that the enemy's defences disappeared as if wiped out by a sponge.   Four

minutes later it stopped, and the tanks and infantry
moved forward. Rawlinson advanced at 4.20,
Débeney some twenty minutes later.

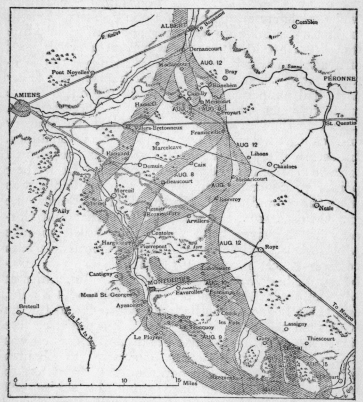

The Last Battle of the Somme—the Allied Advance,
August 8–15.

In the centre success was immediate and continuous. The Canadians and Australians, pressing

along the two Roman roads, marched steadily towards their final objectives. Long before noon they had taken Démuin and Marcelcave, and were beyond the main Albert-Montdidier highway. Von Hutier was completely surprised. At one point the British tanks took captive a German regimental mess while they were breakfasting ; at another the whole staff of a division was seized ; in some villages the Germans were taken in their billets before they knew what had happened, and parties of the enemy were made prisoner when working in the harvest fields. The Canadian cavalry passed through the infantry and captured a train on the line near Chaulnes. Indeed that day the whole British cavalry performed miracles, advancing twenty-three miles from their points of concentration. Only on the flanks was there any hindrance. North of the Somme the 3rd Corps carried the woods of Gressaire and Chipilly in the river bend ; but they failed to take Morlancourt, and before nightfall a vigorous German counter-attack recovered Chipilly. So, too, Débeney on his three miles of front had difficulties at Morisel, in the Avre valley. This fell about 8 a.m., and there began a long fight for Moreuil and for the woods on the edge of the crest. When these were taken the enemy resistance broke, and Débeney was able to bring up his wing level with the British centre. That night the new line ran, from left to right, west of Morlancourt, along the slopes just west of Chipilly, just west of Framerville, and thence through Caix, Beaucourt, and Rozainvillers-Plessier to Pierrepont. The whole of the Amiens outer defence line had been gained except at Le Quesnel, and that fell during the night. The Allied front was within four miles of Chaulnes, and the salient of Montdidier had become dangerously sharpened.

This conspicuous success was due to the brilliant tactical surprise and the high efficiency of the new tanks. But it was also due in some degree to a clearly-marked deterioration in the quality of the German infantry on that part of the front. The machine-gun detachments especially did not display their old tenacity. The Allied casualties were extraordinarily small, one Canadian division, which was in the heart of the battle, losing only 100 men. Débeney had mastered the difficulties of the Avre valley, but the British left north of the Somme was still awkwardly placed owing to the loss of Chipilly. On the morning of Friday, 9th, however, the 3rd Corps, with the assistance of *Aug. 9.* a regiment of the 33rd United States Division (Major-General Higginson), made a fresh attack, captured Morlancourt, on the Ancre, and the high ground beyond it, took Chipilly village, and cleared the whole of the Chipilly bend. In the centre the Allied front was advanced—largely by the brilliant work of the cavalry — to the outskirts of Méricourt and Proyart, and thence lay by Méharicourt, Rouvroy, Arvillers, and Contoire to Pierrepont, on the Avre. This front seriously outflanked Montdidier on the north, but there was more to follow.

For that afternoon Humbert's Third French Army struck in on the south flank of the salient between Montdidier and the Matz. Humbert had received no reinforcements, and had only the troops which at the moment were holding the line ; but his attack was the extra blow needed to complete the work of Rawlinson and Débeney on the north. He took the villages of Le Tronquoy and Le Fretoy, and rung the knell of the enemy in Montdidier. The Germans did not appear to realize their danger, for Débeney and Humbert pushed on through the darkness of the night, and by the morning reached Faverolles and cut the road to Roye, by which alone retreat was possible. During Saturday, the 10th, the Montdidier garrison surrendered, *Aug.* 10. and large quantities of material fell into Allied hands. All day the British and the French pressed forward, and by nightfall were six miles east of the town. Rawlinson was close on Lihons, Débeney was in La Boissière, and Humbert held Fécamps and Conchy.

That day's work had important consequences. It put Chaulnes at the mercy of the Allies, for the place was now under direct observation not 3,000 yards away. Roye itself was under their guns, though at long range. The great Amiens-Paris railway was completely freed for traffic, as was also the other line which ran up the Avre valley to Montdidier. Prince Rupprecht's reserves had been drawn into the battle, and the original seven German divisions on the front had now grown to sixteen. Von Hutier inside the salient was severely straitened in his communications, and had now no line of lateral supply not directly threatened. Foch had repeated his tactical performance of 18th July on the Marne. He had freed his own communications and cut the enemy's, and the heights of Lassigny, towards which Humbert was striving, exactly paralleled that Hill 205 above Rozoy the taking of which by Mangin had driven von Boehn back to the Vesle.

During the night of the 10th Rawlinson advanced

astride the Somme and carried the high ground north of the river between Etinehem and Dernancourt, thus widening the battle front. On Sunday, the 11th, von Hutier flung in fresh divisions to check the British advance. He *Aug. 11.* retook the hill west of Lihons, but was driven off it, though he still held part of the town. He struck also against Humbert, and checked the speed of his progress. Next day, the 12th, Rawlinson advanced south of the Somme, tak- *Aug. 12.* ing Proyart and clearing Lihons; and Débeney made some small gains south - west of Roye. The following day Humbert made progress east of the Matz, and took the iso- *Aug. 13.* lated western outlier of the Lassigny range and the village of Gury. On the 14th he was in Belval, north of the heights, and his *Aug. 14.* right wing carried Ribécourt, on the Oise. On the 15th the whole of the Lassigny *massif* was in his hands, and he had direct ob- *Aug. 15.* servation over the plain to the north, and the communications of all the enemy's southern front in the salient.

The first phase of the Allied offensive had now reached its close, for we were in the old battle area, whose tangled wilderness gave unrivalled opportunities for defence, and the enemy had been heavily reinforced. He had a moment of respite ; but it had been won at the expense of his waning reserves. Since 8th August he had employed thirty-five divisions. He had lost the use of Chaulnes, and of the lateral railway from Péronne to Roye, and the fall of the Lassigny range made a further retreat inevitable. In all the west Ludendorff had now only sixteen fresh divisions in reserve, of which eleven belonged to Prince Rupprecht's group. His chance of a counterstroke had gone for ever, and the most he could hope for was to hold the line of upland between Arras and the Oise till he could make an orderly retreat to the Siegfried Line for winter quarters. For that purpose he created a new army group under von Boehn, which took position between Prince Rupprecht and the Crown Prince, from Albert to Soissons. At the same time he was busy shortening his front on the Lys and the Ancre, and by the 15th we were in Locon and Calonne, in the first area, and had regained Beaumont Hamel, Serre, Puiseux, and Bucquoy, in the second.

The mental condition of the enemy has been described by Sir Douglas Haig : " Buoyed up by the hope of immediate and decisive victory, to be followed by an early and favourable peace, constantly assured that the Allied reserves were exhausted, the German soldiery suddenly found themselves attacked on two fronts and thrown back with heavy losses from large and important portions of their earlier gains. The reaction was inevitable and of a deep and lasting character." Between the 8th and 15th the Allies had taken over 30,000 prisoners, of whom 22,000 had fallen to Rawlinson's army. With thirteen divisions of infantry and three of cavalry, the British Fourth Army had engaged and defeated twenty German divisions. On the 15th mass was said in Amiens Cathedral for the final deliverance of that city.

Foch had no intention of affording Ludendorff a leisurely retreat. It was his business to hustle him as soon as possible from what he had chosen as his intermediate line — the Bapaume ridge and the Somme south of Péronne. The fighting of the 16th and 17th convinced him that Débeney and Humbert had for the moment reached the limits of fruitful advance. *Aug. 16–17.* Roye was still in German hands, though Débeney's position on Cæsar's Camp prevented any use of the place by the enemy. It was time for a new blow in a new quarter. At six in the morning of Sunday, 18th August, Mangin, with *Aug. 18.* the Tenth French Army, struck between the Oise and the Aisne.

It was a strictly limited operation on a short section of ten miles. Mangin advanced for about a mile, took 1,700 prisoners, and occupied the plateau west of Nampcel. It was an adroit performance, for von Boehn, much harassed by requests for reinforcements everywhere, disregarded the business as only a local attack. He withdrew his troops there to the battle zone and waited. But next day Mangin pressed in on a broader front. His men were very weary, having been long in battle; but the indomitable spirit of their general lifted them forward, and he varied his hour of attack so cunningly that he wholly confused the enemy. On the 19th he took Morsain. On the 20th, on *Aug. 19–20.* a front of sixteen miles, he approached the Ailette, taking 8,000 prisoners and 200 guns. He had established himself firmly on the western part of the Heights of the Aisne, and threatened alike the German line on that river and their line west of the Oise. Three divisions were spared by von Boehn from his reserve, including the Bavarian Alpine Corps, but they were too late to save the critical

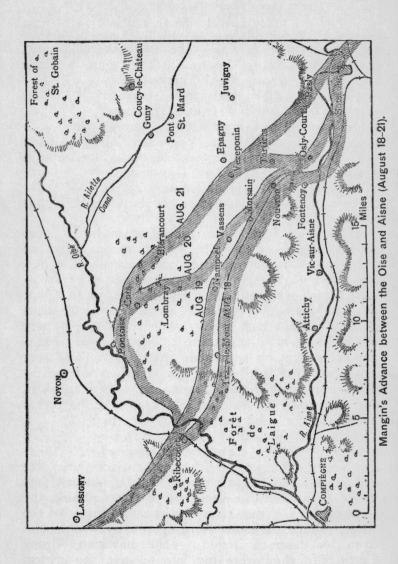

Mangin's Advance between the Oise and Aisne (August 18–21).

Forest of St. Gobain

Coucy-le-Château

Guny

Pont St. Mard

Epagny

Juvigny

R. Ailette

Canal

R. Oise

Béthancourt

AUG. 21

AUG. 20

AUG. 19

Lombray

Vézaponin

Pardieu

Osly-Courtil

Nesy

Nampcel

AUG. 18

Vassens

Morsain

Nouvron

Fontenoy

Vic-sur-Aisne

Pontoise

NOYON

Attichy

Forêt de Laigue

R. Aisne

LASSIGNY

Ribécourt

COMPIÈGNE

Miles

0   5   10   15

78

ground. The result was that by the evening of the 20th the whole front was closely engaged on the hundred miles between the Avre and the Vesle, and von Boehn and the Crown Prince had every man they could muster involved in its defence. It might well have seemed impossible to Ludendorff that the energy of the Allies could find a new battle-ground. He was still far from grasping the relent-less assiduity of Foch's plan. On the night of the 20th, Mangin having done his work, held his hand. On the morning of Wednes-   *Aug.* 21. day, the 21st, Byng struck with the British Third Army.

Haig's reason for this movement was the awk-ward salient now held by the enemy owing to Raw-linson's success south of the Somme, a salient which might be shattered by a blow on its northern side. He wished to turn from the north the line of the Somme south of Péronne as a step towards the main objective Cambrai-St. Quentin. Again, north of the Ancre the ground was less shell-pitted and more suitable for tanks. His aim was by a limited advance to recover the Arras-Albert railway, and two days later to deliver a general attack north of the Somme with the Third and Fourth Armies.

There was never a more complete surprise. All week the enemy had been slowly falling back from his uglier salients north and south of the Lys and south of Arras. The British were again in Merville and Outtersteene, and the Germans on the Ancre were feeling their way towards a securer position for the defence of the Bapaume Ridge. But Byng struck before they were ready, and his purpose was that of Haig on July 1, 1916. He sought to turn the

uplands by an advance north of the Ancre, an enterprise which had failed in the earlier battle, with the
result that the British had been compelled to resort

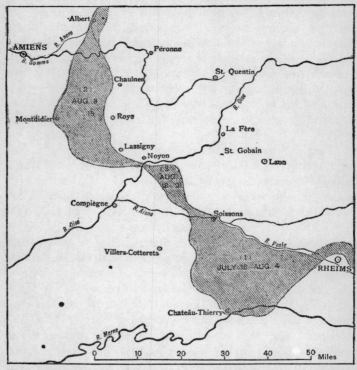

Sketch Map showing the ground regained and the New Front
reached in the first stages of the Allied Offensive.

to a frontal attack.   This time the plan was subtler,
for the turning movement was not an isolated action
but one part of a vast co-ordinated engagement.
The possession of the plateau around Bucquoy and

Ablainzevelle gave us an advantage which we had not possessed in 1916.

It was a thick morning when Byng advanced at 4.55 a.m.　the weather of 8th August and of 21st March.　On a front of nine miles between Moyenneville and Beaucourt, the 42nd New Zealand and 37th Division of Harper's 4th Corps, and the 2nd and Guards Divisions of Haldane's 6th Corps, broke through the enemy front at the first rush.　Then the 5th, 63rd, and 3rd Divisions passed through and completed the work, and the 21st Division cleared the Ancre bank.　Beaucourt was taken, and Achiet-le-Petit, Courcelles, and Moyenneville—names known too well to us in the old Somme fighting—and by the evening we had advanced between two and three miles to where the enemy made a stand along the Albert-Arras railway.　It was sufficient, for Sir Douglas Haig did not need to hasten.　He was still only " nourishing the battle."

Next day, the 22nd, the left wing of Rawlinson's Fourth Army, the 47th, 12th, and 18th Divisions of the 3rd Corps, with the 3rd Australians and the 38th on either flank, came into *Aug.* 22. action between Albert and the Somme, and had a like success.　Albert was recovered by the 18th Division, and the village of Méaulte, and our line was pushed two miles beyond Méaulte to the slopes looking towards Fricourt.　Meantime Humbert had taken Lassigny town on the 21st, and von Boehn was withdrawing to the south bank of the Oise everywhere between Guny and Pontoise ; while farther west the French had reached the line of the little river Divette.

The ground was now prepared for the main

operation.   The Germans were in retreat on a wide
front, and it was our business to confuse and
cripple their withdrawal.   On the 23rd
Aug. 23. Byng and Rawlinson, on the thirty-three
miles of line between Lihons and Mercatel, made
steady progress.   At 4.45 a.m., south of the Somme,
the 32nd and 1st Australian Divisions advanced two
miles, taking Chuignolles and Chuignes, and over
2,000 prisoners.   North of the river the 18th and
38th Divisions of the 3rd Corps and the 5th Corps
pushed east and south of Albert, while the 4th and
6th Corps attacked the Miraumont-Boiry-Becque-
relle line.   Gomiécourt, Ervillers, and Boyelles were
taken, and we won a footing on the Thiepval Ridge.
Byng was now astride the Arras-Bapaume road, and
closing in on the latter place from the north.

That night the Australians took Bray.   On the
24th the whole Thiepval Ridge was cleared by
a brilliant concentric attack, in which
Aug. 24. the 38th Division greatly distinguished
themselves, and Byng was on the edge of Bapaume.
By the 25th we had Mametz, Martin-
Aug. 25. puich, and Le Sars ; but there was a
stiff knuckle of resistance round Bapaume itself.
On the 26th Débeney took Fresnoy, and
Aug. 26– on the 27th he was at last in Roye, and
28. von Boehn was in full retreat between
that town and the Oise.   By the 28th the French
First Army had pushed forward nine miles to the
Upper Somme and the Canal du Nord.

Meantime, on the 26th, Haig had struck again,
this time with Horne's First Army
Aug. 26. astride the Scarpe.   It was a preparation for the next great stage of the British advance.

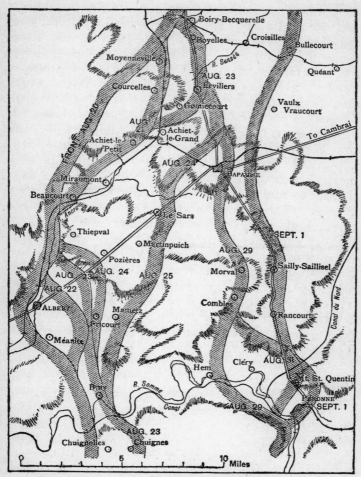

The British Advance across the Ancre and over the
old Battlefields of the Somme.

At 3 a.m. Sir Arthur Currie, with the 51st Division
and the 2nd and 3rd Canadians, attacked cn a five-
mile front. Wancourt was taken, and the old storm
centre of Monchy and Guémappe, and he finished
by nightfall in the outskirts of Roeux, winning as
much in a day as had been won in six weeks in that
area during the 1917 Battle of Arras. Next day the
advance continued, and Roeux and Gavrelle fell.
This was a grave matter for Ludendorff, for he
saw both his line and his reserves shrinking with
a perilous speed—in seven days the British alone
had taken 26,000 prisoners. The Bapaume ridge,
thanks to our brilliant outflanking movements, was
already all but lost, and Horne, on the Scarpe,
threatened to turn the Siegfried Line itself. In
that region the British were already beyond the
front they had held on 21st March. But he still
clung to his hope of an intermediate stand, to enable
him to withdraw in good order to the Siegfried Line
when the weather broke. His scheme was to take
position on a front which was roughly that of the
Ailette and the Oise, the Upper Somme and the
Tortille.

On Thursday, 29th August, von Boehn was in
full retreat to this line. To hold it, he had to retain
Péronne ; but he cannot have hoped that
Aug. 29. he could retain it long. He was fighting
for time—time to get back to the Siegfried positions
without too great a loss in men and guns. Once
there, in that great fortified zone seven miles deep,
he believed he could stand fast for the winter.
Beyond that he did not calculate, for the German
Staff was living from day to day. That day Rawlinson had Combles and Morval, and Byng's New

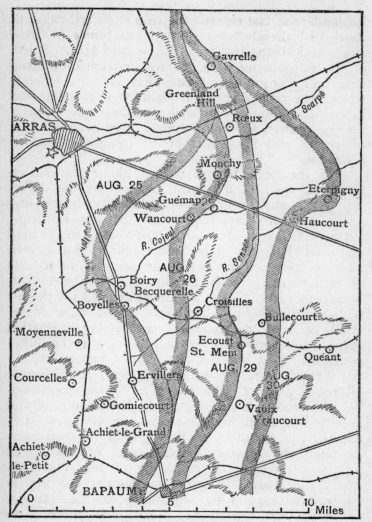

The Last Battle of Arras.

Zealanders at last entered Bapaume.   Farther north
Byng had already been twenty-four hours in Croisilles, and Horne had taken Greenland Hill.   South
of the Somme we held the western bank opposite
Brie and Péronne, and occupied Hem.   Débeney
was on the river line to our right, and Humbert was
in Noyon.   The fall of Bapaume was a grave matter
for the enemy, for it lost him a large accumulation
of stores and it opened up to Byng the road to
Cambrai.

On the 30th Horne moved along the Arras-
Cambrai road, and found the enemy resistance
Aug. 30.   stiffening.   Nevertheless, by the evening
the Canadians were in the skirts of
Ecoust-St. Mein and Haucourt, and the British
on their left had taken Eterpigny.   Horne was
now in close touch with the famous Drocourt-
Quéant Switch, which, it will be remembered, had
been constructed to link up the Siegfried Line proper
with the old German front south of Lens, after the
Battle of Arras had destroyed the northern Siegfried
pivot.   Farther south we reached the edge of Bullecourt, and took Bancourt and Vaulx-Vraucourt.   In
the French area Débeney, Humbert, and Mangin
all made ground.   But the great blow was struck
by the 2nd Australians, with Rawlinson.   By a
superb operation conducted in the darkness they
crossed the Somme on the night of the 30th, and
captured the German trenches east of Cléry.   At
Aug. 31.   five in the morning of the 31st they
rushed Mont St. Quentin, the key of
Péronne, taking 1,500 prisoners at the expense
of some 200 casualties.   That day there were
violent counter-attacks against all the new British

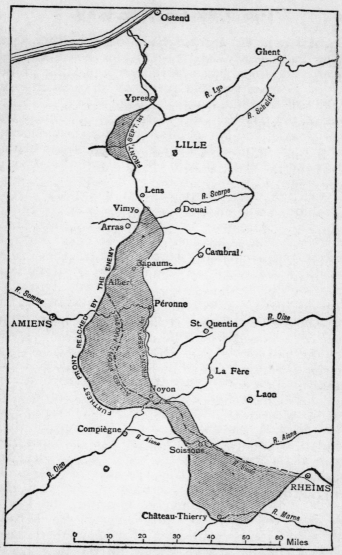

Ostend

Ghent

Ypres

R. Lys

R. Scheldt

LILLE

FRONT, SEPT. 1st

Lens

R. Scarpe

Vimy

Douai

Arras

Cambrai

Bapaume

Albert

R. Somme

Péronne

St. Quentin

R. Oise

AMIENS

FRONT REACHED BY THE ENEMY

ALLIED FRONT, AUG. 8th

FRONT, SEPT. 1st

La Fère

Laon

Noyon

FURTHEST

Compiègne

R. Aisne

Soissons

R. Aisne

R. Oise

R. Vesle

RHEIMS

Château-Thierry

R. Marne

0   10   20   30   40   50   60 Miles

**Sketch Map showing the ground regained by the Allies
up to the end of August 1918.**

87

line between the Scarpe and the Somme, but they were repelled with ease, and Marrières Wood, north of Péronne, the scene of the famous stand of the

Sept. 1. 9th Division in March, was taken. On 1st September the Australians entered Péronne, while we gained a long string of villages to the north—Bouchavesnes, Rancourt, Sailly-Saillisel, and Bullecourt. Mangin that day pushed north of the Ailette to the west of Coucy-le-Château, and Débeney advanced east of Nesle. In Flanders we retook Bailleul station, crossed the Lawe River, and were about to recapture Kemmel Hill. Ludendorff's intermediate position had gone, and he was once more a wanderer.*

He still struggled to find a resting-place short of the main Siegfried Line, but clearly there was no such position in the southern sector, once the Upper Somme had been crossed. In the north, however, he had the line of the Canal du Nord, a water line which he hoped would be an obstacle too difficult for the tanks to cross. His problem now was not to stand, but how to find the means of retiring. The ceaseless pressure of the Allies delayed his going, and unless he found some intermediate defence, he might never reach the Siegfried zone. He hoped, by means of the Canal du Nord, to check Byng, while to the north and south his men retired before Horne and Rawlinson behind the Drocourt-Quéant Switch and the main Siegfried front.

But he had not reckoned with Foch. On Mon-

---

* In the actions which may be collectively called the Battle of Bapaume 23 divisions of the British Third and Fourth Armies defeated 35 German divisions, taking over 34,000 prisoners and 270 guns.

day, 2nd September, while Rawlinson was advancing swiftly east of Péronne, and Byng was beyond Croisilles and Bullecourt, *Sept. 2.* the right wing of Horne's First Army, Sir Arthur

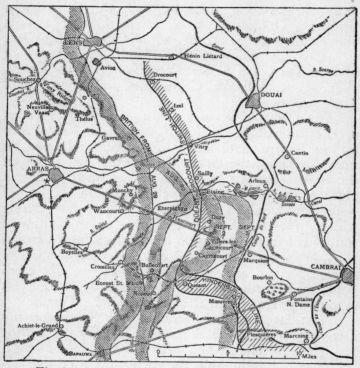

The break through the Quéant-Drocourt "Switch" of the Hindenburg Line (Sept. 2 and 3).

Currie's Canadian Corps, including the 21st Division and the 1st and 4th Canadians, and the left wing of the Third Army, Sir Charles Fergusson's

17th Corps, comprising the 52nd, 53rd, and 63rd Divisions, attacked at 5 a.m. astride the Arras-Cambrai road against the Drocourt-Quéant Switch. It was, as the Germans well knew, the key of their whole front, and they had no less than eleven divisions on the nine miles between the Sensée and Quéant. The attack went clean through all the lines of one of the strongest positions in the West, and took six miles of the Switch, the villages of Etaing, Dury (with the important Hill of Dury), Villers-les-Cagnicourt, Cagnicourt, and Noreuil, and 8,000 prisoners.*

The feat was beyond doubt one of the greatest in the campaign, and it made Ludendorff's plan for an intermediate stand impossible. He had no time for counter-attacks, but hurried his troops in the south behind the Canal du Nord, and, in place of the old Switch, put his trust in the line of water and marsh in the Sensée valley east of Etaing which protected Douai, and which was continued southward from Marquion by the Agache River and the Canal du Nord. By the evening of the 4th our troops were on the canal bank, and found the enemy entrenched on the east side everywhere from the Scarpe to the Tortille.

Sept. 4.

Next day, south of Péronne, both Rawlinson and Débeney crossed the Somme. The former by the evening held the line Athies-Doingt-Bussu, and the latter the line Berlancourt-Guivry-Marest. Mangin was now well north of the Ailette, while his right wing was moving east-

Sept. 5.

* In the whole Battle of the Scarpe between 26th August and 3rd September the British took over 16,000 prisoners and some 200 guns.

ward along the Chemin des Dames, and the French
and Americans of the Sixth and Fifth Armies had
driven the Germans from the Vesle, and stood on
the crest between that stream and the Aisne. In
Flanders we had recovered Neuve Chapelle and
Fauquissart, and north of the Lys Plumer's front
ran from Voormezeele by Wulverghem to Ploegsteert. Lens had been evacuated, but not yet
entered by Horne's troops.

The German front now presented a curious spectacle. The flank of the Siegfried zone had been
turned, but the attack was temporarily checked by a
water line. Farther south the enemy attempted to
hold the Canal du Nord to cover his retreat, but
this front had also been turned on 4th September
by the passage of the Tortille River and the Canal
north of Moislains by the British. South, again,
von der Marwitz and von Hutier were falling back
at their best speed to the Siegfried zone with no
chance of an intermediate stand. Meantime Humbert was working his way up the right bank of the
Oise, and Mangin's pincers were feeling at the St.
Gobain *massif*, which played to the south of the
Siegfried zone the part which the Drocourt-Quéant
Switch had been meant to play in the north. Here,
however, the French had a difficult problem, for the
gap between the St. Gobain Forest and the Oise
and the valley of the Ailette were alike too narrow
for an easy advance. Farther east the enemy hold
on the Aisne heights was endangered. The whole
front, which Ludendorff had vainly hoped to establish for the winter in impenetrable defences, was now
a thing of angles and patches, and parts of it as fluid
as wax under flame.

For a week the Allied armies were occupied only in pressing the German retreat. They struck no great blow, for their immediate task was to secure

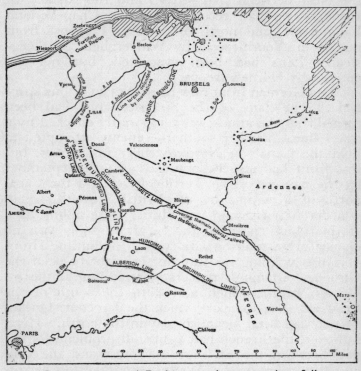

German prepared Positions and more or less fully entrenched Lines, Autumn of 1918.

the kind of front from which they could launch that final battle for which Foch had been preparing since July. Douai was covered by the water line, Cambrai and St. Quentin by the Siegfried zone, and

Laon by the difficulties of the St. Gobain *massif*. Foch had no intention of doing the obvious thing, and delivering a direct attack against sectors on which the enemy would be prepared to meet him. His tactical method was to secure surprise, and strategically his attacks were co-ordinated after the fashion of pincers.

On the 6th Rawlinson advanced seven miles east of Péronne, while Byng reached the western end of Havrincourt Wood. Débeney took Ham, and Humbert pushed two miles beyond *Sept.* 6. Chauny and approached Tergnier. Mangin occupied the lower forest of Coucy, and Dégoutte broadened his front towards the Aisne. On the 7th Byng took the greater part of *Sept.* 7. Havrincourt Wood, and Rawlinson was in Beauvois and Roisel, while Humbert took Tergnier, and crossed the St. Quentin Canal, and Mangin, on the Aisne plateau, pressed north of Vauxaillon. By the 10th Rawlinson was for the most part in the old British reserve lines constructed *Sept.* 10. prior to 21st March, Byng and Horne were beyond our front of that date, while from La Fère to the Ailette von Hutier was back on the German line from which his offensive had begun. The enemy had drawn in his front between the Sensée and the Oise, and from the Scarpe to the Aisne was holding practically a straight line. The result of this was to shorten his front by seventy miles, as compared with the 14th of July, which meant a saving of over thirty divisions. Nevertheless, he was hard pressed for men. Since March he had lost more than one and a half millions, and as reinforcements he had only the 1920 class, already partly drawn upon,

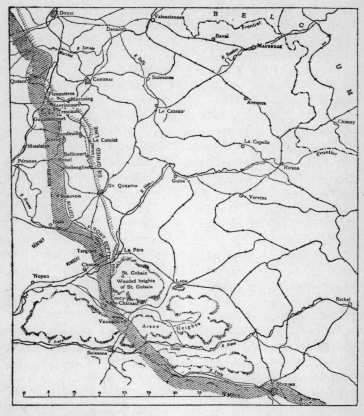

General Situation and Operations on the Front from Douai to the
Aisne in the first part of September.

(The map shows the Allied front, Sept. 10. German communications
and the hinterland of their big salients are also shown.)

100,000 men scraped up from the interior and
the lines of communication, and the 70,000
wounded who returned every month from hospitals.

These reserves were far too few, the more so as their *moral* was clearly declining, and Ludendorff laboured to strengthen every natural defence, such as his northern pillar on the Passchendaele and Wytschaete heights, and to increase by inundations the depth of the water line. He also set about preparing positions well to his rear, and evacuating the civilian population from Douai, Cambrai, and St. Quentin. He had cause for his anxiety, for the whole complexion of the war had changed. Between March and May 1917 the British had forced the Germans back to the Siegfried zone, taking in the process 21,000 prisoners and 200 guns. In 1918, starting from a front many miles farther west, they had performed the same feat in one month, and had 70,000 prisoners and 700 guns to their credit.

North of Havrincourt the enemy was behind the Canal du Nord, and south of it the Siegfried Line ran along the La Vacquerie and Bonavis ridges to the Scheldt Canal, and thence to St. Quentin. In front of that line he held strong forward positions about Havrincourt and Epéhy, which must be taken before the main zone could be assaulted. Accordingly, on the morning of Thursday, 12th September, Byng struck with the 4th *Sept.* 12. and 6th Corps between Trescault and Havrincourt. He took both villages, and cleared the ground for the coming battle. That same day, far to the south, Foch began a new action. His aim was to wipe out the St. Mihiel salient, and open the gate to the Woëvre and the vital railway which fed the enemy on the Aisne and the Oise.

The German position at St. Mihiel, like most salients, was the relic of an unsuccessful offensive.

The great German plan in 1914 had included an
enveloping movement by the Gap of Nancy and
the Heights of the Meuse, as well as by the Sambre
and the Oise. The movement failed, but it left in
the third week of September 1914 a sharp salient
running from Fresnes due south over the wooded

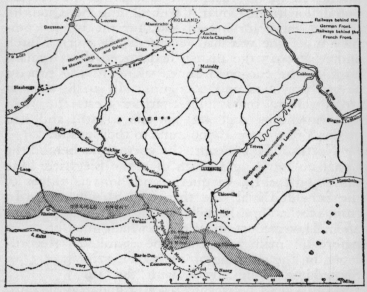

Sketch showing the Strategic Importance of the St. Mihiel Salient
and Verdun with reference to the German Communications.

hills to a bridgehead on the west bank of the river
opposite St. Mihiel, and thence east to Pont-à-
Mousson and the Moselle. This triangle was some
fifteen miles long on its northern side, and twenty-
five on its southern. It was the sharpest on the
whole front; but owing to the curious blind nature

of the country, and to the fact that within it there ran to the apex a sheltered avenue for communications, it had so far been retained by the enemy. It was vigorously assaulted by the French in the spring of 1915, both from north and south, but it was never seriously threatened. For offensive purposes it was of value to the Germans, for it threatened at long range the main line from Bar-le-Duc to Nancy, and it entirely cut the railway running down the Meuse valley from Commercy to Verdun. The result was that the Verdun corner was always an isolated part of the French front, and it was largely for this reason that the Crown Prince launched his attack there in February 1916. Defensively it was important as protecting Metz and the Briey mines.

There was no section of the front where a considerable advance by the Allies would have more profound strategical results. Owing to the Ardennes, the main communications of the enemy with Germany were sharply divided into two. There was a northern system from Liége through the Belgian plain, which served everything as far south as St. Quentin ; and there was a southern system through Trèves and Luxemburg, and through Mayence and Metz, which supplied the front from Laon to Lorraine. If the Allies advanced to the key junction of Longuyon the whole southern system would vanish ; if they cut the main lateral line anywhere it would be grievously put out of gear. The plain of the Woëvre was a nerve centre of the German battle-line.

On 11th September the army group of von Gallwitz had six divisions on the forty miles between Fresnes and Pont-à-Mousson, *Sept. 11.* but since these divisions were not at full strength,

XXIII.

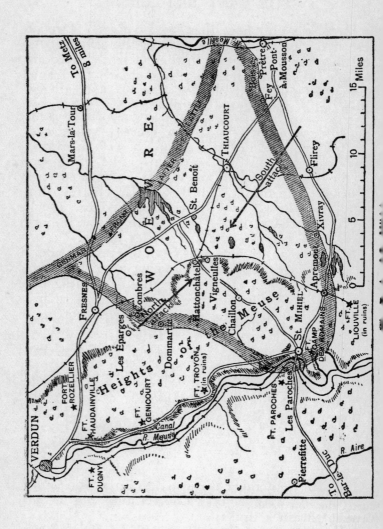

his force was not more than 50,000 men. Two of these divisions were in the apex of the salient. As local reserves he had two further German divisions and one Austro-Hungarian. Ludendorff's extreme shortage of men had decided him to evacuate the salient, and the withdrawal would have begun on the 12th. But he had delayed too long, for Foch was aware of his plan and struck while he was in the act of retirement.

By this time the American divisions were no longer exclusively brigaded with the French and British corps.* The First United States Army had been created under the command of General Pershing himself. At the most the American troops had had six months' experience on the battle-ground, and, judging by the time which it took Britain and France to master the ritual of modern war, the experiment did not lack boldness. Yet it was right that it should be made, for America's superb war effort must culminate as soon as possible in the appearance of her own armies under her own generals. In this, the first major action of America in the field, the French Staff were called in to assist in the scheme, and various seasoned French units were added to the American troops. On the night of the 11th eight American divisions, six in line and two in reserve, lay on the southern front of the salient.† On the northern front were one American

* Three American corps had been so far engaged in the main battle—the 1st (General Liggett) on the Marne and Ourcq, the 2nd (General Read) on the Somme, and the 3rd (General Bullard) on the Vesle.

† The six in line on the south were the 1st, 2nd, 5th. and 42nd, with two of the new National Army, the 89th and 90th.

division and one French, and in the centre opposite the apex at St. Mihiel was the 2nd French Colonial Corps.

At one o'clock on the morning of the 12th the American artillery opened on the eleven-mile front from Fey-en-Haye to Xivray. At five o'clock the first wave of attack crossed the parapets, accompanied by flotillas of tanks. An immense number of Allied airplanes accompanied the advance, and not an enemy machine was seen in the sky. The main attack was from the south, and it moved fast through the narrow lanes and thick woods on the rim of the salient, while the northern attack south of Fresnes struggled southward to join hands. By 10 a.m. the Americans were in Thiaucourt, and had cut the railway within the salient, which meant that the German divisions at the apex were caught between two fires. Meantime the northern attack had taken Combres and reached Dommartin-la-Montagne, while American cavalry were scouring the by-paths of the forests. All day the battle lasted, and early on the morning of the 13th September the northern and southern forces met at Vigneulles,* and the salient had disappeared. For three days the battle continued, and at the close of it the Heights of the Meuse were entirely cleared of the enemy, and the Allied line ran from the Meuse below Pont-à-Mousson, north of the Bois-le-Prêtre, three miles to the east of Thiaucourt, two miles east of St. Benoit, two miles east of Fresnes, and thence along the eastern foot of the Meuse heights to the old Verdun front

Sept. 12.

Sept. 13.

* The 26th Division from the north won the race, closely followed by the 1st from the south.

at Bezonvaux. Already the advance guard of the Americans were under the fire of the fortress guns of Metz.

Fifteen thousand prisoners and over 200 guns had been taken, together with a mass of every kind of stores. The losses of the Allies were very small. Two American divisions had only 300 and 600 casualties apiece, while one division of French cavalry, which took 2,500 prisoners, had only four men killed. The retirement of von Gallwitz was not brilliant, and his communications seem to have fallen into dire confusion.

The destruction of the St. Mihiel wedge was an achievement of the utmost significance. It proved, if proof were needed, the quality of American troops organized in the largest units and acting under their own commanders. Strategically, it vastly assisted the Allied communications, and restored in that area the power of attack at any moment and in any direction. In truth, in that angle of our front which had its apex at Verdun the Allies were now in the position which the Germans had held in the northern salient before the March offensive. They could strike at their will east into Lorraine, or north down the Meuse and into Champagne, and till the attack was delivered the enemy could not tell which side of the salient was their objective. In that angle lay the First United States Army, and other American armies would follow, so that the concentration of the great new Allied reserves had taken place in a region which menaced more than any other the whole existence of the German front. No enemy salient any longer remained as an advance guard in the West.

Something still remained to be done in the north
for in certain sections Haig was not yet in close

Sept. 13. enough touch with the Siegfried zone
On the 13th Byng advanced in the Gouzeaucourt and Havrincourt area ; on the 15th Raw-

Sept. 15– linson took Maissemy, and on the 17th
17. Holnon.   Meantime, on the 14th, Mangin and Dégoutte had attacked north of
the Aisne and along the Vesle, and the former took
Allemant and Laffaux Mill, and next day Vailly an
the key position of Mont des Singes.   On the 18th

Sept. 18. Byng and Rawlinson struck on a front
of thirteen miles between Holnon and
Gouzeaucourt, and made an advance of some two
miles, while a counter-attack between Trescault and
Mœuvres was repulsed during the afternoon.   Next

Sept. 19. day Byng retook Mœuvres, the greater
part of which had been lost on the 17th
On the 18th Débeney, fighting on a front of six

Sept. 18– miles west and south-west of St. Quen-
19. tin, took Savy Wood, and on the 19th
Humbert increased his ground east of the
Crozat Canal.   All this time Plumer and Horne
were steadily making local gains in their area to
prepare the way for the coming battle.

Thereafter there was a lull, but on the 24th Raw-

Sept. 24. linson pushed forward between the Omi-
gnon and St. Quentin, and took Selency.
South of St. Quentin Débeney had been steadily
creeping on, and by the 24th had taken Vendeuil,
Dallon, and Essigny, and reached the right bank of
the Oise.   The stage had now been set, and Byng,
Rawlinson, Débeney, and Humbert from the Scarpe
to the Oise were close up against the last German

defences, while Mangin had fought his way to the edge of the Chemin des Dames.

Foch was now ready for his supreme effort. Since 15th July he had reduced the enemy's strength by half a million, and with the aid of the American reserves had increased his own by the same number. Ludendorff had no longer sufficient troops to defend his long western front. He could only save a breakdown in one part by thinning another, and if the attacks were simultaneous he could not repel them. His one hope was his water-line and the Siegfried zone, continued to the south and east by the Brynhild and Hunding Lines—lines to which the Allies had not yet advanced. The Siegfried zone, as General von Ardenne about this time told his countrymen for their comfort, was not a line, but a fortressed quadrilateral, 38 miles by 25, "a granite wall of 24,000 square kilometres." Ludendorff issued to his divisions elaborate instructions about their tactical precautions against tanks, but he relied chiefly on his prepared defences. These, he hoped, would enable him to stand with a minimum garrison, till such time as the advent of winter took the edge off the Allies' ardour.

But before Foch struck news came of great doings in the East. On 12th September Franchet d'Esperey moved forward in the Balkans, and on the 19th Allenby began his whirlwind advance in Palestine. Germany was already drawing in all her far-flung detachments for the defence of the West; she was pleading with Austria for support; and Turkey and Bulgaria were left to their own resources. The moment had come for the Allies to press in everywhere on the yielding fortress.

Sept. 12 and 19.

CHAPTER CLXI.

BULGARIA MAKES PEACE.

Malinov becomes Premier of Bulgaria—Bulgaria's Policy—The Salonika Front up to September 1918—The Italians in Albania—Franchet d'Esperey's Plan—Allied and Bulgarian Dispositions—The Attack of 15th September—Bulgarian First and Second Lines carried—The Serbians cross the Tcherna—British and Greeks attack at Lake Doiran—General Bulgarian Retreat—Fall of Prilep—Bulgaria sues for Peace—Capitulation signed 30th September—Its Terms—Effect in Germany—Allies advance to the Danube—Flight of King Ferdinand—Effect on Strategy of the War—The Position of Turkey.

ON 15th June M. Malinov succeeded M. Radoslavov as Premier of Bulgaria. There was no popular movement behind the change; it was devised and executed by King Ferdinand, with the concurrence of the fallen Premier ; and *June* 15. its motive was to give the Government a spurious air of reformation in the event of negotiations with the Allies. M. Malinov was a politician with an ambiguous record, having been by turns Russophil and Germanophil ; his chief characteristic was that, whatever faction he belonged to, he kept a foot in the other camp. For honest politics there was scant hope in any class of Bulgaria's public men. Scarcely one but had subscribed to her wildest demands for territorial acquisitions in

Greek and Serbian Macedonia ; scarcely one but had affirmed with every emphasis of rhetoric his undying devotion to the cause of the Central Powers.

Yet in June, in spite of Germany's apparent triumphs in the West, Bulgaria was beginning to grow anxious. She looked with uneasy eyes on Turkey's new arrogance, which led her to defy Germany in her Transcaucasian policy; and the question of the Dobrudja was becoming rapidly a bone of contention between all the partners of the Teutonic League. By the Peace of Bucharest Constanza and the greater part of the Dobrudja had been placed under a *condominium* of her allies, and she could get no assurance that her will would ultimately prevail. She was quarrelling bitterly with Turkey over Thracian questions, and there also Germany seemed inclined to temporize with Constantinople. Bulgaria, herself skilled in political treachery, saw too clearly the signs of the same thing in her masters. She sought to establish her autocracy in the Balkans, but she had no desire to be herself a part of the greater autocracy of Berlin. Ferdinand, who dabbled in the classics, may have remembered the Roman historian's phrase : " *Germani sociis pariter atque hostibus servitudinem imposuerant.*" * Above all, he was a shrewd observer, and judged rightly the weakness of Germany's whole position. So, while he was loud in his protestations of loyalty to the Teutonic League, in which all his Ministers joined, he was casting about for some cover should the skies fall. To quote M. de Kallay's famous

* " The Germans had imposed slavery on friend and foe alike."—Tacitus, *Hist.*, IV., p. 73.

saying, he was looking for the cart filled with straw in case he might have to jump from the window.*

The Allied front in the Balkans had been all but stagnant since the futile offensive of May 1917. In December of that year the Commander-in-Chief, General Sarrail, who had been an unrelieved failure, had been recalled, and his place taken by General Guillaumat, the former commander of the French Second Army. Throughout the early part of 1918 there had been a considerable readjustment of the Allied troops. Units had been withdrawn from the French and British commands for the front in the West, but the Italians had strengthened their force in Albania, and the new Greek Army had been immensely increased, so that it represented the largest Allied contingent. On 30th May *May 30.* the troops raised by Venizelos showed their quality by attacking the Bulgarian positions just west of the Vardar, on a front of seven and a half miles, advancing one and a quarter miles, and taking 2,000 prisoners. The movement was carried out by the Seres Division, which had the humiliation of Fort Rupel to avenge, and it gave them command of the Liumnitsa valley in which Ghevgeli stood.

In June, General Franchet d'Esperey succeeded Guillaumat; and during the summer, by a number of local actions, the position of the Allied front was eased and strengthened. Meantime the *moral* of the Bulgarian forces was not improving, desertions were frequent, and an offensive planned to take place west of Lake Ochrida had to be postponed for this reason. During July the French and Italians moved south-west of Ochrida in the direction of Elbasan,

* See Vol. IX., p. 89.

their purpose being to straighten the front between the Adriatic and the lake. The important road junction of Berat was taken by the Italians, and over a thousand prisoners. The failure of the Austrian

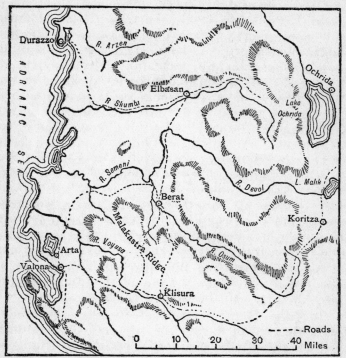

Scene of the Operations in Albania, July and August 1918.

attack in Italy led to a steady activity by both sides in Albania. Towards the close of July an Austrian counter-attack drove General Ferrero back to Berat, thereby endangering the French on his right. Between 22nd and 26th August further counter-

attacks retook Berat and forced Ferrero back some
Aug. 22–
26.
five miles to the Malakastra ridge between the Voyusa and the Yanitsa, which
was the last defence of the harbour of Va-
lona.   This withdrawal necessitated a further retreat
of the French left wing.   Thereafter, the Albanian
front was quiet, and the interest of Europe in the
Balkan battle-ground languished.   Its difficulties
were so notorious, the demands of other areas so
urgent, that it was generally believed that the war
would end with the opposing forces much in their
present positions.

This expectation was to be dramatically reversed.   The Allied High Command perceived that,
so soon as Germany was gravely jeopardized in the
West, there must come a weakening of the allegiance
of her Eastern allies ; for their hope of military
support from her would be gone, and the bribes for
which they had espoused her cause would become
the most worthless of promissory notes.   A vigorous
attack upon Bulgaria and Turkey would, at its worst,
complicate Germany's military problem, and at its
best might put these discontented tributary states
out of action.   In the case of Bulgaria the best was
scarcely to be hoped for, so formidable seemed her
mountain defences.   But a bold offensive might
disintegrate her political unity, and bring to a head
the dissatisfaction of her people and her armies with
what promised to be a campaign of barren sacrifice.

The enemy front was held from left to right by
the II. and I. Bulgarian Armies east of the Vardar,
the XI. German Army (Bulgarian in constitution,
but with a German Staff and a German General)
west of the Vardar, and an Austrian detachment in

Albania. Facing it from east to west lay the British and Greeks east of the Vardar; the French and Serbians (the latter including Yugo-Slav regiments) between the Vardar and Monastir; an Italian detachment, under General Mombelli, west of Monastir; a further French contingent, and then Ferrero's Italians to the Adriatic. Of the total Allied forces, Greece supplied nine divisions, France eight, Serbia five, Britain four, and Italy, apart from her Albanian army, had one and a half divisions at Monastir.

The key to the Bulgarian front was Uskub, for, if that place were won, the communications would be cut between the two parts of the enemy force. An advance against it by the narrow trench of the Vardar valley was out of the question, and it could be taken only by a turning movement from the east or the west. On the east such an operation was impracticable, because of the great barrier of the main Balkan range running from west to east. On the west there was better hope, for there the ranges ran irregularly with a general direction of north to south. In the autumn of 1916 the Allies had taken Monastir; but their advance could not be continued, since east of the town was the great bend of the Tcherna, containing the Selechka Mountains, and while the enemy held these it was impossible to advance towards Prilep and the Babuna Pass, which led to Uskub. The first stage in any action must be to clear the Tcherna bend and the Selechka range.

Franchet d'Esperey resolved to make his attack, not from Monastir, but from the east in the space between the Tcherna and the Vardar. In that area, north and north-east from Lake Ostrovo, the Allied front lay roughly along the Kaimakchalan and Dobropolye ranges, which formed the old Serbian frontier ; but in certain vital parts the Bulgarians held the crest, and had created along the south slopes an apparently impregnable position. Franchet d'Esperey's plan was to take the enemy by surprise with an attack on a narrow front, and in the event of success to extend his area of assault on both flanks and make a push for the Tcherna. He argued that if he could carry the first and second Bulgarian lines on this side the river, the enemy's resistance might be so weakened as to permit of a real break through ; for, though the Bulgarian communications were better than those of the Allies, they were fighting in a sense on exterior lines, and it might be possible by a swift advance to split their front. To puzzle the enemy as to the area of the main attack the British 27th Division on 1st September made a feint attack in the Vardar valley.

On Saturday, 14th September, the Allied guns bombarded heavily the line which ran north-east from Kaimakchalan. Early on the morning of Sunday the 15th, the Serbians, under *Sept.* 15. Mishitch, with the French on their left, attacked the seven-mile front between Mount Sokol and Vetrenik. They were immediately successful. With a fury hoarded through two years of difficult waiting, the Serbs pressed up the steep hillsides, won the crest, and carried all the enemy's first line. The French were stayed for a time at the razor back of Sokol, but early on the 16th this *Sept.* 16. was taken, and, according to plan, the front of attack was enlarged on both sides to some sixteen miles. That day the Allies went five miles forward, and through the enemy second lines ; the Yugo-Slav Division fighting with the Serbs had reached the vital crest of Koziak, nearly 6,000 feet high, and were looking down on the affluents of the Lower Tcherna ; more than 3,000 prisoners and 24 guns had been taken at the expense of few Allied casualties.

It was one of those assaults the impetus of which grows with each mile of advance. On the 17th the Allies were twenty miles *Sept.* 17. beyond their starting-point, and their front had stretched to a width of twenty-five miles. On the 18th the Serbians had reached and crossed the Tcherna, and were pushing *Sept.* 18. towards Prilep by the eastern skirts of the Selechka Mountains, while their cavalry had entered Poloshko, and their right wing was approaching the Vardar itself. A little more and the road and railway would be cut, which formed the immediate connection between the enemy's right and left armies. Meantime, the British and the Greeks facing the Bulgarian I. and II. Armies made it certain that no reserves would be sent westward, for on the 18th they attacked east and west of Lake Doiran, while the Greek 1st Corps of three divisions pinned the enemy down on the Struma.

The Doiran battle was a hard struggle, for the enemy was prepared, and knew the place for the key of his whole front. General Milne had but two corps, the 12th and the 16th, both now fallen below one-half of their normal establishment. West of the lake lay the 26th and 22nd British Divisions, the Greek Seres Division, and a French regiment, the whole under Lieutenant-General Sir H. F. Wilson. East of the lake was the Cretan Division and the

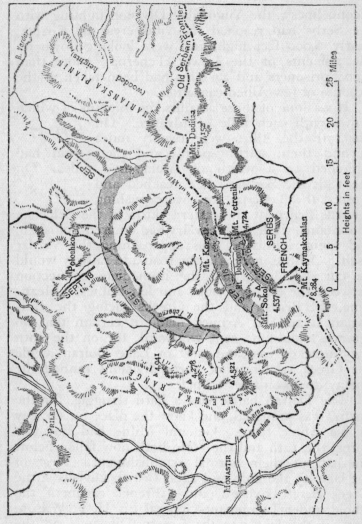

D'Esperey's Victory on the Serbian Frontier Range and the Push towards Prilep (September 15-18, 1918).

British 28th Division, both under the other corps commander, Lieutenant-General Sir C. F. Briggs. On the 18th the Allies won ground in both areas, but not their whole objectives. The height called the Grand Couronne, which had baffled us the year before, still repelled our efforts. On the 19th the attack was repeated, but still *Sept.* 19. the front held. Meantime, to the west the whole line was in action from Monastir to the Vardar. The Serbians were across that river and far north of the Tcherna, and the enemy was retreating in complete disorder, burning the villages which he abandoned. By the 22nd the Bulgarians had fallen back from the Doiran front, *Sept.* 22. closely pursued by the British and the Greeks. By the night of the 23rd the Serbians were in Gradsko, and since the 15th had *Sept.* 23. advanced forty miles—beyond doubt one of the great exploits of the campaign. The British and Greeks were pressing east of the Vardar, across the Belesh Mountains, towards the Strumnitza; the French were approaching Prilep; and Mombelli's Italians were moving north and east of Monastir into the Tcherna bend. Next *Sept.* 24. day French cavalry entered Prilep, and found huge quantities of abandoned stores.

The Bulgarian position was now most serious. The direct communications of their armies were completely severed; more, their broken right wing had now but one way of retreat open—the road from Prilep by Kirchevo and Uskub. By the evening of the 25th the Serbians had the Babuna *Sept.* 25. Pass and the town of Ishtip; they were close on Veles, and Uskub was almost within their grasp. The enemy front was cut in two, and the halves driven into a divergent retreat. Its right wing, the XI. Germany Army, was being pressed north-east towards Kaikandelen. Its left wing, the I. and II. Bulgarian Armies, was pushed north to the Strumnitza, and the British * had entered Bulgaria at Kosturino, a hundred miles south of Sofia. The Austrians in Albania had their flank in the air.

Moreover, the enemy was making but a poor defence. The spirit had clearly gone out of him, and he was being flung from post to pillar at the Allies' will. He was manifestly beaten and demoralized, and in the main he owed his condition to the superior prowess of his opponents. The conduct of every section of the Allied command had been superb, and especial mention should be made of the Greeks and the Serbians. M. Venizelos' new levies had behaved like veterans, and had shown a fighting quality scarcely revealed in their race since the great age of Hellas. As for the Serbians and the Yugo-Slavs, they had advanced with the patient and relentless fury of men who have to avenge a martyred people and a ruined land. They swarmed over precipitous mountains as if they had been level lawns ; they broke through the strongest defences like steel through wax ; by sheer indomitable courage they routed the enemy wherever and in whatever numbers they found him. The crumbling Teutonic League was faced by men who had already gone through the nether pit of suffering, and for whom nothing mortal had any terrors.

* The Derbyshire Yeomanry, the leading troops of the 16th Corps, who had been brought from the right to the left of the Anglo-Hellenic Army.

For Bulgaria the end had come. She saw no prospect of aid from her allies, and, now as ever a devotee of *realpolitik*, she resolved to make the best of a bad business. On the night of Thursday the

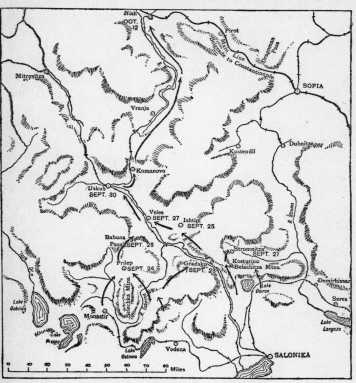

The Allied Advance into Serbia.

26th, a Bulgarian staff officer appeared under a flag of truce at the British Headquarters. *Sept. 26.* Speaking on behalf of Todorov, the Bulgarian Commander-in-Chief, he asked for a suspension of hostilities for forty-eight hours, to permit the arrival of authorized delegates to discuss the conditions of peace. General Milne referred the request by telephone to General Franchet d'Esperey, who refused the armistice but undertook to receive

Sept. 28. the delegates. On the evening of Saturday, the 28th, General Lukov, Commanding the Bulgarian II. Army, the Bulgarian Minister of Finance, and M. Radev, the ex-Minister,

Sept. 29. arrived at Salonika, and next day were received by Franchet d'Esperey. They accepted without demur the Allied terms. These were : that the Bulgarian army should be immediately demobilized and its arms and equipment placed in Allied custody ; that all Greek and Serbian territory at present occupied by Bulgaria should be at once evacuated ; that all Bulgarian means of transport, including her railways and her ships on the Danube, should be placed at the Allies' disposal ; that Bulgaria should cease to be a belligerent except with the Allies' consent ; that her territory should be available for their operations, and that strategic points should be occupied by British, French, or

Sept. 30. Italian troops.* On the morning of Monday, 30th September, these conditions were ratified by the Allied Governments. At noon the armistice was signed at Salonika, and Bulgaria ceased to be a participant in the war.

Meantime, in the past few days the Allied armies had been sweeping forward. On the

Sept. 27– 27th the British took Strumnitza, and
30. advanced north and east along the river valley. On that day the Serbians captured Veles

* See Appendix IV.

and on the 30th French cavalry entered Uskub. Farther to the west the French and Italians reached the Elbasan-Ochrida road, and in Albania Ferrero advanced and took Berat.

The news of Bulgaria's defection brought consternation to Berlin. At first the German view was that Malinov had engineered it without the consent of the king and the people ; but this argument was speedily dropped when it became apparent that it was the people and the army who had forced the step, and that the views of Ferdinand mattered little to anybody. Then came brave talk of holding the Danube front, and the name of Mackensen was brought forward as a bogey to check the Allied rejoicings. But Mackensen was in no position to help. He had four divisions in Rumania, and there were some thirty German and fourteen Austro-Hungarian divisions in Russia, much depleted and of poor quality. The Central Powers were not so beloved on that front to make it possible to send reinforcements to the Danube, and even if they had, they could not hope to check Franchet d'Esperey's advance. Germany had perforce to acknowledge defeat in that quarter, and do nothing.

Events marched swiftly in the Balkans. On 4th October Ferdinand abdicated in favour of the Crown Prince Boris, and retired to his estates in Hungary. The new king *Oct. 4.* issued a proclamation announcing that he would respect the constitution, and was " imbued with the spirit of democracy; " but his reign was destined to be as short as that of the other monarchs of the Teutonic League. The Allies advanced to the Danube, meeting with no resistance except from the broken

Austro-German fragments now littered throughout
Serbia.   On 12th October the Ser-
Oct. 12.   bians entered Nish, their ancient capital.
There had been a brilliant naval raid on Durazzo by
Italian and British cruisers on 2nd October; on the
7th the Italians occupied Elbasan, and on the 14th
they took Durazzo.   On the 19th, twenty-
Oct. 19.   four days after the launching of the
offensive, the Allies reached the Bulgarian shore of
the Danube.   By the end of the month the Serbians
were in Belgrade, and the Balkan States south of the
Danube and the Save were virtually cleared of the
enemy.

The downfall of Bulgaria was such a *peripateia*
as rarely occurs in a campaign.   In an area which
had been, by universal consent, written down as
incapable of producing a military decision, a hetero-
geneous Allied force moved against defences, elabo-
rated during three years, in what was little more than
an exploratory operation.   There was no vital strategic
objective within forty miles, and those miles were
made up of precipitous mountains and unfordable
rivers.   Yet in three days the formidable enemy was
in flight; in a fortnight he had made peace on terms
of complete surrender; and in three weeks the Allied
cavalry were watering their horses in the Danube.
Bulgaria's power of resistance had decayed at the
heart.   The Salonika campaign, which for three
years had seemed to be a fruitless divergent adventure, found an abundant justification.   The Central
Powers had been since 1914 a beleaguered fortress,
and it is in the way of such fortresses to fall suddenly.
To the besiegers the walls look as stout as ever and

the garrisons as alert, but they cannot read the hearts within; and lo! when they attack for the hundredth time with a somewhat weary resolution, the flag falls and the gates are opened.

Bulgaria had made little of her huckstering. Soured by the injustice of the old Treaty of Bucharest, and led by men without vision, she had deliberately chosen the path of dishonour and the easy advantage. She had already paid a heavy toll in loss of men, in famine, and in a sordid bondage to Germany. She was now to pay the further penalty of surrendering her own will as a nation and submitting humbly to justice. In her conduct of the war she had shown revolting brutality to Serbia and her Balkan neighbours; but on the whole she had behaved well to prisoners of the Western Allies, and, apart from her initial treachery, her record was less black than that of her colleagues. For one man there could be no pity. Her wretched king was one of the meanest figures that ever disgraced a throne. He fled to his refuge beyond the Danube, followed by the hatred of his subjects and the contempt of the civilized world.

The immediate military consequences of Bulgaria's surrender were enormous for the strategy of the war. The southern frontiers of Austria and Rumania were thrown open to an Allied invasion. The subject-races of Austria-Hungary were put in a new position of vantage in their struggle for independence. Above all, the direct communications were cut between Germany and Turkey. No longer could the " Balkanzug " start from Berlin on its four days' journey to Constantinople. It was true that Germany, owing to her command of the Black

Sea, could still keep in touch with the Bosphorus through South Russia and Rumania, and, though Turkey was now outflanked, she was not yet surrounded. Had Germany the will to send support she still had the routes, provided that Turkey had the will to resist.

But Turkey was following fast upon Bulgaria's heels, and already that will had almost gone. For *Sept. 19.* on 19th September Allenby had begun his amazing advance, and on the day when Bulgaria signed the capitulation he was already at the gates of Damascus.

CHAPTER CLXII.

THE LIBERATION OF THE EAST.

T HE capture of Jerusalem on December 9, 1917, left a curious situation. The Turkish Army was split into two parts, with its right wing holding a line curving south-east from about three miles north of Jaffa, and its left running in a semicircle north and east of Jeru- *Dec.* 9, salem astride the Nablus and Jericho 1917. roads, about six miles distant from the city. Between the two wings lay a patch of rocky hill country, with no lateral communications except those far in the rear. Clearly the next step in Allenby's cam-

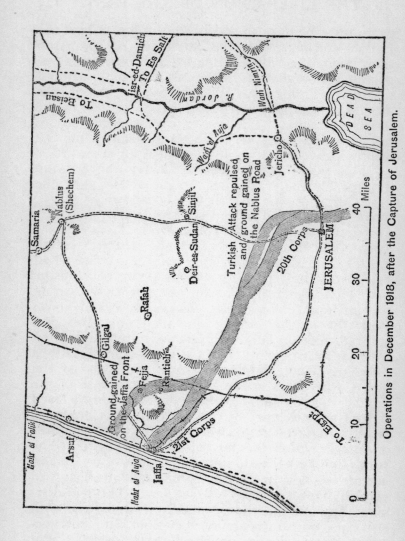

Operations in December 1918, after the Capture of Jerusalem.

paign must be to push east of the Jordan and cut the
Hedjaz railway, with the assistance of the Arab
army from the south. But in that intricate campaigning ground an advance was impossible without
careful preliminaries. When a move came it was
swift and sudden, but it had been led up to by
long preparation. His first care must be to secure
his advanced bases at Jaffa and Jerusalem, for the
enemy was too close to both of them for comfort.

This work was performed during the last ten
days of December. On the night of the 20th the
21st Corps, on the British left, began to *Dec. 20–*
move. The 52nd (Scottish Lowland) *30.*
Division crossed the El Auja stream in
spite of its swollen current, established its footing
on the northern bank, and next day constructed
bridges and brought over its guns. On the 22nd the
54th (East Anglian) Division, on the right, swung
forward and took the villages of Rantieh and Fejja ;
while the 52nd passed beyond their objectives, and
secured high ground that denied any observation
over Jaffa harbour to the enemy. These operations
drove the Turks eight miles from Jaffa, and gave the
21st Corps elbow room. Meantime the task of the
20th Corps, on the British right, had been delayed
by the wild weather of the week before Christmas.
On the night of 26th December the enemy opened
an attack astride the Jerusalem-Nablus road. The
60th (London) Division bore the brunt of it ; and an
assault was also made on the line held by the 53rd
(Welsh) Division east of Jerusalem. The two divisions beat off the enemy, and by noon of the 27th
the 74th and 10th (Irish) Divisions had counter-
attacked, and driven in the Turkish right. That

evening the enemy's attempt had wholly failed, and on the 28th the 20th Corps made a general advance northward. By the night of the 30th it had progressed on a twelve-mile front to a depth running from two to three miles. The result of the operations was that not only had the enemy attempt to retake Jerusalem been signally defeated, but the area held by the British around Jaffa and Jerusalem had been substantially increased, and their main line of lateral communication, the Jaffa-Jerusalem road, put out of danger.

Any further progress northward was out of the question till highways had been improved and the railway from the south brought nearer the front. Allenby's next step must be to secure his right flank by driving the enemy beyond the Jordan, a step which was necessary both as a preparation for a northern advance and to secure a starting-point for an attack upon the Hedjaz line. The land between Jerusalem and the Jordan valley was no easy country to operate in. It fell steeply in a succession of stony ridges and deep-cut glens to the great trench more than 1,000 feet below sea-level. The work was entrusted to the 60th and 53rd Divisions, and the Australian and New Zealand Mounted Division was attached to the 20th Corps for the time being.

Feb. 19, 1918. On February 19, 1918, the 60th Division advanced, and by 9 a.m. had carried El Muntar, the most conspicuous crest among the ridges. Behind it the mounted troops were able to assemble in cover, and on the 20th Talaat ed Dumm was taken, which the Arabs call the Hill of Blood. All day the two infantry divisions crept forward, and the cavalry assisted

Feb. 20.

in a terrain such as cavalry has rarely operated in. At 8.20 on the morning of the 21st the Australians rode into Jericho, patrols *Feb. 21.* were pushed forward to the banks of the Jordan, and the Turks retired across the river. It had been a most difficult piece of work, performed through appalling country in the worst of weather. So impossible was the ground that one battery of field artillery took thirty-six hours to cover eight miles.

Allenby's right flank was now secure, but he must broaden his base before he could undertake an attack east of Jordan against the Hedjaz railway. He must seize the high ground on the north bank of the Wadi el Aujah, which enters the river north of Jericho, and thereby control the approaches by the road from Beisan; and he must push north of Jerusalem on both sides of the Nablus road so as to prevent the use by the enemy of all the northern routes to the lower Jordan valley. The 20th Corps was accordingly disposed in two parts. Its right wing endeavoured to secure the Jordan to a point north of the Wadi el Aujah; then came a gap which was sufficiently protected by the intricate nature of the country; while its centre and left were directed along the Nablus road to the line Sinjil-Deir es Sudan. It was arranged that the 21st Corps should make a small movement to conform. The total advance contemplated was one of seven miles on a front of twenty-six.

This stage in the operations began on 8th March. At first it went swiftly; but on the 9th resistance stiffened, and the 20th Corps had some heavy fighting before, on 11th March, *Mar. 8–11.* they obtained all their objectives. Next day the 21st

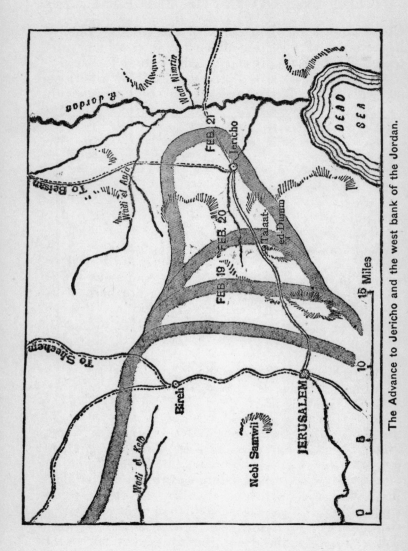

The Advance to Jericho and the west bank of the Jordan.

Corps completed their share of the work. Allenby had won a very strong defensive line, which protected his flank in any movement beyond Jordan.

The way had now been prepared for a serious attempt on the Hedjaz railway, in conjunction with

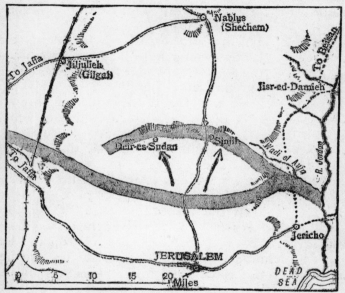

The Advance on the Nablus Road.

the Arab army from the south. The latter force, under Sherif Feisal, the son of the King of the Hedjaz, was based on Akaba, and since the beginning of the year had been pushing north up the Hedjaz line till it was within seven miles of Maan, while isolated detachments were well to the north-west of that place, and had raided and cut the railway. Tafile, fifteen miles from the south-east corner of

the Dead Sea, had been taken by the Arabs, and
held till enemy reinforcements, including a German
battalion, reoccupied it in March. Allenby's first
plan was for a raid on the line, which would damage
it by the destruction of the viaduct and tunnel near
Amman, and might, by forcing the recall of the
Tafile and Maan garrisons, open the way for Sherif
Feisal.

Amman lay thirty miles north by east of Jericho.
Beyond the Jordan was a mile or so of marsh and
scrub; then clay ridges deeply cut by gullies; and beyond them the stony and swampy plateau of Moab.
Amman itself lay in a pocket of the tableland, through
which ran the Hedjaz line. The expedition, which
was entrusted to the 60th Division, the Australian
and New Zealand Mounted Division, the Imperial
Camel Brigade, and brigades of light-armoured
cars and mountain artillery, started on the night of
Mar. 21. 21st March in a deluge of rain. Moving
down the Valley of Achor, the troops
found themselves faced with a river in roaring flood
and severe Turkish fire from the scrub on the left
bank. Swimmers managed to reach the farther
shore with tow-ropes, and by 7.45 next morning
Mar. 22. the leading battalion had crossed. By
8.30 a bridge was completed, but it was
not possible to enlarge the bridgehead so long as
daylight lasted, owing to the violence of the enemy
Mar. 23. fire. Early on the morning of the 23rd
a New Zealand regiment managed to
cross, and, galloping northward, drove off the Turks
from the bank. That day three bridges were built,
and by 10 p.m. the 60th Division and most of the
cavalry were east of the river.

On the 24th the 60th Division, working its way up the gullies, carried the position at Shunet Nimrin, which protected the pass leading to Es Salt, and advanced four miles along *Mar. 24.* the Amman road, while the mounted troops followed the tracks to Ain es Sir and Naaur. The weather was an unceasing downpour of rain; all wheeled transport had to be sent back, and the horses could barely keep their footing on the muddy slopes. The cavalry reached Naaur on the evening of the 25th and Ain es Sir on the morning of the 26th. The last dash for the railway now *Mar. 25–* began, the Australians aiming at the line *27.* north of Amman, the New Zealanders at the line south of it, and the Camel Brigade at Amman itself. By the evening of the 27th the New Zealanders reached the railway; but the Camel Brigade was checked a mile west of Amman, and the Australians were also held, though one of their demolition parties blew up a bridge north of the town.

On the 28th a brigade of the 60th Division came up, and a general attack was made on the Amman position, but without success. Things went no better next day, for the Turks *Mar. 28–* had received reinforcements. At two in *30.* the morning of the 30th the attack was renewed; but since artillery could not be brought up, owing to the state of the roads, it was clear that success was impossible. Moreover, enemy forces from the north were threatening our rear at Es Salt, for the trans-Jordan advance had created an acute salient in the British front. Accordingly, Allenby *April 2.* withdrew his troops, and by 2nd April the whole force had recrossed the Jordan, except

XXIII.

9

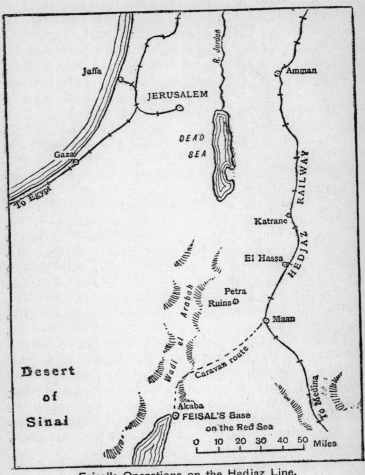

Feisal's Operations on the Hedjaz Line.

for a garrison left on the east bank to hold a bridgehead.

One result of the operations had been to concentrate all available Turkish troops, including part of the garrison of Maan, for the defence of Amman. This gave Sherif Feisal his opportunity. His patrols cut the Hedjaz line north and south of Maan, and on 13th April he carried Senna, and on the 17th the station of Maan itself. *April* 17. There, however, he was checked, and being short of ammunition, fell back on Senna. Meantime, he had made havoc of large sections of the railway both south and north of Maan.

The British withdrawal behind the Jordan allowed the Turks to reoccupy the strong Shunet Nimrin position, from which on 11th April they made heavy and futile attacks on our bridgehead. Allenby resolved to try and cut off the forces at Shunet Nimrin, which were some 5,000 strong, and to endeavour to hold Es Salt till Feisal could come up from the south, with the object of denying the enemy the use of the coming harvest. The 60th Division was to attack at Shunet Nimrin, while a mounted force, consisting of the better part of the Desert Mounted Corps and the Imperial Service Cavalry, was to move northward from Ghoraniyeh to Es Salt, cut the communications of the enemy at Shunet Nimrin, and occupy Jisr ed Damieh in the north, from which the flank attack had come that compelled our previous retirement.

The movement began on 30th April, when the 60th Division captured the outworks at Shunet Nimrin, but could not carry the main *April* 30. position. The cavalry took Es Salt by the evening,

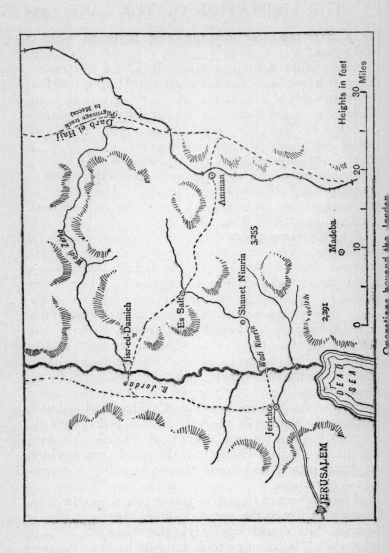

Operations toward the Jordan

132

and left an Australian Brigade to guard its flank in the direction of Jisr ed Damieh. Early next morning, 1st May, this brigade was attacked by the 3rd Turkish Cavalry Division *May 1.* and part of the 24th Division, and was driven back with a considerable loss of guns and transport. This put the cavalry at Es Salt in an awkward predicament, for they were cut loose from their base, since Shunet Nimrin had not fallen. Accordingly, it was arranged to attack the latter point again on 2nd May, the 60th Division advancing from the west and the cavalry from Es Salt in *May 2.* the north-east. But on that day the cavalry had to fight a defensive battle at Es Salt, and so could give little assistance to the 60th Division, which made no headway. As the promised Arab assistance had not been forthcoming, there was nothing for it but to withdraw. By the 4th of *May 4.* May the British troops, except for the bridgehead garrison, were again west of the Jordan.

For the time being Allenby had to hold his hand. The grave situation on the Western Front made it necessary for him to reorganize his forces, for all white troops that could be spared were ordered to France. Early in April the 52nd Division had gone, to be followed immediately by the 74th. Presently, nine regiments of Yeomanry left, ten more British battalions, and a number of siege batteries and machine-gun companies, and in May a further fourteen British battalions. To replace these losses the Indian 7th (Meerut) and 3rd (Lahore) Divisions arrived from Mesopotamia, and a number of Indian cavalry regiments and infantry battalions were dispatched from India. In July and August a further batch of British battalions was replaced by Indian units. All this meant a reduction in fighting strength, and complicated provisions for readjustment and training. The summer could therefore witness no British offensive on a large scale.

Nevertheless, there was a good deal of activity. Between the 9th and 11th of April the 21st Corps *April 9–11.* on the British left advanced three miles on a front of twelve, taking among other places the village of Rafat. On 8th June they again *June 8.* attacked on the coast, and deprived the enemy of important observation points. During July and August there were many successful raids by Indian infantry and cavalry. In July the Turks, stiffened by German battalions, made a vigorous attempt to break into the British salient which had its apex at the Jordan bridgehead. On *July 14.* the 14th they attacked its northern flank at Abu Tellul, on the Jericho-Beisan road, and after a momentary success were driven out by the 1st Australian Light Horse Brigade, with a loss of 276 Germans, including 12 officers. A thrust at the same time against the Jordan bridgehead was anticipated and frustrated by the fine charge of an Indian cavalry brigade. During these months, too, the Turks failed to restore the Hedjaz line north and south of Maan, and Medina was definitely cut off from the north.

The stage in the Palestine campaign which we have just recorded was in the main a stage of preparation, intermediate between the brilliant advance on Jerusalem and the still more brilliant operations which were presently to bring Allenby to Damascus and Aleppo. It had been most arduous campaigning, partly owing to the drenching rains of the early spring, and partly to the natural difficulties of the Jordan trench and the hills of Moab. Of its immediate results let Allenby speak :—

" On 12th December the enemy still remained within four miles of Jerusalem. He is now twenty-two miles from the Holy City. To the east he has been driven across the Jordan, and his communications to the Hedjaz raided. His losses between December 12, 1917, and May 31, 1918, were considerable, the number of prisoners amounting to 330 officers and 6,088 other ranks. His one attempt on a large scale to assume the offensive and retake Jerusalem failed, and was turned into a defeat, accompanied by a considerable loss of territory."

We come now to what must rank as the most dramatic tale in the whole campaign, an exploit undertaken at the precise moment when its chances were brightest and its influence on the general strategy of the war most vital, perfectly planned, perfectly executed, and overwhelming in its success. The little campaign, which began three years before on the banks of the Suez Canal, had grown slowly to a major operation. In face of every difficulty the Allies had crept forward, first across the Sinai desert, then after long delays through the Turkish defences of the south, and then in a bold sweep to the gates of the Holy City. It had been always, so to speak, a campaign on sufferance, working only with the margin of strength which could be spared from the greater contest in the West. But it had moved patiently to its appointed end, for it was in the true tradition of those dogged elder wars of Britain which had created the Empire. Our feet might be stayed for a season or retire, but in the long run they always moved forward. The Last Crusade was now approaching its climax, and the Crusaders would have startled the soul of St. Louis and Raymond and Richard of England could they have beheld that amazing army. For only a modest portion of it was drawn from the Western peoples. Algerian and Indian Moslems, Arab tribesmen, men of the thousand creeds of Hindustan, African negroes, and Jewish battalions were among the liberators of the sacred land of Christendom.

In September the Turkish Army of Syria, under the German General Liman von Sanders, held a front from the coast north of Jaffa through the hills of Ephraim to a point half way between Nablus and Jerusalem, and thence to the Jordan and down its eastern bank to the Dead Sea. On their left flank, at a considerable distance, the Arabs of Sherif Feisal were threatening the neighbourhood of Maan. The Turkish dispositions were, from west to east: the VIII. Army, under Jevad Pasha, comprising the 22nd and Asian Corps (the 7th, 20th, 19th, 16th, and 46th Divisions); the VII., under Fevsi Pasha, comprising the 3rd and 20th Corps (the 1st, 11th, 26th, and 53rd Divisions); and east of the Jordan, the IV., under Kutchuk Jemal Pasha, which included the 2nd and 8th Corps (the 28th and 62nd Divisions). All these units were greatly below establishment. With a ration strength of over 100,000, they had in line only some 32,000 rifles, 4,000 sabres, and 400 guns, and the garrison of Maan and the posts on the Hedjaz railway gave them a further 6,000 rifles and 30 guns. Their general reserve was small—3,000 rifles and 30 guns, distributed between Tiberias, Nazareth, and Haifa. Against this force Allenby had two divisions of cavalry, two mounted divisions, seven infantry divisions (the Meerut, Lahore, 53rd, 54th, 10th, 60th, and 75th—the British divisions having now a large admixture of Indian troops), an Indian infantry brigade, four extra battalions, and the equivalent of a French infantry brigade—a total of 12,000 sabres, 57,000 rifles, and 540 guns. The situation had been reversed since the days of Gaza. Moreover, Liman von Sanders' command had behind it a record of failure ; and above it, as above the whole Teutonic League, the skies had darkened.

It was the Allied interest to strike soon, for beyond the enemy front lay the plains of Sharon and Esdraelon, which would become swamps with the first winter rains. Allenby's strategic plan could not be in doubt. It was difficult to join hands with Feisal if the communications of any force east of the Jordan were liable to be cut by the enemy transferring troops from the west to the east bank, and this danger remained so long as the Turks controlled the crossing at Jisr ed Damieh. If, however, the enemy west of the Jordan were defeated, this obstacle would be removed, and the IV. Army east of the river must either retreat or be isolated. The communications of the VII. and VIII. Armies were very imperfect, running mainly through Beisan to Damascus. This meant that the VIII. Army, on the enemy's right, had no direct communication (all the routes trending north-east by El Afule and Beisan to the junction of the Palestine and Hedjaz lines at Deraa) except by the road along the western shore of the Sea of Galilee. Now, behind the Turkish front lay the hills of Samaria, stretching to the sea at Mount Carmel, and beyond these the

Plain of Esdraelon and the Valley of Jezreel. If, therefore, the front of the VIII. Army could be broken and our cavalry sent through, they might ride over the coastal Plain of Sharon, cross the hills, and reach Esdraelon and Jezreel before the enemy could make good his retreat. Once El Afule and Beisan were in our hands the VIII. and VII. Armies would be cut off; and if Deraa, east of the Jordan, could be reached by Feisal, the Turkish armies would cease to exist. Allenby, therefore, determined to thin his front elsewhere, and concentrate his energies on breaking up the VIII. Army in the Plain of Sharon and opening a road for the cavalry. He was playing not for a local success, but for final and absolute victory, and he was preparing to use his cavalry as that arm had not been used since the outbreak of the war.

He made his dispositions with extreme care. Opposite the VIII. Army was the British 21st Corps, under Lieutenant-General Sir Edward Bulfin, now comprising the Lahore, Meerut, 54th, 60th, and 75th Divisions, the French detachment and the 5th Australian Light Horse Brigade. Behind it lay the Desert Mountain Corps, under Lieutenant-General Sir Harry Chauvel, waiting to exploit its success. The 20th Corps, under Lieutenant-General Sir Philip Chetwode, lay astride the Nablus road and along the Jordan valley. It now contained only two infantry divisions (the 53rd and the 10th), and most of the cavalry had gone to Bulfin's area. In order to screen their departure, Major-General Sir Edward Chaytor, with the Australian and New Zealand Mounted Division and various other infantry and cavalry units, was ordered to demonstrate eastward,

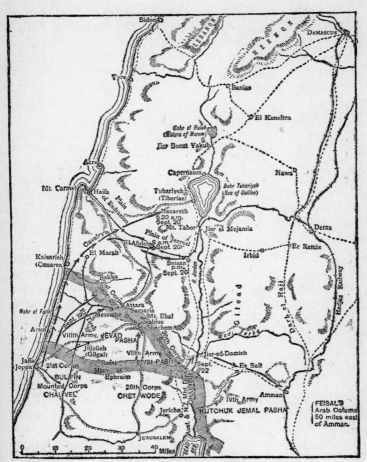

The Decisive Battle.

as if an attack were contemplated beyond the Jordan. This led the enemy to keep the IV. Army in position, and to refrain from strengthening his threatened right wing. Finally, a mobile Arab column, under Feisal, supported by a French mountain battery and British armoured cars, assembled fifty miles east of Amman for the advance on Deraa. Our complete pre-eminence in the air prevented the Turkish aircraft from detecting these preparations. When our attack was launched, it fell everywhere with the shock of an utter surprise.

At 4.30 on the morning of Thursday, 19th September, the 21st British Corps made its attack, its *Sept.* 19. dispositions being, from left to right, the 60th Division, the Meerut, the 75th, the Lahore, the 54th, and the French detachment. Progress on the right in the foothills was necessarily a little slow, but the centre and the left, in the Plain of Sharon, swept clean through the enemy's defences. His first positions fell at once. Presently the 60th Division were at the Nahr Falik (the stream by which, in September 1191, Cœur de Lion's English horsemen won their great victory), and were wheeling to the right against Tul Keram, leaving the coast road clear for the cavalry. By 11 a.m. the 75th Division had taken the ridge of El Tireh, and the Lahore Division had taken Jiljulieh (Gilgal), and were pressing into the foothills. The VIII. Army was in utter rout, pouring along the roads to Nablus and Messudie, desperately harassed by our airmen and mounted troops, while the main body of our cavalry was riding for Esdraelon to cut them off in rear.

That night Chetwode advanced with his 20th

Corps to close the roads leading to the lower Jordan valley. The Turkish VII. Army fought well, but the 53rd and 10th Divisions that night and the next day slowly pressed forward towards Nablus. On the 20th Bulfin, with the 21st Corps, *Sept.* 20. moved through the mountains of Samaria, and by the evening reached the line Bakka-Beit Lud-Massudie Station-Attara. The enemy resistance was stiffening in that difficult country, and he was showing his traditional tenacity in defence. Apparently he did not realize that already his doom was sealed.

For the cavalry had fulfilled their task to the full. By noon on the 19th their leading troops were eighteen miles north of the old front *Sept.* 19. line, and wheeling north-east towards Esdraelon and Jezreel. That afternoon they were through the last barrier of the Samarian hills. The 14th Cavalry Brigade was in El Afule by eight on the morning of the 20th; by 5.30 a.m. the *Sept.* 20. 13th Cavalry Brigade had reached Nazareth, and taken 2,000 prisoners, including part of the staff of Liman von Sanders, who only escaped by the skin of his teeth. That night the 4th Cavalry Division reached Beisan, eighty miles from its starting-point, and seized the railway bridge over the Jordan, while the Australian Mounted Division took Jenin, and so closed the last outlet from the south. In thirty-six hours the trap had been shut. The 21st Corps held the line Samaria-Attara, the 20th Corps the high ground north-east of Nablus and Mount Ebal, and the cavalry the whole hinterland to the north. Between them lay the remnants of the Turkish VIII. and VII. Armies, with no possible way of escape except by the roads south-east to the Jordan crossing at Jisr ed Damieh.

Every track and road was choked with the rout, camps and depots were in flames, and our airmen steadily bombarded each section of the retreat. At *Sept. 22.* 1.30 on the morning of the 22nd the New Zealand Mounted Rifles Brigade, and the West Indian battalions from Chaytor's force, seized the crossing at Jisr ed Damieh, and deprived the two Turkish armies of their last hope of retreat. They were being relentlessly driven by the Allied infantry into the arms of the cavalry. It remained *Sept. 24.* only to reap the fruits of success. By the 24th the two armies had for the most part passed into our hands, with such of their stores as remained undestroyed. Meantime, while the 4th Cavalry Division and the Australian Mounted Division were collecting the fragments, the Desert Mounted Corps had occupied Haifa and Acre, for it was necessary to clear the coast route as soon as possible to provide bases for the next advance.

There now remained of all Liman von Sanders' forces only the IV. Army, east of the Jordan. Till the third day of the battle it had shown no signs of moving, though the west bank of the river was falling steadily under our power. On the morning *Sept. 23.* of the 23rd it began its retreat towards Es Salt and Amman, closely pursued by Chaytor's horsemen, and ruthlessly bombed from the air. That night the New Zealanders entered Es Salt, and two days later Amman fell. Maan had meantime been evacuated. Chaytor and Feisal had now joined hands, and the Arabs pressed the fleeing Turks northward along the Hedjaz railway.

Chaytor remained at Amman to intercept the retreat
of the 2nd Turkish Corps from the Hedjaz, and on the 28th duly added this *Sept.* 28.
unit to the list of captures.

The game was wholly in Allenby's hands. His
next step was to move on Damascus, and so intercept what was left of the Turkish IV. Army in its
northward flight. Chauvel and the Desert Mounted
Corps were ordered to advance in two columns, one
by the south end of the Sea of Galilee and Deraa,
the other round the north end by Capernaum and
El Kuneitra. On the 25th Tiberias was *Sept.* 25.
occupied, and the Australian Mounted
Division concentrated there. On the afternoon of
the 25th the 4th Cavalry Division moved out of
Beisan on its 120-mile ride, and the Australians left
the following day by the northern route. The left-
hand column had a stiff fight at the crossing of the
Jordan, and again at El Kuneitra ; but they made good
progress round the skirts of Mount Hermon, and
by 10 a.m. on the 30th were twelve miles *Sept.* 30.
south-west of Damascus. The right-hand
column had meantime gained touch at Er Remte with
the Arab forces, whose vanguards by the 27th had
entrenched themselves seventeen miles north of
Deraa, across the line of the Turkish retreat. Next
day Feisal took Deraa, and the 4th Cavalry Division
and the Arabs pushed northward. On the 30th
the Australian Mounted Division had closed all the
northern and north-western exits from Damascus,
and the 5th Cavalry Division lay in the *Oct.* 1.
southern outskirts. At six in the morning
of 1st October Feisal and Chaytor entered the city.

It was the twelfth day from the opening of the

attack. Three Turkish armies had melted away, over 60,000 prisoners and between 300 and 400 guns were in Allenby's hands, and the dash for Damascus had destroyed the faintest expectation of

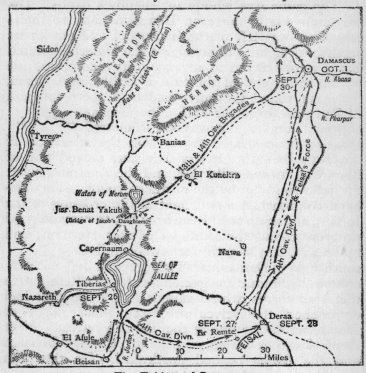

The Taking of Damascus.

an enemy stand. All that remained was a mob of 17,000 Turks and Germans, of whom perhaps 4,000 were effectives, fleeing north without discipline or purpose. Of the many brilliant episodes of those marvellous twelve days, perhaps the most brilliant was the converging movement of Chauvel's Desert Corps and Feisal's Arabs on the most ancient of the world's cities. Damascus had been an emporium when Tyre was young, and she was still a mighty city centuries after Tyre had become a shadow. Rich in holy places—for is it not on that minaret called the "Bride" of her great Mosque that, according to popular belief, the Lord will take His stand at the Day of Judgment?—she had one shrine of peculiar interest for this last Crusade. Within her walls lay the tomb of Saladin, the greatest of those who fought in Palestine the battle of Asia against Europe. One of Feisal's first acts was to remove the tawdry bronze wreath with which the German Emperor, in 1898, had seen fit to desecrate the sleeping-place of the great Sultan.

Allenby did not rest upon his laurels. His next objective was the line Rayak-Beirut, for he wanted a port and a railway running inland, to shorten his communications. On 6th October Rayak was occupied without trouble by the *Oct. 6.* Desert Mounted Corps, and the junction with the broad-gauge line to Aleppo was won. Meantime the Meerut Division had been marching north along the coast from Haifa through Tyre and Sidon, and on the 8th occupied Beirut *Oct. 8.* amid the enthusiasm of the inhabitants. The rest was a triumphal procession. The Desert Corps reached Baalbek on the 11th, and, riding down the valley of Orontes, took Homs *Oct. 11–13.* on the 15th. The 21st Corps, following the coast, occupied Tripoli on the 13th, thereby providing a shorter supply line for the cavalry at Homs.

The next and last stage was Aleppo, that great mart through which, in the Middle Ages, the wealth of Asia flowed to Venice and the West. The 5th Cavalry Division and the armoured cars were sent forward, and after a few small brushes with the

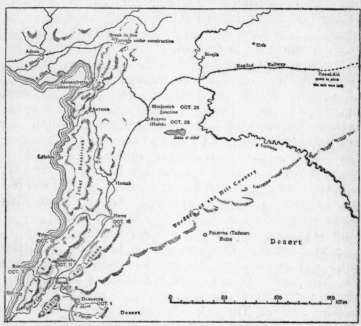

Operations after the Capture of Damascus.

enemy, reached the place on the 25th, where they were joined by an Arab detachment.

Oct. 26. Next day the town was cleared and occupied, Liman von Sanders having fled to Alexandretta. Our cavalry patrols advanced fifteen miles and occupied Muslimie Junction, thereby cutting

the Bagdad railway. Since 19th September the
Allies had moved their front 300 miles to the northwards. They had taken over 75,000 prisoners and
huge quantities of stores. They had entirely destroyed the Turkish armies in Syria, and driven the
enemy back behind the Cilician Gates. They had
cut, too, the much prized line which was to link
Berlin with the Persian Gulf. The Turkish empire,
and all the hopes that Germany had built on it, were
crumbling under the deadly pressure from the south.

It was the moment for General Marshall to move
in Mesopotamia. One British column advanced up
the Tigris, and another along the Kifri-Kirkuk-
Altun Keupri road. The left column forced the
Turkish force on the Tigris steadily back, cut off its
retreat by means of an enflanking cavalry movement,
and on 30th October compelled its sur- *Oct. 30.*
render. It numbered 7,000 men, under
its general, Ismail Hakki. In the meantime the
right-hand column had taken Kirkuk on the 25th
and advanced to Altun Keupri. The resounding
events in Syria had weakened the enemy resistance
everywhere, and its echoes were heard in Persia and
Transcaspia. Mosul was now within General Marshall's reach, but when he entered it on *Nov. 3.*
3rd November it was without opposition.
For Turkey, like Bulgaria, had followed the path of
wisdom, and surrendered to the Allies.

On the 3rd of July the Sultan Mahomed V. died.
He was an old and feeble man at his best, and had
never been more than a puppet in the *July 3.*
hands of the Committee of Union and
Progress. His successor had not been many weeks on

the throne before he gave signs of some independence
of character. The estrangement between Enver

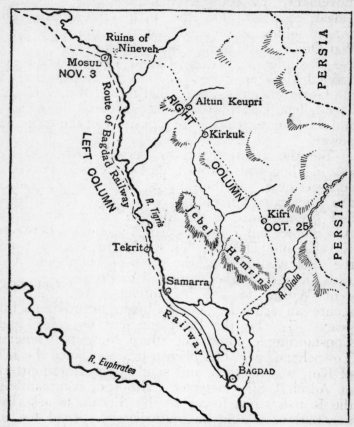

The Advance to Mosul.

and Talaat was increasing, and as Germany's prospects darkened in the West the policy of *sauve qui
peut* began to have supreme attractions for Turkey's

governors. The defection of Bulgaria, and Allenby's exploits in Syria, gave impetus to the movement. On 10th October Enver and *Oct.* 10. Talaat resigned. On the 11th Izzet Pasha, an honest soldier, succeeded Enver at the War Office, and Tewfik Pasha, a colour- *Oct.* 11. less ex-diplomat, became Grand Vizier. Javid re- mained Minister of Finance, and the constitution of the Government suggested that though Enver might have fallen, Talaat was still active behind the scenes, and the Committee still the repository of the supreme power.

But the situation was too serious to be met by any juggling with Cabinet appointments. Turkey's end was near, and the blindest of the Young Turks was constrained to admit the truth. The British and French were at the Maritza and marching on Adrianople, and a Greek corps was moving between Kavalla and Drama. Presently the enemy from the west would be at the gates of Stamboul. On 14th October Turkey appealed to Presi- dent Wilson to use his influence to *Oct.* 14. secure an armistice and to begin negotiations for peace. To this the President sent no reply, and Constantinople could not afford to wait. General Townshend, who had been a prisoner since the fall of Kut, was released, and sent to the headquarters of Admiral Sir Somerset Calthorpe, commanding the British naval forces in the Ægean, to ask that negotiations should be immediately opened for an armistice. Admiral Calthorpe stated the condi- tions on which this would be granted, and during the last week of October the Turkish plenipoten- tiaries arrived at Mudros. On the 30th an armis-

tice was signed, and from noon on the 31st hostilities ceased. The main terms were the
opening of the Dardanelles and the Black
Sea, the immediate repatriation of Allied
prisoners, the demobilization of the Turkish Army,
the severing of all relations with the Central Powers,
and the placing of Turkish territory at the disposal
of the Allies for military purposes.*

Oct. 30–31.

The surrender of Turkey brought to an end the
hopes of the Central Powers of using gains in the
East to redress the balance in the West. It shattered
the whole fabric of bluff and intrigue built up labori-
ously during the past four years between the Baltic
and the Indian Ocean. It left Germany with no
crutch to lean on but her Western armies. We turn
now to that battlefield where, long before Turkey
signed the armistice, the fate of those armies had
been decreed.

* See Appendix VII.

CHAPTER CLXIII.

THE BREAKING OF THE GERMAN DEFENCES.

Ludendorff's Position on 25th September—The Two Danger Points—German and Allied Dispositions—Foch's Plan—Pershing and Gouraud Attack on 26th September—Difficulty of Pershing's Terrain—Haig attacks towards Cambrai on the 27th—The Nature of the Siegfried Zone—The Belgian Attack on the 28th—Attack of Mangin and Berthelot—Haig's Attack on the 29th—The Storming of the Scheldt Canal—Débeney enters St. Quentin—Ludendorff's Position—German Retreat between the Lys and Arras—Gouraud crosses the Arne—Haig's Attack of 8th October—End of the Siegfried Zone—The British approach Le Cateau—Fall of Cambrai—Pershing attacks East of the Meuse—Summary of the Battle—Germany in Defeat.

O N the 25th of September the Germans between the North Sea and the Moselle held a position difficult, indeed, but not hopeless. They still possessed many of the chief points of vantage in the West—the Ypres ring of hills, the Wytschaete-Messines ridge, the St. Gobain *massif*, the main part of the Aisne heights, the uplands about Rheims, and a strong line covering the road down the Meuse valley. They had the waterline in front of Douai, and the Siegfried system still intact, covering Cambrai and St. Quentin; while its extension, the Hunding and Brynhild zones, defended the country between the Oise and the Aisne and the positions in Champagne. Their

Sept. 25.

151

worst anxiety was on behalf of their left, for at all costs the Allies must be warded off Mezières and Longuyon and the vital railway of the south.   There, accordingly, Ludendorff had strengthened his forces, for he believed that the American attack at St. Mihiel would be followed by an advance into Lorraine.

His second main preoccupation was his centre from Douai to St. Quentin.   He could not afford to lose Cambrai, because it was the road and railway junction which supplied the Siegfried zone, and he had some cause for nervousness, since in front of it was a gap in the water defences.   The Siegfried zone itself must be maintained, for behind it lay the great railway from Lille by Valenciennes and Hirson to Mezières, on which his position was based.   If this were breached his whole battle plan would be in ruins.   Therefore he laboured to keep his left and centre at maximum strength, for, in spite of his experiences in August and September, he could not conceive the possibility of an assault by the Allies on every section.

The dispositions of the opposing forces on the eve of the final struggle may be briefly recapitulated. The German group commands remained as before —Rupprecht on the right, von Boehn and the Imperial Crown Prince in the centre, and von Gallwitz on the left.   From the north the order of their armies was as follows : the IV., under von Armin, from the sea to the Lys ; the VI., under von Quast, to a point north of Arras ; the XVII., under Otto von Below, in front of Douai and Cambrai ; the II., still under von der Marwitz, but about to pass under von Carlowitz, to St. Quentin ; the XVIII., under von Hutier, astride the Oise ; the VII., under von

Eberhardt, north of the Aisne ; the I., under von Mudra, north of Rheims ; the III., under von Einem, in Champagne ; the V., presently to be under von der Marwitz, north of Verdun ; and, covering

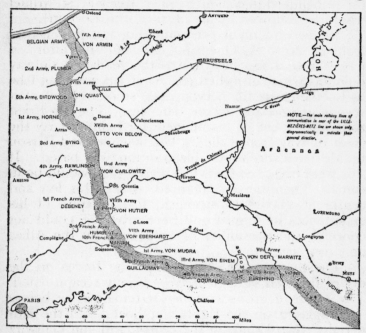

General Situation and Distribution of Army Commands in the Last Week of September, 1918.

Longuyon and Metz, a special detachment, under Fuchs. The Allied forces from left to right were : the Belgians north of Ypres ; the French Third Army, under Humbert, which had been withdrawn from the Oise ; the British Second Army, under Plumer, to the Lys ; the new British

Fifth Army, under Sir William Birdwood, in front of Lens and Lille ; the British First Army, under Horne, opposite Douai ; the British Third Army, under Byng, before Cambrai ; the British Fourth Army, under Rawlinson, to St. Quentin ; the French First Army, under Débeney, to the Oise ; the French Tenth Army, under Mangin, on the Ailette and the heights of the Aisne ; the French Fifth Army, now under Guillaumat, in front of Rheims ; the French Fourth Army, under Gouraud, in Champagne, west of the Argonne ; the United States First Army, under Pershing, between the Argonne and the Meuse ; and the nucleus of the United States Second Army, east of that river, looking towards Briey.

The Allied Commander-in-Chief had compelled Ludendorff to conform to his will, and to make his chief concentration within the outermost bend of the great salient, leaving much of the rest very weak, in spite of all efforts at reinforcement. The German High Command was in this dilemma : they had two sections of acute importance, Lorraine and the Siegfried zone, and with shrinking forces both had to be maintained against an opponent with far greater strength in guns and men. Defeat in either quarter would be fatal, but the defences of both were still strong. Ludendorff pinned his faith to the seven miles of the Siegfried system and the masked and tortuous terrain through which the Meuse flowed to Mezières.

Foch made his plan cunningly, so as to exploit every weakness in the enemy's position. He withdrew secretly the First United States Army* from its old

* This army was largely composed of divisions still untried. The only veteran divisions were the 4th and the 77th.

battle-ground to the west bank of the Meuse, and left the new Second United States Army in its place. He aimed at striking almost simultaneously against each of the danger points. Pershing, with Gouraud on his left, would attack west of the Meuse in the direction of Mezières. If he succeeded, the enemy would be forced back towards the Ardennes. At the same moment other French armies would press towards Laon and Hirson, and the British would attack the Siegfried zone, break through it, and cut the main German communications. Simultaneously the Belgians and the British left would advance in the north, where the enemy was weak, in the direction of Ghent, so as to clear the Belgian coast and complicate any retirement. The strategy was that of a general pressure on all parts of the salient, and the vital elements were the attacks of Pershing and Gouraud in the south and of Haig in the centre. For, if the first made retreat imperative, and the second destroyed the machinery of retreat, a comprehensive disaster must follow. In this scheme the British were cast for the most difficult *rôle*. They had to attack in the area where the enemy's defences were most highly organized and his forces were strongest. If the Siegfried zone held, the German *moral* might well recover and a new era of resistance open. Nor should it be forgotten that Haig's armies had borne the heaviest share of the summer fighting, and that every division had been sorely tried. Yet the attempt must be made, for it was the essential part of the whole strategy, and the measure of the difficulty was the measure of the honour in which Foch held the fighting quality of his British allies.

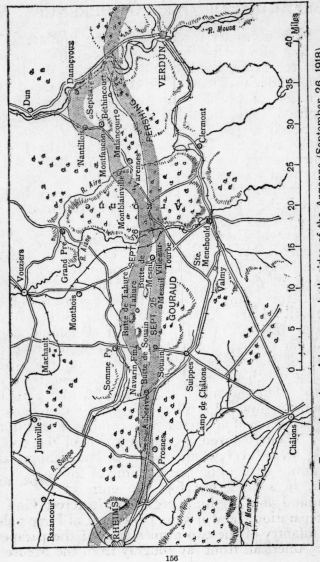

The Franco-American Advance on both sides of the Argonne (September 26, 1918).

It is necessary to emphasize the importance of the task allotted to the British forces, for it sets in high relief the courage and insight of the British Commander-in-Chief. So difficult seemed the operation of breaking at one bound through the Siegfried Line, that the British Government was compelled to put the responsibility of the decision wholly upon Sir Douglas Haig. Even the French Generalissimo was dubious as to its feasibility. The movement was undertaken on Haig's initiative; he bore the sole burden of it; and therefore to him belongs the full credit of what was destined to be one of the decisive actions of the war.

Foch resolved to begin on his right flank, where the enemy was waiting for the expected thrust towards Metz, while the main American forces had been moved to the left bank of the Meuse. There he hoped for a surprise, though he was aware of the strength of the continuation of the Siegfried defences through Champagne. If Pershing could push far enough down the Aire he would turn the flank of the whole enemy position on the Aisne, against which Gouraud would be pressing from the south. On the night of Wednesday the 25th the Americans opened artillery fire on the east bank of the Meuse, as if an attack were coming in that quarter. Then followed a bombardment of the enemy back areas everywhere between the Suippe and Verdun. At 2.30 on the morning of the 26th, in a cold, wet fog, the guns of *Sept. 26.* Gouraud and Pershing began the severest kind of "preparation," and at 5.30, on a front of forty miles, the infantry of the two armies crossed the parapets. The American front lay roughly from the Meuse to the Argonne, the French from the Argonne to the Suippe, and the length of each was twenty miles.

The first rush took Gouraud's six corps of attack through the front positions, which had been ceaselessly strengthened ever since the Champagne battle of September 1915. Places famous in that action fell into his hands—Navarin Farm, Tahure, and the Buttes of Tahure, Souain, and Mesnil. His average advance was some three miles, for he was operating in most difficult country, that series of long, low ridges, each of which was tunnelled and fortified to the last degree of elaboration. His attack was a complete surprise ; and by the evening he had broken the back of a position which von Einem had thought impregnable. Pershing had, to begin with, the easier task, and his progress was more rapid, for before night fell he had put seven miles of enemy ground behind him. He swept over the Forges brook, and into the region of wooded hills, not yet desecrated like those of Verdun. The Americans, fighting with superb dash and resolution, took Malancourt, Béthincourt, and Septsarges, were held up for a little by machine-gun fire from Montfaucon, encircled and carried the place, and by the evening were also in Varennes, Montblainville, Nantillois, and Dannevoux. In Montfaucon they had won the commanding observation point of the whole district, from which, in the old battles at Verdun, the fire of the German heavy guns had been directed. Von Gallwitz hurried every man he could spare to stop this breach, for he argued correctly that Gouraud's advance was a containing battle, and that the Americans were the spearhead. There was no German general reserve, so he had to borrow troops where he could from other parts of the front. But it seemed wise to borrow them, for Foch was clearly directing his main effort on the Meuse.

Next day the enemy knew more of Foch's mind, which thought not in terms of isolated thrusts, but of linked and cumulative actions. For that day, Friday, 27th September, Haig struck *Sept. 27.* towards Cambrai. To appreciate the importance of the stroke it is necessary to sketch the nature of the Siegfried zone, before which were drawn up the armies of Horne, Byng, and Rawlinson. Its northern limit was the southern end of the water-line which protected Douai. North and south of Mœuvres the enemy had the Canal du Nord as an extra defence to cover that gap between the water-line and the Scheldt Canal, which offered an avenue of approach to Cambrai. But the strongest part of the zone was opposite Rawlinson's front, between St. Quentin and Bantouzelle, where the Scheldt Canal formed the outworks of the system. The principal German trenches were on the east bank, but on the west bank lay advanced posts skilfully sited, so as to deny the attack effective artillery positions. The canal gave cover for resting troops and shelter to the garrisons of the outpost line during a bombardment. The configuration of the whole section was most curious. From Vendhuile south to Bellicourt the canal passed through a tunnel 6,000 yards long, which was connected by shafts with the trenches above. North of Vendhuile the canal lay in a deep cutting, the sides of which were honeycombed with dug-outs, and the edges studded with armoured machine-gun emplacements. From

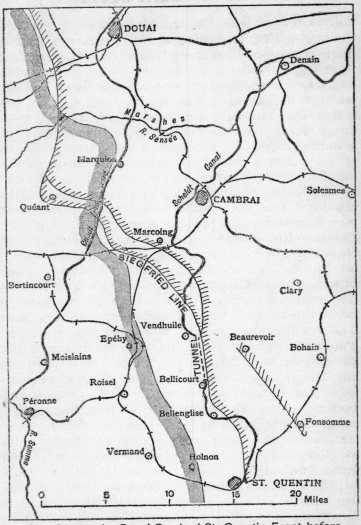

Situation on the Douai-Cambrai-St. Quentin Front before
Haig's Advance on September 27.

Bellicourt south to Bellenglise the cutting became shallow, till at the latter place the canal was almost on the ground level, while south of Bellenglise it was dry. From Bellicourt southward the enemy had two heavily wired trench lines, nearly a mile west of the canal, while north of Vendhuile his positions were on the east bank. These were, so to speak, the outpost and battle zones of the system; but it ran back for a distance of from five to seven miles, a belt of country containing many subsidiary lines and numerous fortified villages, and culminated in what was known as the Beaurevoir-Fonsomme line, a double row of trenches analogous to the front position. East of that there was open country.

Haig had selected the southern section between Vendhuile and Holnon, held by the Fourth Army, as the main area of attack. But there the Siegfried defences were at their strongest, and a long "preparation" was necessary. He therefore decided to attack first with the First and Third Armies from Vendhuile north to the water-line, in order to puzzle the enemy as to the quarter in which the chief blow would be delivered, and to enable the two armies to get forward so as to simplify Rawlinson's task. On the night of the 26th a heavy bombardment opened between St. Quentin and the Sensée. The night was very wet, but before dawn the clouds departed, leaving clear air and a rain-washed sky. At 5.30 a.m. on the 27th, just as light was breaking, Byng and Horne advanced on a front of thirteen miles, between Gouzeaucourt and Sauchy-Lestrée. The dispositions from right to left were the 4th, 6th, 17th, and Canadian Corps. The key of the problem was the debouchment on a nar-

row front in the Mœuvres area, for the Canal du
Nord north of that place was too strong to be
passed in the face of the enemy. But if the canal
could be crossed there, the northern sector might be
turned by an attack fanning out from the bridgehead. This task was entrusted to the 63rd Division,
and the 4th, 3rd, and 1st Canadians.

Just at dawn these divisions stormed the canal,
and swung forward on Graincourt, Anneux, and
Bourlon—the storm centre of the first battle of
Cambrai—while our engineers built bridges in their
rear. At Graincourt there was a stubborn fight;
but the 63rd Division took the place by the evening,
while the 4th Canadians took Bourlon, and the 3rd
Canadians Bourlon Wood. On their right the
57th and 52nd Divisions were east of Anneux, and
close upon Fontaine-Notre-Dame. Farther south
the Guards and the 2nd Division made good progress, and the 3rd Division took Ribécourt and
Flesquières, while on their right the 5th and 42nd
Divisions had established a flank between Ribécourt
and Beaucamp. In the left centre the 1st Canadians
and the 11th Division had taken Sains-lez-Marquion,
Haynecourt, and Epinoy, and on the extreme left
the 56th Division was in part across the canal and in
part moving towards Palluel. That evening we had
taken over 10,000 prisoners and 200 guns; we were
everywhere across the Canal du Nord, and were
close on the Scheldt Canal south of Cambrai.

Next day Gouzeaucourt fell, and Marcoing and
Fontaine-Notre-Dame, and at Marcoing we reached
Sept. 28.   the east bank of the Scheldt Canal, while
        farther north we were in Sailly and Palluel
and Aubencheul-au-Bac. Cambrai was now menaced

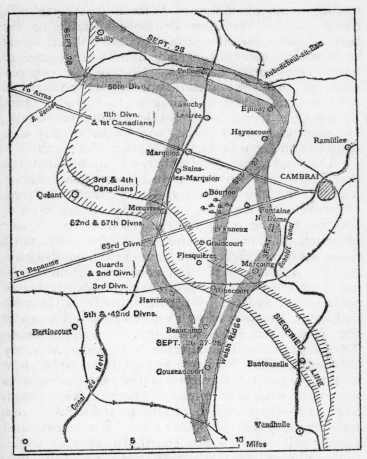

Haig's Advance on Cambrai, September 27 and 28.

on two sides, and the defences of the gap had been destroyed. The great road-and-rail junction was out of action, and Douai was also threatened by the turning of its water-line on the south.   Worse still, the crossing of the Canal du Nord by tanks on the back of tanks, and the passing of the Scheldt Canal at Marcoing, had broken Ludendorff's confidence in his outer Siegfried defences.   He was now engaged hotly in two vital areas, and, having no general reserves, and being unwilling to take troops from Rawlinson's front, he could look only to the St. Gobain and Aisne sections, and to the already thin lines of von Armin and von Quast in the north.

That day, 28th September, he found that the cup of his misfortunes was in no way full.   For at 5.30 that morning it was von Armin's turn.   A force, commanded by the King of the Belgians, made up of his own army, part of the French Third Army under Humbert, and the 19th and 2nd Corps of Plumer's Second Army, attacked on a front of twenty miles from south of Dixmude to Ploegsteert Wood.   In the northern area there was a preliminary bombardment of some hours, assisted by British ships from the sea ; in Plumer's section of four and a half miles south of the Ypres-Zonnebeke road, there was no warning " preparation."   The advance was instantaneously successful.   The Belgians, led by their King, who all day was in the forefront of the battle, fought as men fight who have much to avenge.   Von Armin had no more than five divisions, and could make little stand.   The Belgians took Zonnebeke and Poelcappelle, and cleared Houthulst Forest ; while, under Plumer, the 14th, 35th, 29th, and 9th Divisions, supported by the 41st and 36th, pressed far beyond the limits reached in the Third Battle of Ypres, and took Zandvoorde and Becelaere.   On their right, the 31st, 30th, and 34th Divisions cap-

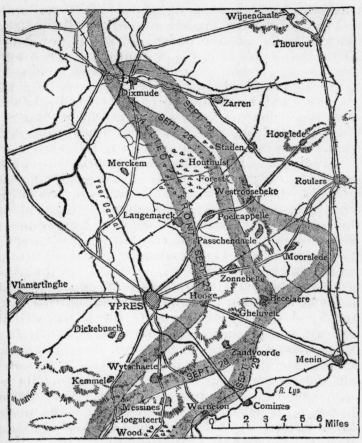

The Allied Advance in Belgium.

tured Wytschaete, and reached the crest of the ridge. Next day the Belgians beat off *Sept.* 29. all counter-attacks and went through the second enemy position, carrying Dixmude, Pas-

chendaele, Moorslede, and part of Westroosebeke,
and reached the Roulers-Menin road ; while Plumer
cleared Ploegsteert Wood, took Messines, and held
all the left bank of the Lys from Comines westward. Over 10,000 prisoners and some hundreds
of guns remained in the Allied hands.

Ludendorff's perplexities had thickened. Gouraud was still pressing on, and was now some two
miles north of Somme-py and within half a mile of
Monthois, while Pershing was close on Brieulles.
The Americans found their task laborious in that
confused countryside, and their difficulties were increased by their ardour, for at first they neglected to
clear the ground behind them—that *nettoyage* which
their allies had learned from bitter experience.
Also, as was natural with a new army, the staff and
transport work was scarcely adequate at the start to the
fighting quality of their men. It looked as if the gate
of the Meuse might be harder to unlock than Foch
had imagined. But Cambrai and Douai were in dire
peril, and there was imminent risk of the whole
German front being outflanked on the north by
King Albert's advance. Ludendorff dared not thin
the St. Quentin section where Rawlinson was waiting, and his hope of reinforcements from von Eberhardt and von Mudra had gone. For, on the 28th,
the day of the Belgian attack, Mangin and Guillaumat
had struck between the Ailette and the Vesle.

The new attack began modestly, but by the
second day it had reached a depth of three and a half
Sept. 28. miles, Italian divisions fighting gallantly
in the centre. By the 30th Mangin's
front ran from Bourg by Braye-en-Laonnais to
Filain, and then along the south bank of the Ailette

to a point west of Anizy-le-Château, while Guillaumat to the east had taken Montigny *Sept.* 30.
and Revillon. That day, too, Gouraud
had carried, after a hard fight, the hill called Mont
Cuvelet, which commanded the whole Aisne valley
as far as Vouziers.

On the 28th no part of the German front was
disengaged, except the Siegfried zone from Vendhuile southward.   There and there only could
reinforcements be found to support the cracking
lines in Flanders, on the Aisne, and on the Meuse.
But on the 29th that hope vanished, for *Sept.* 29.
Haig delivered his crowning blow on
the German defences. He struck at the strongest
part, and it crumbled before him.

For two days the guns of the Fourth Army had
not been silent ; the enemy's garrisons were forced
into tunnels and deep dug-outs, and the bringing up
of food and ammunition was made all but impossible.
The Germans were therefore in a state of confusion
and fatigue when Haig struck at ten minutes to six
on the morning of Sunday the 29th. The area of
attack was from Marcoing to St. Quentin. The
right wing of the Third Army, the 5th and 4th Corps,
advanced between Marcoing and Vendhuile, and
the left wing of Débeney's French First Army between St. Quentin and Cerizy. But the main
thrust was that of the centre, Rawlinson's Fourth
Army, on the twelve miles between Holnon and
Vendhuile, its dispositions being, from left to right,
the 3rd Corps, the 2nd United States Corps (Major-
General G. W. Read), and the 9th Corps. The 3rd
Corps had the section of the Scheldt Canal where
the cutting was deep ; the Americans had the tunnel

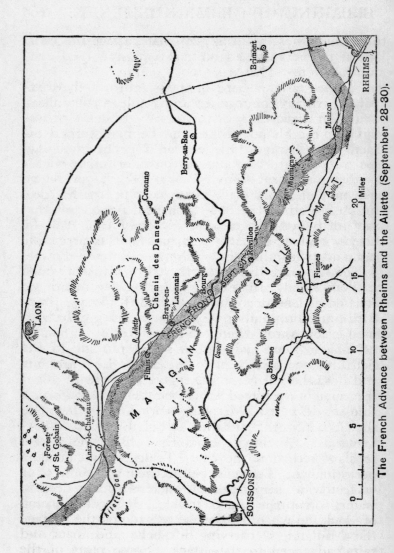

The French Advance between Rheims and the Ailette (September 28–30).

area ; and the 9th Corps had that part of the canal where it approached ground level and curved eastward.

This action was one of the greatest of the campaign, whether we regard the difficulties to be faced or the strategic value of the gains. Ludendorff was fighting for his last hope, and he had warned his men accordingly. One captured order reminded his troops that " our present position is our winter position." Another ran thus : " There can be no question of going back a single step farther. We must show the British, French, and Americans that any further attacks on the Siegfried Line will be utterly broken, and that that line is an impregnable rampart, with the result that the Entente Powers will condescend to consider the terms of peace which it is absolutely necessary for us to have before we can end the war." Germany was already busy with peace proposals, and she had nothing to bargain with except those defences in the West.

The key of the position was the angle of the Scheldt Canal where it turned east to Le Tronquoy and held the village of Bellenglise in its bend, for if the canal were forced there, the defences on either side would be turned. The work was entrusted to the 46th (North Midland) Division, under Major-General G. F. Boyd, which had had a long and brilliant record in the war. Theirs was an amazing performance. The canal before them was some 50 or 60 feet wide, sometimes as much as 10 feet deep in water, sometimes a mere trickle. It was a morning of thick fog when behind the tornado of the barrage the Midlanders, carrying life-belts and mats and rafts, advanced to the attack. Some parts of the canal were impossible, so the crossing had to be made on a narrow front. Swimming or wading, and in some cases using the foot-bridges which the enemy had left undestroyed, they passed the canal west and north of Bellenglise, swarmed up the farther wall, and took the German trenches on the far bank. Then, fanning out, they attacked in rear the positions to the south, capturing many batteries still in action. That day this one division took over 4,000 prisoners and 70 guns.

South of the Midlanders the 1st and 6th Divisions pressed along the west side of the canal bend, over the Thorigny ridge, and reached the west end of the small tunnel at Le Tronquoy. There they found on their left the 32nd Division, which had passed through the 46th and had taken the villages of Lehaucourt and Magny-la-Fosse on the east bank. Meantime, on the Midlanders' left, the 2nd United States Corps had done nobly in the tunnel section between Bellenglise and Bony. On its right the 30th U.S. Division (Major-General Lewis), men from Tennessee and the Carolinas, broke through the main Siegfried defences and took Bellicourt and Nauroy. North of them the 27th U.S. Division (Major-General O'Ryan) reached Bony, and fought a desperate fight for the possession of that village. All day the American front was hotly engaged, bodies of the enemy holding out at the strong points of the intricate system; but by the evening they had cleared the area with the help of the 5th and 3rd Australian Divisions, who came up in support. On Rawlinson's left, the 12th and 18th Divisions of the 3rd Corps advanced around Vendhuile.

The Third Army to the north made good prog-

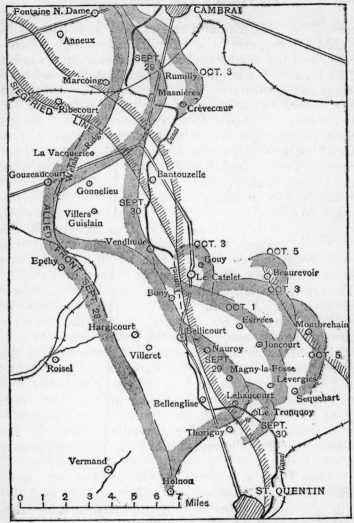

The Allied Advance between Cambrai and St. Quentin
(September 29–October 5)

ress. The New Zealanders cleared Welsh Ridge and took La Vacquerie ; the 62nd Division took Masnières ; and the 63rd, on their left, crossed the Scheldt Canal east of Cantaing, and reached the southern skirts of Cambrai. Farther north the Canadian Corps took St. Olle and Sancourt, and reached the environs of Cambrai from the north-west. Meantime, on the right of the battle, Débeney took Cerizy and Urvillers and crossed the St. Quentin-La Fère road. Already both Cambrai and St. Quentin were gravely outflanked.

It had been foggy all day, and that night the wind rose and the rain fell. On Monday the 30th
Sept. 30. it was still cloudy. That day the Fourth Army pressed through the gap in the main Siegfried defences. The 1st and 32nd Divisions took Thorigny and Le Tronquoy and the Le Tronquoy tunnel, while the enemy evacuated Villers Guislain and Gonnelieu, and withdrew behind the Scheldt Canal. The position now was that we were close up to the west bank of the canal between Vendhuile and Crèvecœur ; north of Crèvecœur, in the great bend of Cambrai, we were on the east bank ; and from Vendhuile to Le Tronquoy we were well to the east of the canal and through the chief Siegfried trenches. But at Cambrai the German resistance had stiffened. The Canadians were in the suburbs of Proville and Tilloy, but they could only advance slowly.

On Tuesday, 1st October, Rawlinson again attacked in conjunction with Débeney. The latter
Oct. 1. had hitherto fought chiefly with his right wing. He now flung forward his left, broke through the Siegfried Line, and took Gauchy,

while his vanguard entered St. Quentin and held the city as far as the canal, though the enemy still resisted in the eastern suburbs. Byng also advanced, and his right, the 3rd and New Zealand Divisions, took Crèvecœur and Rumilly. The Canadians were still battling fiercely in the northern and western skirts of Cambrai. In five days eleven German divisions had been brought up against them, for if they advanced another half mile Cambrai must fall. Rawlinson took Levergies with the 32nd Division; and the Australian Corps captured Joncourt, Estrées, and Bony, and pushed their line well to the north and east of this last village. The record of that corps was one which it would be hard to parallel. They had been fighting continuously since July, and had advanced in a straight line from Villers Bretonneux, till now they were half-way to the French frontier. Whatever new task was laid upon them they performed it with an apparently effortless mastery.

The greatest battle in history was now approaching its climax. The whole 250 miles of front from the Meuse to the sea were ablaze. The Belgians and Plumer were threatening Lille from the north. Cambrai was outflanked, St. Quentin had fallen, and the larger part of the main Siegfried Line had gone, while the Allies were battling through the fortified zone to the last defences of Beaurevoir. Mangin had regained the west part of the Chemin des Dames, and Guillaumat had reached the Aisne and cleared all the land between that river and the Vesle. Gouraud was through the first position in Champagne, and close on the final Brynhild Line. Pershing, though his advance was naturally slower,

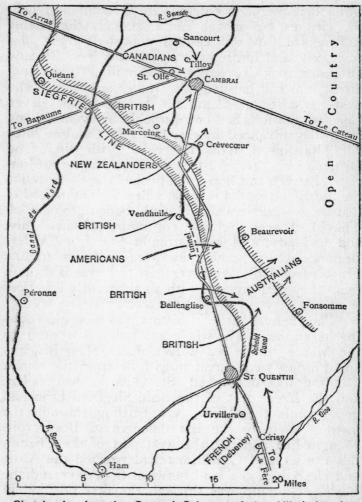

Sketch showing the General Scheme of the Allied Attack,
the Forcing of the Siegfried Line and the Scheldt Canal,
and the Envelopment of Cambrai and St. Quentin.

174

was feeling for a blow at the most deadly spot of all. Germany's man-power was quickly shrinking, and already, owing to the disbandment of units, she had only 183 divisions in the West, most of them far below strength. Wounded men coming out of hospital were returned direct to the front without passing through the field depôts. Her home depôts were empty, and her only reserves, apart from her 1920 class, were returned prisoners of war from Russia, who were mutinous and incompetent. From 15th July till the last day of September the Allies in the West had taken more than a quarter of a million prisoners, over 3,600 guns, and 25,000 machine guns. It needed but one effort more to break through the last defences, and leave the enemy, baffled and depleted, to meet the onset of the Allies in a war of movement.

Ludendorff could not have withdrawn even had he wished it. He retired, indeed, on the one moderately quiet section of the front, that of the British Fifth Army, between the Lys and Vimy. On 2nd October there was a *Oct. 2–4.* general falling back between Lens and Armentières, and Birdwood reoccupied Douvrin, La Bassée, Lorgies, and Aubers. By the night of 4th October he was on the line Fresnoy-Sallaumines-Vendin le Vieil-Wavrin-Erquinghem-Houplines.

On Thursday, 3rd October, Rawlinson attacked on the eight-mile front between Sequehart and Le Catelet. The 32nd Division took Se- *Oct. 3.* quehart, the 50th Gouy and Le Catelet, and the 2nd Australians broke through the northern part of the Beaurevoir-Fonsomme line, the last works of the Siegfried zone. We were now peeping into open country. That day the British were again in Armentières, and Lens was clear of the enemy. On the 5th the villages of Montbrehain and Beaurevoir were captured. This compelled the enemy to leave the upland, called the La Terrière plateau, in the bend of the Scheldt Canal between Le Catelet and Crèvecœur; and his withdrawal enabled Byng's right, which was still on the west bank between Crèvecœur and Vendhuile, to cross and come into line with Rawlinson.

Oct. 5.

The position by 7th October was therefore as follows : Haig had crossed the Canal du Nord and the Scheldt Canal; he had broken through all the front Siegfried Line and was pressing upon the last defences, in one section being actually beyond them. The time was therefore ripe for a great movement on the broadest possible front which should destroy the whole zone. For, in the words of the official dispatch, "nothing but the natural obstacles of a wooded and well-watered country lay between our armies and Maubeuge." In the action, which began on 26th September, thirty British and two American infantry divisions and one British cavalry division had engaged and defeated thirty-nine German divisions, and taken over 36,000 prisoners and 380 guns.

Oct. 7.

Nor was the prospect brighter for the enemy on other parts of the front. Pershing had attacked again on the 4th, advancing at one point nearly three miles, while Gouraud on the 3rd had reached the southern bank of the Arne and compelled a withdrawal of the German right. Next day the enemy began to retire on the whole front

Oct. 4.

between Rheims and the Argonne, and by the 6th had withdrawn everywhere to his final positions on the northern banks of the Arne and the Suippe. On the 6th Gouraud crossed the Arne at several points—an achievement of su- *Oct. 6.* preme importance, since it turned all the German positions on the Rheims heights and compelled an extensive retreat. With these positions gone the St. Gobain *massif* and Laon itself were in acute danger. The Belgian advance in the Ypres sector continued steadily but slowly, for the nature of the ground greatly complicated the supply problem ; indeed, this difficulty was only surmounted by dropping food and ammunition for the advanced troops from airplane squadrons. Meantime, Débeney at St. Quentin was now four miles east of the canal. If Pershing could get forward in time there was every chance of the retreat becoming a rout.

The great movement was begun early on Tuesday, 8th October, by Haig. It was a wild, wet autumn morning when Byng at 4.30, and Rawlin- son at 5.10, attacked on a 17-mile front, *Oct. 8.* from south of Cambrai to Sequehart, while Débeney extended the battle four miles farther south. The enemy resisted desperately, but no gallantry had power to stay the rush of the Allied infantry and the deadly penetration of their tanks. The whole Siegfried zone disappeared in a cataclysm. On the right the 30th United States Division took Brancourt and Premont ; and, following the front northward, the 66th and 25th Divisions captured Serain ; the 38th, Villers Outreaux and Malincourt ; the New Zealanders, Lesdain and Esnes ; the 3rd, 2nd, and

63rd, Seranvillers, Forenville, and Niergnies ; while, on Byng's extreme left, the 57th Division forced their way forward in the southern part of Cambrai, which the Germans had previously set on fire. By the evening Haig and Débeney had advanced between three and four miles, and the Siegfried zone was no more. The enemy was falling back to the Oise and the Selle, and for a moment his organization had been broken. Every road converging upon Le Cateau was blocked with transport and troops, and our cavalry were galloping eastward to confuse the retreat. On that day we took over 10,000 prisoners and nearly 200 guns.

During the night the Canadian Corps forced their way at last into Cambrai from the north, and joined hands with the 57th Division in its streets.

Oct. 9.   Next day, Wednesday the 9th, Byng and Rawlinson again advanced and pressed the retirement. Cambrai was occupied, and the Canadians pushed three miles east of the town. Bohain was in our hands, Caudry was outflanked, and our advance guards were within two miles of Le Cateau, the old battlefield where, on August 26, 1914, Smith-Dorrien and the 2nd Corps had saved the British Army. All day our cavalry had been hustling the enemy and cutting off his rearguards. By the 10th the Germans

Oct. 10.   had found a temporary lodgment on the line of the little river Selle, and Haig's front ran from Riquerval Wood along the west bank to Viesly, and thence by St. Hilaire and Avesnes to the Scheldt at Thun St. Martin. Débeney, in the meantime, had pressed east and south-east of St. Quentin, and held the west bank of the Oise-Sambre Canal as far north as Bernot. The lateral railway from St. Quentin by Busigny to Cambrai was wholly in our hands.

Subsidiary to this main action vital progress was made on other parts of the front. On the 8th

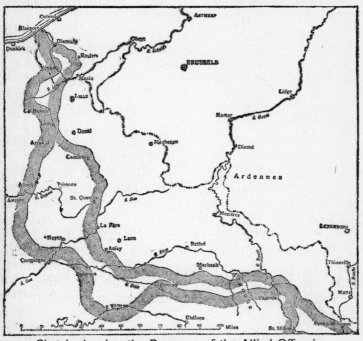

Sketch showing the Progress of the Allied Offensive
up to October 9, 1918.

Gouraud was two miles north of the Arne. Pershing, in order to clear his right flank for a further advance, attacked on the east bank of the Meuse and moved forward nearly three miles on a front of six, taking over 3,000 prisoners. By the 10th he had cleared that bank as far as Sivry, and his

left and centre were able to advance and seize the
Grand Pré defile, through which ran a lateral railway that for some days had been denied to the enemy.*

Oct. 11.   Gouraud took Challerange, and by the
11th Mangin and Guillaumat had occupied the whole of the Chemin des Dames.

The battle of 8th to 10th October may be
reckoned the determining action in the campaign.
Consider what had happened in the fifteen days
since the 26th of September. Foch had played on
the whole front a crescendo of deadly music. First
came the attack of Pershing and Gouraud ; the
next day Haig broke through the main defences of
Cambrai ; next day Plumer and the Belgians were
through the Ypres front, and Mangin and Guillaumat
were advancing between the Ailette and the Aisne ;
next day Haig smashed all but the last lines of the
Siegfried zone ; a few days later Birdwood was
pressing the enemy retreat between Arras and the
Lys ; on 4th October Gouraud reached the Arne ;
on the 8th the British and Americans swept through
the Siegfried zone to open country, and Cambrai
fell ; on the same day, in the south, Pershing and
Gouraud, Mangin and Guillaumat were advancing
in a linked movement. The death-blow had been
struck to the remnant of Germany's military power.
Lille must go, and Laon and the St. Gobain heights
were as good as lost. The whole southern Hunding
and Brynhild positions, where they had not been
already broken, were outflanked from the north.
Foch's conception, indeed, had not been wholly

* On October 9th Pershing handed over the direct command
of the First Army to Lt.-General Liggett, and constituted the
Second Army east of the Meuse under Lt.-General Bullard.

realized. He had set Gouraud and Pershing too hard a task, and they were not far enough forward when the Siegfried zone fell to pin the enemy to the trap which had been prepared for him. Nevertheless, on 8th October Germany was finally beaten.

The main attack had been that of the British and Americans under Haig, and the battle of October 8–10 was rightly described by Foch and the French Staff as " a classic example of the military art." It had no defect either in plan or execution. The enemy was fairly and squarely defeated in a field action. He was defeated, but before that date he was already crumbling ; for though, on paper, twenty divisions of British infantry, one of American infantry, and two of British cavalry, routed twenty-four German divisions, an immense preponderance in strength was on the Allied side. The German units were depleted, weary, and disheartened, and their organization was cracking. Ludendorff's strategic position was so desperate that no local stand could save him. There was talk of a German retreat to the Meuse, but it was an idle dream. Even had it been possible to conduct such a retirement without crippling losses, with the Allies pressing in on every quarter, the Meuse was no line to abide on. It was a river with the tangled mass of Ardennes behind all its centre, and the two narrow guts of Liége and Longuyon at either end as the sole communications with the Rhine. Had Foch's plan succeeded in its entirety, by 10th October Ludendorff would have been brought to the eve of surrender. But the day of doom was merely postponed. Long before her broken divisions reached the Meuse Germany would be on her knees.

APPENDICES

APPENDIX I.

THE AUTUMN OF 1917 AND THE SPRING OF 1918 IN MESOPOTAMIA.

GENERAL HEADQUARTERS,
MESOPOTAMIAN EXPEDITIONARY FORCE,
15th April 1918.

SIR,

I assumed the command of this force on the 18th November last on the death of the late lamented Lieut.-Gen. Sir Stanley Maude, and now have the honour to submit a report on the operations in Mesopotamia from October 1st, 1917, till 31st March of this year.

2. The last dispatch of General Maude covered the period April 1st to September 30th, 1917, and concluded with the operations which resulted in the capture and occupation of Ramadi on the Euphrates. At the commencement of the period covered by the present dispatch this force was opposed on the north-east by Turks, who were holding the hills known as Jebel Hamrin, while up the Tigris they were entrenched in front of Daur, and the left wing was secure at Ramadi.

3. At the beginning of October it was decided to clear the Turks from the left bank of the Diala, and occupy the Jebel Hamrin, astride of that river, in order that the control of the canals might be in our hands. This operation was entrusted

to the corps then under my command. I decided, as a preliminary operation, to drive the Turks out of their forward positions on the right bank of the Diala, where they were holding a line near Deli Abbas, and after that to hold them in front whilst my main attack developed from the southeast against their left flank. These measures had the desired effect of dislodging the enemy from a very strong position with extraordinarily few casualties in my force ; but, owing to the Diala being at that time of year fordable in innumerable places, the bulk of the Turks evaded capture, destroyed their bridge at Kizil Robat, and retreated to the right bank of the river. All our objectives were gained, and a position astride the Diala gorge, protecting the headworks of the canals, was seized and consolidated.

To ensure a perfect system of communication in the new forward area considerable work was necessitated. The main canals, *i.e.*, Khalis, Mansuriya, Khorassan, Mahrut, Haruniya, and Ruz, as well as their numerous distributaries, were rapidly bridged—often at more than one place—and this mobile bridging equipment was subsequently replaced by more permanent structures capable of carrying heavy loads. Seventy-five bridges of various sizes were built in this area alone, and the Jebel Hamrin, which prior to our occupation was a roadless tangle of hills, was gradually pierced by a very complete and convenient number of roads suitable for wheeled traffic. These roads have involved heavy work, not only in digging but in rock-cutting through the hills and in metalling over the sandy flats.

4. Whilst the operations referred to in para. 3 were in progress, the 18th Turkish Army Corps on the Tigris undertook a counter demonstration against our troops on that line, and in the middle of October advanced as far as El Huweslat, 8 miles north of Samarra, where they proceeded to entrench themselves. General Maude decided to attack before they had time to consolidate their position to any great extent, and on the 24th October, after a night march, our leading

division on the Tigris front captured El Huweslat, which the Turks had evacuated in haste, and then pushed north to Daur, supported by our cavalry. This position was captured on 2nd November by the 28th Infantry Brigade, who by pressing on with vigour caused the Turks to evacuate also their second line of trenches. The cavalry endeavoured to press round the western flank, but were met with heavy artillery fire, under cover of which the Turks withdrew to Tekrit. Although by this time our infantry had already marched 30 miles in twenty-four hours, it was decided to push on to Tekrit, and on 5th November the 8th Infantry Brigade assaulted the hostile position at that place, capturing the whole of their objectives and repelling two counter-attacks in force. The enemy suffered heavily, and many prisoners were taken. Meantime the cavalry, supported by the 19th Infantry Brigade, had pushed round the flank, and in the afternoon a spirited attack by the infantry, coupled with a charge by the Cavalry Brigade on the flank, threw back the Turks in disorder, who fled panic-stricken under cover of strong rearguard positions, which had previously been prepared for some miles in rear, and which held up our pursuit. During the following night the enemy withdrew the whole of their forces to Shoreimiya, and burnt large quantities of ammunition and stores. Their losses were estimated at 2,000, including 300 killed, and considerable booty fell into our hands.

The Turkish position was found to consist of an intricate system of trenches, many of which had been well and deeply dug, with numerous machine-gun emplacements, and its capture at a moderate cost redounds to the credit of all ranks.

The main portion of our troops were then ordered back to Samarra.

5. On the 19th November 1917 the army in Mesopotamia received the news of the death from cholera of our beloved and revered Chief, Lieut.-General Sir Stanley Maude, K.C.B., C.M.G., D.S.O. Needless to say, it was a bitter blow to the whole Force that he of all men should have been singled out

by this fell disease, which was not in any way in epidemic form.

General Maude, whose genius had altered the whole face of affairs in Mesopotamia, was an almost irreparable loss: he had taken over an army whose moral had been severely tried by their failure to effect the relief of Kut, whose health had been sapped by a very trying climate, and consequently he had a very difficult task to restore its fighting efficiency; but in a few months, by his hard work and great gifts of organization, clearsightedness, determination, and above all by his intense sympathy with and love of his soldiers, a very different state of affairs came into being. Strongly backed by the efforts of H.E. the Viceroy and the Government of India and by the War Office he thoroughly reorganized the transport services, and the troops were well fed and made as comfortable as circumstances permitted, though training and discipline were never relaxed. When he considered that all was perfectly ready, and not until then, he moved, and from that time this Force never looked back. When, therefore, I had the honour of being appointed as his successor, the moral of the army was magnificent, whilst organization and training had reached a high level of efficiency. The Turkish Army, on the contrary, was low in moral, and desertions from it were numerous and frequent; on the Tigris and Euphrates they had retreated out of rapid striking distance, and only on our right flank was there a good opportunity of hitting them. Towards the end of November, therefore, I determined to attack that part of the 13th Turkish Army Corps which was holding the Diala river above Mansuriya, the passes over the Jebel Hamrin, and Kara Tepe.

The Turkish forces were well placed for defence, and the task set to our troops included the forcing of the passages of the Diala and Nahrin rivers, as well as the Sakaltutan and Abu Zenabil passes through the Jebel Hamrin.

The operations were entrusted to Lieut.-General Sir R. Egerton, K.C.B., K.C.I.E., whilst an independent force of cavalry under Major-General L. C. Jones, C.M.G., M.V.O., was ordered to demonstrate up the Adhaim river and prevent strong reinforcements being brought down against our attacking force from the line Tuz Kermatli-Kirkuk.

The passage of the Diala was successfully forced by night, but it was found that the Turks had flooded the whole of the low-lying ground on the right bank above its confluence with the Nahrin river, and this proved a serious obstacle. In spite, however, of the bad going, the whole of the Turkish position between Mirjana and the Nahrin river was occupied on the 3rd December, the Turks falling back northwards. During the same time an infantry brigade advanced north-west along the Jebel Hamrin and drove the enemy towards the Sakaltutan pass and Nahrin river, while another infantry brigade cleared Kishla Suhaniya, capturing 44 prisoners and two field guns. During the night the Turks withdrew, and we occupied the Sakaltutan pass, and devoted the following day to a forward concentration of troops and supplies, all of which had been delayed by the unavoidable difficulties of ground and weather.

On the 5th December a combined column pushed forward against Kara Tepe ; but progress was slow, and it was not until midday of the 6th that an assault, carried out by one infantry brigade, coupled with a flank attack by another infantry brigade, captured the position. The majority of the Turks fled, and the hilly nature of the ground, coupled with the bad going, saved them from heavy punishment. In their retreat through Kifri they set fire to their dumps of coal and the Kifri coal mine. Two hundred and forty-nine prisoners were taken, and over 100 dead were buried by us. The features of the day's fighting were the determination and dash of the infantry, their close support by the artillery, and the valuable co-operation of the flying corps with both. During these operations our troops received valuable assistance from the Russian detachment under Lieut.-Colonel Bicharakhov. On the 8th December the troops were withdrawn from the forward areas, but the Sakaltutan and Abu Zenabil passes were held, and a bridgehead established at Kizil Robat, with a view to further action in the future. Our casualties were very small, in spite of the difficulties of terrain, and the operation reflected great credit on the commanders and staffs concerned, as well as on the regimental officers and men.

On the 9th December Khanakin was occupied and the communications in that area improved.

6. On the Euphrates, Ramadi had been captured in September, and the months from October to December were occupied by the troops in that area in consolidating their forward positions and in establishing a sense of security amongst the surrounding tribes. Offensive measures were of a minor kind, and consisted of raids against hostile shaikhs, some of whom were smuggling food to the Turks, of air raids, and of reconnaissances along both banks of the river and into the desert on either flank. Several bridges were thrown across the river Euphrates, and the development of the forward area was taken in hand so as to relieve the strain on transport which had to bring supplies by road from Baghdad until the railway was completed on 21st December.

During December and January it was evident that the Turks were being reinforced, the bulk of their troops being near Hit, and as their strength grew their patrols were pushed downstream as far as Uqbah and Nafata. I accordingly issued orders to Major-General Sir H. T. Brooking, K.C.B., K.C.M.G., commanding the troops on the Euphrates front, to capture Hit and its garrison as soon as his arrangements were completed and the state of the ground permitted. My opinion was that there would be no difficulty in capturing the town and driving the Turks out of their positions, but that the capture of the Turkish force would be a matter of extreme difficulty, in consequence of their previous experience at Ramadi.

On 19th February troops were pushed forward to Uqbah, which was found evacuated, and it was ascertained that the

Turkish main position was two miles above Hit, behind a depression known as Broad Wadi, while about two-thirds of his troops were fifteen miles further upstream at Salahiya. I did not wish to commit our troops to serious fighting unless I saw a chance of delivering a severe blow against the enemy, and accordingly touch was ordered to be maintained by constant patrolling and reconnaissances, while forward communications were improved and supplies pushed up.

On March 8th it was discovered that the Turks had vacated their Broad Wadi position, and were falling back on Salahiya. The troops were accordingly pushed forward, and the R.F.C., which co-operated by bombing and machine-gun fire, caused many casualties and much confusion amongst the retreating columns of the enemy and their transport. Hit was occupied on the 9th, and Salahiya on the 10th, the Turks retreating to Khan Baghdadi.

I then issued orders to drive the enemy as far as possible from Hit, and to inflict all possible damage on him. To assist in this object additional mobile troops, including a cavalry brigade and light armoured motors, were ordered to Hit, with instructions to move by night and conceal themselves by day, so that the enemy might think that no further advance by my troops was intended ; in many other ways efforts, apparently successful, were made to deceive the Turks as to our intentions.

On the 26th the plan of operations was to make an attack in strength against the enemy's left, and to send the cavalry and armoured motor cars round his right flank. Preparations for this attack were nearing completion when it became evident that the enemy had already commenced to withdraw from their forward positions, but intended to make a stand north-west of Khan Baghdadi. Arrangements for assaulting this position were accordingly made, and under cover of an effective barrage it was carried out at 5.30 p.m., with slight loss.

Meantime the cavalry, after a long and difficult march, gained the Aleppo road where it crosses the Wadi Hauran, shortly after 5 p.m., and cut off the enemy's retreat by road and river. About 11.30 p.m. the Turks launched a heavy attack in the hope of breaking through the centre of the cavalry, but were completely repulsed and lost 1,000 prisoners.

By 5.30 a.m. next morning the infantry columns arrived and completed the defeat, capturing a large number of prisoners, supplies, and munitions of all kinds. An energetic pursuit by the cavalry and by a mobile column in motorcars was then carried out. Haditha was captured without serious resistance, the enemy having no time to destroy his ammunition dumps at that place, and in the evening Khan Feheme was reached. On the 28th Ana was captured and another large dump of ammunition was found in it. The pursuit by motor was continued for 73 miles along the Aleppo road, many prisoners were taken, the Turks in most cases surrendering freely, being worn out and demoralized by the rapidity of our pursuit. The total prisoners taken were the commander and staff of the 50th Turkish Division, the commandant of Ana, two regimental commanders, 213 officers, and 5,022 other ranks, inclusive of Germans. Twelve guns, 47 machine guns, and great quantities of rifles, ammunition, and stores were also captured. The amount of ammunition found at Ana being too large to be brought away, was blown up, and on 30th March the troops were gradually withdrawn down the Euphrates to previously arranged positions.

The complete success of this operation I attribute to the masterly way in which the force was handled by Major-General Sir H. T. Brooking and his very complete preparatory arrangements.

The endurance of the troops, and their determination to get at the enemy, was worthy of all praise, whilst the tactical ability of their commanders was of a very high order. The magnificent work done by the Cavalry Brigade under Brig.-General R. A. Cassels, as well as by the light-armoured motor batteries, both in cutting off the enemy's line of retreat, as well as in the pursuit to and beyond Ana, was a notable feat. Best of all, our casualties were very slight.

7. With the advent of the New Year, the weather, which had been unexpectedly good in December, became consistently wet. Continuous operations on any large scale were rendered out of the question, and the greatest strain was thrown on the lines of communication and supply formations.

On the north-east front a small column was sent at the beginning of January as far as Pai Tak, at the foot of the Tak-i-Girra pass. It met with no opposition, and on its return occupied Kasr-i-Shirin. Towards the end of the month the state of famine to which the Turks had reduced Northern Persia made it incumbent on me to endeavour to open the main trade route via Kirmanshah in order to get supplies to the poor inhabitants of the towns and villages, and to provide them with an outlet for their home manufactures. With this object in view I increased the garrison of Kasr-i-Shirin, and pushed small posts towards Kirmanshah. A large amount of tribal labour was also employed in improving the road, which was in a lamentable state of disrepair. The continuance of wet weather up to the present date, coupled with snow on the high ground east of the Tak-i-Girra pass, has rendered the maintenance of troops along the road a matter of extreme difficulty.

8. In addition to the operations on the Diala, Tigris, and Euphrates, and the activities towards Kirmanshah, to which I have referred, numerous minor operations have been carried out on all fronts. These consisted generally of reconnaissances by cavalry and light armoured motor cars and by bombing raids by the Royal Flying Corps. At the end of March manœuvres under war conditions were carried out on a large scale near Tekrit, but the Turks in that area withdrew northwards before the arrival of our troops.

9. In the time of my predecessor, the Civil Commissioner, Sir Percy Cox, had strongly urged that the whole of the Euphrates line from Feludja to Nasiriya should be brought

XXIII.   13 under military and civil control, but at that time circumstances did not permit of any extension of our military responsibilities. By the middle of December 1917, however, the military position had completely changed owing to the magnificent successes gained by General Allenby in Palestine. I therefore considered that the time was ripe to establish a firm control of the line of the Euphrates, and by that means encourage and assist in the development of the rich agricultural lands in that area. To that end I issued orders for troops to be dispatched from Nasiriya and Baghdad to garrison various villages, thus establishing through communication by river between Basra and Feludja and controlling the development of local resources throughout the lower Euphrates valley. The extension of military control over this area was also desirable in order that the shaikhs of important towns like Kerbela, Nedjef, Hilla, and Diwaniya might be brought more closely into the sphere of British influence and that pro-Turk sympathisers might be expelled.

Care was taken not to establish troops in either of the religious cities of Kerbela and Nedjef, and they were quartered at a distance. The inhabitants of Nedjef are, for the most part, well-disposed, holy people, but there is in addition a proportion of irreconcilables in the town. On 12th January some of these fired on the troops exercising near the town, causing a few casualties. Not wishing to injure a town which is full of sacred memories for Mahomedans, I decided to punish two of the leading shaikhs who were known to be responsible for the offence, and to levy a heavy fine. The shaikhs, however, fled before they could be arrested, and they became outlaws. The fine was paid. After this incident matters seemed to be going on satisfactorily when, on 21st March, to my great regret, the political officer in Nedjef, Captain W. M. Marshall, was murdered. No reason was given for the act, as the deceased officer was universally liked. I immediately ordered a blockade of the town until all those implicated in the murder were given up, and surrounded it by a cordon of military posts joined by barbed wire. While I am prepared to go to extreme measures if necessary in order to exact reparation for so foul a deed, I feel confident that by blockade methods I shall cause all the delinquents to be surrendered. When these have been removed the further punishment of the town will be a matter for subsequent consideration.

Meantime, the development of the Hilla area has proceeded apace. Many hundred tons of seed grain have been planted, and to assist in bringing the harvest into Baghdad a branch line down to Hilla is being made, which is expected to be open for traffic by the middle of May. I have every confidence that this scheme will prove beneficial and enable this Force to be dependent largely on local produce.

10. The riverain tribes of the Euphrates had long been independent, and though the capture of Feludja and Ramadi had produced a very marked effect upon them, and checked any serious attempt at hostile action, nevertheless certain minor punitive operations had been necessitated. These took the form of dispatching small columns of all arms, assisted by river gunboats, by means of which the towers of recalcitrant chiefs were demolished and the tribe in question punished. Five such expeditions were sent out from Nasiriya between November and February, and were uniformly successful. Though of a minor nature, nevertheless they taxed the powers of endurance of the troops employed.

11. A portion of this Force is maintained along the Karun river, primarily to protect the oilfields near Tembi, but also to maintain order in Ahwaz, Shushtar, and Dizful. In this work the troops have been markedly successful. A disturbance occurred at Shushtar on November 2nd, during which the British Consulate was threatened, but it was quickly and easily suppressed, thanks to the energetic action of the officers in responsible positions, and by the rapidity with which the troops employed performed a long and difficult march to the scene of action.

12. The maintenance of the line of communication defences

along both the Tigris and Euphrates has been carried out with marked efficiency. Though the work has at times been arduous, and often more monotonous than that of troops employed in forward areas, the inability of enemy agents to cause even the slightest damage or delay on the lines of communication redounds to the vigilance and credit of all concerned.

On the Tigris the only trouble caused has been due to losses by theft from trains and boats, especially between Kurna and Amara. This district is inhabited by marsh tribes, who in their native swamps are afforded complete immunity against attack by land, as they retreat rapidly into their boats, leaving nothing of value behind.

The tribes between Basra and Nasiriya have been absolutely quiet, and have made no hostile movement.

I have nothing but praise for the patrols, railway guards, and escorts, whose work has brought out qualities of self-reliance and devotion to duty.

The defences at Fao have been consolidated and improved, and the examination service of ships entering the Shatt-el-Arab has been effective. During the six months under review 581 vessels other than British and 8,466 native craft have been examined.

13. I desire to bring to favourable notice the names of my two Corps Commanders, Lieut.-General Sir R. G. Egerton, K.C.B., K.C.I.E., and Major-General (temp. Lieutenant-General) Sir A. S. Cobbe, V.C., K.C.B., C.S.I., D.S.O., who have rendered me every assistance and have commanded their respective corps with ability.

My thanks are also due to the commanders of higher formations and staffs for their loyalty and untiring work, and to the gallantry, endurance, and devotion to duty displayed by regimental officers, non-commissioned officers, and men of all arms throughout the period under review.

Throughout the whole period covered by this Dispatch the work of the R.F.C. has been, as usual, perfectly admirable, and enemy machines, which endeavoured at one time to carry out raids on our camps and communications, were either driven off or brought down. Many reprisals were also carried out on the enemy aerodromes and camps, both by day and night. During all operations the R.F.C. have co-operated with other arms—cavalry, artillery, and infantry—in the closest and most effectual way, whilst the flight of the retreating enemy columns has been harassed by our machines in the boldest manner, both by bombing and machine-gun fire.

14. The extension of the lines of communication to the north-east and north-west, coupled with the opening up of the lower Euphrates, has thrown an ever-increasing responsibility on Major-General Sir George MacMunn, K.C.B., C.S.I., D.S.O., Inspector-General of Communications, and I concur whole-heartedly in the opinion of his ability which was held by my distinguished predecessor.

One of the principal features of the lines of communication has been the rapid development of the port of Basra by the completion of the dockyard and of the first set of wharves, earlier planned, as well as the continuance of the arrangements for improving the working of ocean shipping. A large island at Magill has been raised by dredging to take ocean ships on one side and to load river steamers on the other. The auxiliary annexe of Nahr Umr has also given very great assistance with little outlay of material. All this work reflects great credit on the construction branch of the Port Administration and Conservancy.

The period covered by this Dispatch contains the worst months of low water, when every day was a constant anxiety with regard to river navigation, and the river was kept open only by the most unremitting care of the buoying establishment. The riverborne tonnage has steadily improved, and the organization of the Inland Water Transport has shown a very high state of efficiency.

Considerable progress has also been shown in the development of the railways in all sections of the lines of communication, and in the improvements of the river ports of the Amara and Kut-el-Amara.

15. The high standard of efficiency displayed by all ranks of the Medical Service has been most gratifying to me, and reflects great credit on Surgeon-General A. P. Blenkinsop, C.B., C.M.G., my Director of Medical Services. The health of the troops has shown marked improvement, as compared with the corresponding months of 1916–17. The sanitary organization and administration has steadily progressed, and the standard of comfort and efficiency of the hospitals is most satisfactory.

The Nursing Sisters have, as always, devoted themselves with untiring care and zeal to the welfare of the sick and wounded. Through the generosity and kindness of Her Excellency Lady Willingdon, clubs and convalescent homes for these devoted ladies are being established at suitable centres.

I also wish to take this opportunity of recording my gratitude, and that of all ranks under my command, for the valuable help afforded by the Red Cross Society, which has resulted in the increased comfort of the troops.

16. I was lucky to receive a visit early in March from Lieut.-General Sir E. Altham, K.C.B., C.M.G., Quartermaster-General in India, and Sir Thomas Holland, K.C.I.E., head of the Munitions Board, who were thus able to see for themselves the wants of the country and the results of the efforts made by India to supply our needs.

The work thrown on the Administrative Services and Departments, most of which is primarily due to the long line of communications, has been consistently heavy. In spite of distances traversed over a roadless country, and of interruptions by floods, supplies to the fighting troops have been maintained with the utmost precision. In Transport a salient feature has been the welcome arrival of extra mechanical transport companies, which increased the radius of action of the troops in the large areas over which they had to operate.

The maintenance of these companies reflects great credit on the mechanical transport branch of the Army Service Corps.

Similarly, the mule columns and animal drawn transport have shown a high standard of efficiency. In this connection I would specially mention the assistance rendered by the corps raised by Indian princes, viz., Jaipur, Bharatpur, Gwalior, and Mysore Imperial Service transport.

The Ordnance Services have been conducted and developed with energy and efficiency with a view to making the Force as self-supporting as possible and to the consequent saving of sea transport. To this end boot-repairing shops, disinfecting and repair stations, and other workshops, have been established or extended.

The duties of the Works Department in providing protection for the communications to Baghdad and Baghdad itself against floods have proved long and arduous, and show good progress. It is not, perhaps, realized that in this undeveloped country the only local products are mud bricks, reeds for making mats, lime and bitumen in small quantities, and gravel in isolated localities. Every other requirement, from a constructional point of view, has to be imported. The supply of good drinking water has been well maintained. Automatic suction chlorination is now in general use, and mechanical filtration plants have been or are being erected at all important posts.

The conduct and administration of the Remount Department is most satisfactory, and I consider that the Remount Depôt and attached farm at Baghdad are models of their kind.

Owing to the increased area over which this Force operates, to the amount of animal diseases existing in the territories conquered, and to the consequent danger of the animals of the Force becoming infected, it has been found necessary to increase the Veterinary administrative staff and to form extra veterinary hospitals. The results are most gratifying, and reflect great credit on this Department.

The Irrigation Department, as such, has been recently

constituted, though irrigation work was carried out previously chiefly on the Euphrates. The work done can only be described as extraordinary, and I look forward to a great development in this direction next year. The excellent results already achieved are due to the untiring zeal and energy of all ranks in a country where, until recently, there was no military control.

The period has been one of constant construction work and of steadily increasing demands on the Railway Department. Floods have caused several interruptions, but the service of trains has been maintained with great success in face of difficulties inherent to lines rapidly constructed in a new country, where all material has had to be brought from overseas.

The Department of Local Resources has, in addition to its former duties, taken over the control of grass farms, the feeding of the civil population, and the arrangements for the collection and transportation of the coming harvest. Tanneries, and a poultry farm, primarily to supply hospitals, are being formed. The blockade system has been carefully regulated, and ample evidence is available of severe shortage of supplies among the Turkish troops, resulting in increased desertions and loss of moral. The Department has been conducted with considerable ability.

Agriculture has made great progress, and my especial thanks are due to Mr. C. C. Garbett, I.C.S., first Revenue Officer, for the initiative displayed and the valuable work done by him in this connection. The latest estimate for the coming harvest is most gratifying. I hope, by the institution of a properly constituted Department of Agriculture and by its co-ordination with the Irrigation Department, that a very large increase will be shown next year in the agricultural development of this country.

The Postal Services have had to compete with the ever-increasing wants of this Force, and the Department has worked satisfactorily.

17. The Chaplains of all denominations have continued to devote themselves to the spiritual welfare of the troops, and have carried out their duties to my entire satisfaction. I am indebted also to the Church Army for the provision of tents for social and religious purposes, which have not only afforded opportunities for recreation to the troops, but have assisted the chaplains in their work.

The activities of the Y.M.C.A. have extended considerably during the last six months. There are now a total of seventy centres, and the system of soldiers' clubs has been initiated throughout the country. I greatly appreciate the excellent work of this society in undertaking the management of these recreational centres, which tend so largely to the well-being of the troops.

Considerable advance has been made in Graves Registration, and the special difficulties inherent to this country have been satisfactorily overcome.

To all those ladies and gentlemen who have so generously worked for, and contributed to, the comfort of the troops by the provision of war gifts, hospital ships and launches, and in numberless other ways, I can only, on behalf of this Force, tender our very grateful thanks and assure them that their kindness will never be forgotten.

18. The Directorate of Signals and Telegraphs has had to deal with ever-increasing communications and to improve those already existing in connection with the extension of the area occupied and of the railway system and with the development of the country. In addition the telephone systems have been enlarged and extended, and the work done by the wireless squadrons has been of a high order. The efficiency of this Directorate has been well maintained.

The work performed by the Surveys has assumed very large proportions, but my demands have always been met in the most satisfactory manner, and the Map Compilation Section has been of the greatest assistance.

19. In the working of the civil and political branch of this

Force I have been most ably advised by the Civil Commissioner, Sir Percy Cox, G.C.I.E., K.C.S.I., to whom I am greatly indebted. The military developments on both flanks have involved a corresponding extension of our political responsibilities. The functions of the civil administration consist in the extension of political control, the exercise of influence on agricultural shaikhs and tribes, the levy of revenue in kind, and not least the work connected with Central Arabian politics and the local Arab tribes.

The administration of the Basra Vilayet continues to run smoothly on what are practically peace lines, and satisfactory progress is noticeable in all branches.

20. The Royal Navy has ever been anxious to give me every assistance when called upon, and I am grateful to Rear-Admiral D. St. A. Wake, C.B., C.I.E., and the officers and ratings under his command, for their ready co-operation.

21. Lastly, I desire to record my most sincere thanks to my Staff and technical advisers who have so ably and loyally carried out my wishes.

Major-General W. Gillman, C.B., C.M.G., D.S.O., my Chief of the General Staff, has rendered me most loyal and invaluable assistance, whilst during his absence on an important mission his place was ably filled by Brig.-General T. Fraser, C.B., C.M.G., to whose capable work I owe much both during that period and on previous occasions.

Major-General the Hon. A. R. M. Stuart-Wortley, C.B., D.S.O., my Deputy Quartermaster-General, has had an ever-increasing load of work and responsibility placed on his shoulders owing to the various new directorates which have come into being within the past six months, but his energy and ability have overcome all initial difficulties.

Major-General F. F. Ready, C.B., C.M.G., D.S.O., my Deputy Adjutant-General, has been a tower of strength to me, and I owe much to his painstaking work and sound advice.

The entire absence of friction or discord which has characterized the work of all branches of the Staff has been a source of great gratification to me, and, I feel sure, to the entire Force.

22. As a proof of the gallantry and devotion to duty displayed by regimental officers and men during the period covered by this Dispatch, I have, under the powers delegated to me as Commander-in-Chief, made the following immediate awards for service in the field : Distinguished Service Order 15, Military Cross 109, Distinguished Conduct Medal 33, Military Medal 67, Indian Order of Merit 30, Indian Distinguished Conduct Medal 104.

23. I attach, in addition, a list giving the names of those officers, ladies, warrant and non-commissioned officers and men, whose services are deemed to be deserving of reward and special mention.

I have the honour to be,

Sir,

Your obedient Servant,

W. R. MARSHALL,

Lieut.-General, Commanding-in-Chief,

Mesopotamian Expeditionary Force.

APPENDIX II.

Sir W. R. Marshall's Second Dispatch.

MESOPOTAMIA OPERATIONS DURING THE SUMMER OF 1918, AND THE BAKU EXPEDITION.

WAR OFFICE,
10th February 1919.

THE Secretary of State for War has received the following Dispatch, addressed to the Chief of the General Staff, India, by Lieutenant-General W. R. Marshall, K.C.B., K.C.S.I., Commanding-in-Chief, Mesopotamian Expeditionary Force.

GENERAL HEADQUARTERS,
MESOPOTAMIAN EXPEDITIONARY FORCE,
1st October 1918.

SIR,

1. I have the honour to submit herewith a report of the operations carried out by the Mesopotamian Expeditionary Force during the period extending from April 1st to September 30th, 1918.

2. In my previous dispatch I alluded briefly to the murder of the political officer at Nedjef, but not to the motives which had prompted such an unprovoked crime. The reasons for it have been traced to enemy agency, and amongst the evilly disposed inhabitants of Nedjef a conspiracy, fostered by German gold, had been organized, the heads of it calling

themselves "The Committee of Rebellion." The roots of this conspiracy were in Nedjef, and its branches extended both up and down the Euphrates Valley. To put down this conspiracy, therefore, and to mete out stern justice to those actually concerned in the murder, was from every point of view an urgent necessity. It was not desired to treat the city, which contains one of the most holy shrines of the Shiahs, and is surrounded by a very high wall, in an ordinary way, *i.e.*, by shelling or by direct assault.

A strict blockade was therefore ordered and the outside water supply cut off. Picquets were established round the town with barbed wire connecting them, and these effectually stopped ingress or egress. There were two attempts of the insurgents to break out through the blockade line, but these were effectually stopped, dominating mounds were assaulted and held by our troops, and gradually the blockade line closed in and occupied the bastions of the walls as well as holding the entrance gates. Every consideration was shown to the holy Ulema and to the theological students (most of whom were Persian subjects), and had it been necessary to proceed to extremities all these would have been given an asylum. The loyal inhabitants, under the guidance of the Ulema, determined, however, to rid themselves and their sacred city of these evil-doers, and eventually by 13th April the proscribed persons had been handed over and the blockade was raised. The instigators of the murder and the actual murderers were brought before a military court to answer for their deeds, and as a result of the trial eleven were condemned to death and duly executed, seven others were sentenced to transportation, and three were deported ; in addition, a number of undesirables were sent out of the country. The firmness with which the situation was handled, the fairness with which the law-abiding inhabitants were treated, and the scrupulous care which was taken to avoid damage to holy persons and places created a most favourable impression on all the surrounding tribes, and contributed in no small degree to the subsequent establishment of friendly relations with the somewhat re-calcitrant tribes of the Shamiya, Rumeitha, and Shatra districts.

For this eminently satisfactory ending to a delicate and somewhat difficult situation my thanks are due to the acting Civil Commissioner, to Brig.-General G. A. F. Sanders and the troops under his command, and also to the political officer on the spot, Captain F. C. C. Balfour, M.C.

I subsequently visited Nedjef myself and was received with every token of honour. I attended a meeting at which were assembled the Ulema, the Shaikhs of the district, and the notables of the town, who one and all expressed the most lively gratitude for the measures which had been adopted and their loyalty to Government.

TRIBES IN GERMAN PAY.

3. On the Persian border certain tribes, notably some sections of the Sinjabis, were inclined to be troublesome (another result of German intrigue and gold), and as this tribe has its habitat just to the north of the Quasr-i-Shirin-Kerman-shah road it became necessary to give them a lesson. The Guran confederation (which includes the Kalkhanis) was reported on the 19th April to be about to take action against the pro-enemy sections of the Sinjabis. I decided therefore to support these friendly tribesmen in their action, and dis-patched a small column of all arms to co-operate. On the 25th April a brief action took place with eminently satisfactory results. The Sinjabis were defeated and suffered heavy casu-alties (as well as losing large numbers of animals), and our aeroplanes turned their retreat into a rout.

The effect of this small operation, carried out in severe conditions of weather, has been far-reaching. The pro-enemy chief of the Sinjabis, who was known to be in German pay, was himself wounded, and the German agents were thoroughly discredited ; whilst among the surrounding tribes a profound impression was created in favour of the British, and our line of communications into Persia was safeguarded from serious raiding.

4. Again, with the object of making the Persian line of communication more secure, I considered it advisable to drive the Turks out of the Kara Tepe—Kifri—Tuz Kermatli area and to hold both Kifri and Tuz for the future.

5. The general plan of operations decided upon was to simulate a converging attack upon Kara Tepe and Kifri, but in reality to strike first at the more distant objectives of Abu Gharaib and Tuz Kermatli, with the intention of cutting off and dealing subsequently with any hostile forces south-east and east of these places. This plan was to be carried into effect by means of various columns. Preliminary movements were delayed by rain in the middle of April, but all columns were concentrated at their respective positions of assembly by the 25th of that month. Secrecy was well maintained, and the Turks appeared to be in ignorance of the impending attack. The operations were entrusted to Lieut.-General Sir R. G. Egerton, K.C.B., K.C.I.E., and by the morning of 26th April he had completed the deployment of the troops selected for the operation.

A small column was sent up the Adhaim River to induce the Turks to strengthen and hold their Abu Gharaib defences. On the right a small mixed column, with which were some irregulars, demonstrated on the upper Diala. At Mirjana another small column of all arms was concentrated, and the 6th Cavalry Brigade moved to Umr Maidan and bridged the Lesser Naft River above that place. The main column, consisting of the majority of the 13th Division, with attached troops under Major-General Sir W. de S. Cayley, K.C.M.G., C.B., was at Nahrin Kupri, where the bridge, which had been destroyed by the Turks in their hurried retreat last December, was rapidly put in repair. This column detached forces towards Abu Gharaib and the Lesser Naft, the last-named with orders to move to Abu Alik before dawn on April 27th in order to head off any enemy movement from Kara Tepe in a north-westerly direction. Although the Turks must have been aware of these movements, they evidently failed to appreciate their significance, as they did not commence their withdrawal from Kara Tepe until evening of 26th April.

The night of 26th–27th April was very stormy, and torrential rain fell, making the night march of the detached forces an exceedingly difficult and arduous one. However, in spite of inky darkness, boggy ground and flooded streams, they reached their objectives by daybreak on 27th. The Abu Gharaib position had, however, been abandoned by the Turks, and its retreating garrison was discovered and bombed by our aeroplanes. The detached force on the Lesser Naft came in contact with the Turks retreating from Kara Tepe, and fulfilled its mission by heading them off from their direct line of retreat.

A FINE CAVALRY CHARGE.

The 6th Cavalry Brigade, under Brig.-General P. Holland-Pryor, C.M.G., D.S.O., M.V.O., after an arduous night march, overtook the Turks who had retreated from Abu Gharaib and had taken up a defensive position at Kulawand, covering Tuz Kermatli from the south-east. Feigning a frontal attack, whilst gradually working round the enemy's right flank, our cavalry cut the enemy's lines of retreat and then charged right through his infantry, killing some 200, including two battalion commanders, and capturing 565 prisoners, a mountain gun, and considerable booty. After reconnoitring the Ak Su with cavalry and light armoured motor cars, and finding the trenches south of Tuz Kermatli strongly held, the cavalry fell back on the main column, which was bivouacked four miles south of Kulawand. This retrograde movement was made with the object of inducing the Turks to believe that our forces, as in previous operations, would retire to their original positions. The move evidently had the desired effect, completely deceiving the enemy and inducing him to remain in his position at Tuz Kermatli, and even to reinforce it by bringing up troops from Kirkuk.

The small columns operating on the right had conformed to the general forward movement on the 27th, and before darkness on that date had reached Chaman Kupri and the right bank of the upper Diala respectively. Kifri was occupied unopposed on the 28th, where some 70 sick Turks were found. The coal mines had been flooded, but were otherwise undamaged.

The attack on the enemy position was arranged for the 29th, and was fought in two main parts, viz., on both banks of the Ak Su. On the left bank a detached force attacked the enemy and drove him with loss across the river to Tuz Kermatli, whilst some prisoners and a machine gun remained in our hands.

The main attack, however, was made on the right bank against the Yanijah Buyuk position, and was carried out with great dash by the 38th Infantry Brigade, supported by artillery, machine guns, and low-flying aeroplanes. The Turks made a stout resistance, but the infantry advanced under heavy artillery and machine-gun fire with the greatest rapidity and in the most perfect order. By 7 a.m. the position was carried, and the Lancashire men, pressing on in pursuit, entered Tuz Kermatli, capturing the major portion of the Turkish forces. The cavalry and cyclists took up the pursuit of the remnants, who were endeavouring to get away through the hills, and captured many prisoners and much transport. The enemy suffered severely, over 200 dead being buried by us alone, while 1,300 prisoners, 12 field guns, 20 machine guns, and large quantities of ammunition fell into our hands. Reconnaissances carried out on the 30th showed that the Turks farther north were retiring on Kirkuk, and had withdrawn from Tauq. The task which I had set the troops was therefore satisfactorily completed, and the whole area completely cleared of the enemy.

However, on receipt of instructions to continue the pressure and to capture Kirkuk (130 miles distant from railhead), some readjustment of the troops became necessary in order to make the supply situation at all possible. Further action was also delayed by the state of the weather, which was very stormy and wet during the first week of May; indeed, on the 7th torrential rain caused heavy floods in the rivers, which washed away the temporary bridges. Notwithstanding this difficulty, reconnaissances were pushed forward, and on the 5th May found the Turks holding a position at Taza Khurmatli; but this force, evidently a small rearguard, withdrew at dusk, and the place was occupied by our troops on the 6th. The cavalry pushed on ahead and got astride of the southerly road leading from Kirkuk to Altun Kupri. Some opposition was encountered, but the Turks continued to withdraw, and our main body that night bivouacked seven miles north of Taza Khurmatli, after having done a 28-mile march. During this period the First Corps, to which was attached the 7th Cavalry Brigade, continued to threaten the Turkish positions on the Tigris and to hold the enemy there to his ground.

KIRKUK CAPTURED.

On the 7th our leading troops entered Kirkuk unopposed, the Turks having retired from it during the night of 6th–7th, leaving behind them 600 sick and wounded soldiers, who were in a deplorable sanitary condition, and were suffering greatly from malnutrition. A large amount of ammunition and equipment was also captured. Cavalry patrols pushing forward got into touch with the Turkish rearguard, but the state of the ground precluded any large movements. On the 8th our main body reached Kirkuk, and the Turks withdrew across the Lesser Zab, having prepared the bridge at Altun Kupri for demolition.

7. Difficulties of supply, due to distance and state of the ground, now made it imperative to stop further pursuit. Kirkuk was in an indescribably filthy condition, and starvation was rife amongst the inhabitants; our troops therefore were

kept very busy in sanitary measures, town control, salving and destruction of military material, as well as in the evacuation of prisoners and refugees. For a time a small mobile column was left as a garrison after the main force had been withdrawn, but, though it was politically desirable to continue in occupation of this centre of Kurdistan, military considerations made this impracticable—all possible transport was required to fulfil the *rôle* allotted to us in Persia, and on the 24th May the last of our troops withdrew from Kirkuk. Before the final withdrawal all those of the inhabitants who feared the return of the Turks were evacuated as refugees by their own express desire. Those who took advantage of our offer numbered nearly 1,600, and included Chaldeans, Armenians, and Mohammedans.

Owing to the distance covered by these operations, and to the bad weather which prevailed throughout, the work of the troops was very arduous, and I have nothing but admiration for the good work put in by all arms and the excellent co-operation which was maintained between them. In prisoners alone over 3,000 Turks were taken, whilst our total casualties only amounted to 26 killed and 210 wounded. My thanks are greatly due to the able manner in which the whole sweeping operation was conducted by Lieut.-General Egerton, his staff, and the troops under his command.

8. The rain had continued much later in the year than is usual, and the road into Persia had therefore been impracticable, so that, in spite of urgent calls, I had been unable to send in that direction more than small detachments. The demoralized Russian troops were retreating to the Caspian, and with the exception of Lieut.-Colonel Bicherakov's Partisan Detachment there was nothing to prevent anarchy breaking loose in Persia.

A state of famine prevailed over the whole length of road from Kerind to Kasvin, and the Mission under Major-General L. C. Dunsterville, C.B., was largely engaged in relief work. The Persians, who had suffered greatly from both Turks and

Russians, were, rather naturally, averse to yet another belligerent entering their country, and this point of view was sedulously fostered by enemy agents and propagandists. A great deal of good and useful relief work was undertaken by the Dunsterville Mission, and much of the prevailing distress was thereby alleviated. In this connection I would like to bring to notice the excellent work done by Mr. and Mrs. Stead (American Missionaries) in the neighbourhood of Kermanshah ; there is no doubt that they saved many hundreds of lives by their devotion.

THE CASPIAN COLUMN.

However, by the end of May the road to Hamadan became possible, and, the matter being urgent, I sent forward troops in Ford vans as far as Kasvin to take over that place (which covers Teheran from the north and west) from Colonel Bicherakov, whose detachment comprised the rearguard of the Russian troops evacuating Persia.

9. We were now embarking on an operation of great difficulty. From railhead to the Caspian and Enzeli is, by the road, nearly 700 miles, and this road, west of Hamadan, is unmetalled and traverses rocky passes, swift-running streams, and broad alluvial valleys; bridges had been broken and blown up, so that temporary expedients for crossing had to be devised. One at least of the passes is over 7,000 feet, and the rocky nature of the ground encountered on many stretches of the road wore out tyres with alarming rapidity. The country in the immediate neighbourhood of the road was famine-stricken, and not only was the food situation an anxious one, but much transport was required for the supply of petrol, oil, spare parts, ordnance stores, and the many and varied articles of equipment necessary for maintaining a force in the field.

On 1st June General Dunsterville's Mission arrived at Kasvin, then occupied by Colonel Bicherakov's Partisans some 1,200 strong, together with weak British detachments.

On the 8th June the Russians marched from Kasvin with the intention of proceeding to Enzeli and thence by ship to Baku. A small British detachment accompanied them. On reaching Mandjil three days later this force found the bridge at that place held by a Gilan tribe named the Jangalis, with whom were several German officers. After a vain attempt to parley on the part of the Germans, the Russians attacked, and after capturing the Mandjil bridge pushed on to Resht and Enzeli, assisted by our light armoured cars.

The moral effect of this small action was out of all proportion to its military importance, and for a time kept in order the Jangali leaders, who had previously been bolstered up by a fictitious prestige. The closely-wooded nature of the country round Resht which they inhabit gives them a sense of security which they endeavoured to turn to account by sniping at our convoys which were being sent to Enzeli ; but no serious trouble arose until 20th July, when they attacked a small British detachment at Resht, together with the British Consulate and Bank at that place. After some hand-to-hand street fighting the attack was beaten off, and over 100 Jangalis were killed. Our Hampshire and Gurkha troops fought extremely well, and the Jangalis have not only given no more trouble, but have made an agreement not to assist the Turks any further.

10. During June small detachments were dispatched to Bijar and Miane to keep an eye on the possible activities of the Turks against my lengthy line of communications in Persia, and to establish friendly relations with the local tribes. A further reference will be made to minor operations in these districts (see paras. 15 and 16).

11. On 3rd July Colonel Bicherakov sailed from Enzeli for Alyat, 35 miles south-west of Baku. He had previously accepted the post of Commander-in-Chief of the Red Army of the Caucasus. At this time the Government of Baku was purely Bolshevik, and strongly opposed to British intervention. Various small actions were fought near Baku during

July between the Tartars and Turks on one side, and the
Russians and Armenians on the other ; but, owing to existing
disorganization, the resistance offered, with the exception
of Bicherakov's troops, was ineffective, and proved powerless
to prevent Baku being seriously threatened. On 26th July a
coup d'état took place, the Bolshevik Government being over-
thrown and its place taken by a Centro-Caspian Dictatorship.
The latter at once appealed for British aid, but before it could
arrive Bicherakov was convinced that the fall of the town
was inevitable, and in consequence of repeated acts of treachery
on the part of the Red Guards, drew off his detachment to the
north and moved along the coast of the Caspian towards
Derbend.

DEFENCE OF BAKU.

12. What news filtered through from Baku was now very
meagre, but the Turks were slow to make the most of their
opportunities in occupying the town, and, though a landing
of British troops now seemed impracticable, a small mission
of British officers with one platoon as escort was dispatched
to report on the situation. These landed in Baku on 4th
August. For the time being the appearance of even this small
party of British troops, which received an ovation on marching
through the town, seemed to have an electrical effect on the
citizens and government of Baku, and a Turkish attack on
the following day was repulsed with heavy loss.

Further British reinforcements were sent during the remainder of August, but their numbers were restricted by the
limitation imposed by the great length and difficulties of the
Persian line of communication. On arrival they took over portions of the defended perimeter of the town, and every effort
was made by General Dunsterville and his staff to instil order
into existing chaos. The inhabitants of Baku seemed, however,
to think that it was no longer necessary for them to fight, now
that the British had arrived, and they gave our troops little
or no assistance. On 26th August the Turks attacked with

considerable determination a pronounced salient in the line ; they were well supported by their artillery and charged home with the bayonet. This point was most gallantly held by a British company against odds of five to one, unsupported by local Baku troops who should have been there in reserve. The company suffered heavy casualties before being obliged to withdraw. On 31st August the Turks made two further attacks, which were beaten off with heavy loss by British and Russian troops, who were, however, subsequently compelled to give ground owing to the exposure of their flank resultant on the withdrawal of some Armenian battalions. On 1st September further ground was lost, our troops being forced back fighting against heavy odds without any efficient support from our local Allies. During all these attacks the Turks lost heavily, and it was not till the 14th September that they again attacked, after receiving large reinforcements. On this date they succeeded in scaling the heights, driving out the Armenian troops opposed to them with little difficulty, and thereby causing a readjustment of the British line to save a menaced flank. On this flank three very weak British companies held out all day on the last ridge on the outskirts of the town under heavy shell-fire and against repeated attacks by the main strength of the Turks. From this ridge the town and harbour are completely dominated, and its possession was of great importance.

An attack by the enemy on the centre was brought to a standstill by rifle-fire. A counter-attack by British, Russians, and Armenians in this vicinity failed through the British and Russians losing all their officers as well as sustaining heavy casualties in the ranks, while Turkish artillery fire arrested the advance of the Armenian troops at an early stage. Throughout the day the North Staffordshire Regiment had fought with great gallantry, and were ably supported by the men from the Royal Warwick and Worcester Regiments, as well as by the Dunsterforce armoured cars, which were boldly handled and accounted for large numbers of the enemy.

At 4 p.m. it became evident that the Turks, who had been attacking since dawn, were fought to a standstill, and could do no more than occupy the positions they had gained. Had an effective counter-attack now been possible, it is more than doubtful if the Turks could have withstood it, but every British rifle was in the line, and the Russian and Armenian troops were by this time incapable of any further effective action. The town was at the mercy of the enemy, who occupied all the high ground, and could shell the shipping in the port at ranges of 3,000–5,000 yards.

It was decided, therefore, to evacuate the British detachment. This decision was communicated to the Baku Government. By 8 p.m. all sick and wounded had been carried on board. Troops and guns were then embarked, and by 10 p.m. all were on board the three ships which had, since our arrival at Baku, been ear-marked for our use. These three ships sailed without lights, closely followed by another in which it had been possible to collect explosives and ammunition. This latter ship was hit by gunfire from the guardship at the mouth of the harbour, but the others slipped away unscathed, and all four arrived safely at Enzeli.

This British detachment had denied to the enemy for a period of six weeks the town of Baku with its very valuable oilfields, and had caused heavy casualties to the Turks, who were compelled to bring up a force of considerable numerical superiority before the capture of the place could be effected.

ASSYRIANS AT URMIA.

13. I referred earlier in the dispatch to a detachment at Bijar. A road runs through this place to the Urmia district, where it was known that the Assyrians, Nestorians, and Jelus had been successfully resisting the Turks during the earlier summer months. In July it was decided to get into communication with these tribes by aeroplane, and to send them by convoy assistance in the shape of ammunition, machine guns,

and money. This convoy reached Sain Kala on 23rd July,
but the Assyrians were 10 days late in meeting it, and their
eventual arrival coincided with the occupation of Urmia by
the Turks, who drove all the Assyrians out, massacring many
and pursuing them along the road to Sain Kala until checked
by our advanced troops. The whole of the Assyrians who
survived—men, women, and children—then poured along the
Sain Kala-Bijar road from 3rd August onwards, and eventually
over 50,000 arrived at Bijar, whence they were evacuated
unmolested to Hamadan. Large numbers unfortunately died
from cholera and privation on the way. After a few days'
rest and food all were evacuated in batches of 3,000 at a time
down the Persian line of communication to Bakuba, where a
large refugee camp had been formed. Men capable of bearing
arms were organized into a fighting force, and others were
employed at work on the roads and elsewhere. Their feeding
on the way threw a great strain on my supply staff, and practically denuded the reserves of supplies which had been collected for our winter use. The able manner in which this
undisciplined mob of men, women, and children, were dealt
with reflects great credit on the staff of the Persian line of
communication.

14. I had also kept a detachment at Miane, on the Kasvin-
Tabriz road, and by the end of August I received information
that the Turks in Tabriz were collecting transport, and pre-
sumed that their intention was to endeavour to raid my
vulnerable line of communication in the direction of Kasvin.
I have already recounted the difficulties of sending troops
and maintaining them in North Persia, and every man I
could spare from there had been hurried to Baku. Consequently I had only extremely weak parties between Kasvin
and Tabriz. On 5th September the Turks attacked an advanced post of irregulars on the road some 45 miles north-
west of Miane. This was driven in, and during the next few
days my advanced troops gradually fell back fighting before
superior numbers of Turks, who occupied Miane on 9th Sep-

tember, and took up a strong position to the south of it. By this time, however, I had been able to push reinforcements forward, and brought the Turkish advance to a standstill.

GUARDING THE OILFIELDS.

15. My relations with the Bakhtiari Khans, to whom are entrusted the safeguarding of the oilfields near Ahwaz, have remained most cordial, and in order to coerce the Kuhgalus, a tribe who had been causing the friendly Ilkhani of the Bakhtiari some annoyance, and at the same time restore security along the Ahwaz-Ispahan road, I placed during June and July a section of mountain artillery at the disposal of the Ilkhani. The results were pre-eminently satisfactory, and it is worthy of record that this section of an Indian mountain battery in the hottest season of the year covered a distance of 395 miles in 28 marching days, and returned with men and animals in excellent condition.

16. The defence of the line of communications on both Tigris and Euphrates have been ably performed. Trouble from riverain tribes is now almost unknown.

17. In so far as the climate has permitted, progressive military training has been carried out by all formations since the cessation of active operations in May last. A special feature of this has been the development of schools of instruction.

RESTORING PROSPERITY.

18. Uninterrupted progress has been made in the opening up and development of the country. It must be remembered that in the tract of country watered by the Middle Euphrates the tribesmen have never felt the weight of our arms, and, unlike those on the Lower and Upper Euphrates, have never seen our troops in any numbers.

From the Hilla district, which is now connected with

Baghdad by a broad gauge railway, some 70 per cent. of the cereals available for the force are derived. The extensive agricultural and irrigation projects in this region bid fair to restore to this once fertile tract the prosperity it enjoyed when Babylon was at her zenith.

The manufacture of prepared bitumen and lime continues at Hit on a large scale. Some 4,000 tons of bitumen and 5,350 tons of lime have been exported during the past four months, and it has been found possible, after meeting all Government demands, to allow of private enterprise in this industry.

19. The opportunities afforded to the Royal Navy during the period under review have been few, but Commodore D. Norris and the officers and ratings under his command have invariably displayed a spirit of ready co-operation in accordance with their high traditions.

20. The hot weather in Mesopotamia of necessity limits the sphere of activity of the Royal Air Force. Notwithstanding this, many fine long-distance flights have been undertaken and valuable reconnaissances and much photographic work performed. Some idea may perhaps be gained of their wide range of action when I say that since the conclusion of the Kirkuk operations aeroplanes have been employed on various missions at places as widely separated as Samawa, on the Middle Euphrates, and Baku, in Trans-Caucasia. In fact, wherever troops have operated, the pilots and observers of the Royal Air Force have invariably contributed in no small measure to their success, and their boldness and intrepidity are fully recognized by the Army.

21. Great progress has been recorded in the development of the port of Basra and in the reclamation of low-lying areas in its vicinity. There is now a continuous wharf, 3,300 feet in length, adequately equipped with electric cranes.

22. The Directorate of Signals and Telegraphs has had many difficulties to contend with, more especially in connection with the extension of the area now controlled by the Force. These have been promptly overcome, and communica-

tion well maintained at all times. During the period, no fewer than 850 miles of telegraph line, carrying 1,700 miles of wire, have actually been erected, while 375 additional miles are now under construction.

There has been, too, a considerable extension in the use of wireless telegraphy, and a complete chain of wireless stations has been established throughout the area now in occupation.

23. Surveys and the Map Compilation Section have always risen to the occasion, and have continued to produce a large output of admirable work.

HEALTH OF THE TROOPS.

24. The period April 1 to July 13 shows a distinct improvement in the health of the troops as compared with the corresponding weeks of last year :—

	Last year.	This year.
Average weekly admissions on account of sickness. Ratio per cent. of ration strength .	1.73	1.45
Average weekly wastage (death and invaliding) on account of sickness. Ratio per cent. of ration strength	0.31	0.16

These figures indicate a very considerable saving to the Force, which has been achieved by unremitting care paid by the Medical Authorities to sanitary and medical requirements, and to the constant devotion to duty shown by the Nursing Services.

The Red Cross Society has continued to attend to the needs and comforts of the sick and wounded in a most praiseworthy manner.

Ministration to the spiritual welfare of the troops by Chaplains of all denominations continues satisfactorily, and the work of Indian Assistant Chaplains is much appreciated amongst Indian Christians.

Considerable progress in the recording of Christian graves has been made, and cemeteries are being well maintained.

26. The physical and moral recreation of the Force is being attended to, and I am satisfied that the steps taken in forming a Central Recreational Committee will have a beneficial result.

In April we had the honour of a visit from Their Excellencies Lord and Lady Willingdon, who have, throughout the campaign in Mesopotamia, done so much for the benefit of all members of the force. Their visit was a source of genuine pleasure to all, and they were enabled to see for themselves some of the results of their unremitting labours on our behalf.

27. The difficulties of the administrative departments and services have naturally increased with the extended area now occupied by the Force.

Local resources have been developed in a very satisfactory manner, and good results achieved. The harvest, though later than was anticipated, has been bountiful, and it is confidently expected that in the future the Force will be self-supporting as regards barley and fodder.

Supplies have been satisfactorily maintained and delivered to the troops with a regularity which is worthy of all praise, when it is remembered that not a single metalled road exists throughout the length and breadth of Mesopotamia.

The work of the Transport, particularly of the Mechanical Transport, has been extremely arduous. Immense wear and tear to vehicles has been caused on the Persian road, and it reflects great credit on all concerned to have kept so many vehicles in working order. It is safe to say that a line of communication of such a length has never previously been kept up.

The development and opening up of new lines by the Railway Department during the period has been most marked. Allusion has already been made to the broad gauge line to Hilla. A narrow gauge extension thence to Kifl on the other branch of the Euphrates has since been opened to traffic.

IRRIGATION PROJECTS.

The Board of Agriculture was constituted some three months ago, and has already proved of value in co-ordinating with the Political Department the work of the two recently established Directorates of Irrigation and Agriculture. Considerable irrigation projects are in hand, with the object of increasing the food development of the country, but the scope of these is limited by the labour available for the works and the number of cultivators available for the ultimate production of crops.

28. The period under review has been, owing to the extreme heat during the greater part of it, one of inactivity for the large majority of the troops, and I was enabled to send a large number of officers and men on leave to India. Leave camps at various centres had been kindly arranged for by Army Headquarters in India, to which the British troops were sent ; the Indian troops were, of course, able to visit their own homes. The General Officer Commanding Ceylon also made arrangement for the reception of a large number of British officers, and his efforts in this respect have been much appreciated.

Urgent cases (treated for precedence on their merits) were granted leave to the United Kingdom, but transport difficulties naturally confined this privilege to a selected few.

The country has gone ahead, and is being further developed, and the inhabitants are showing by their behaviour that they appreciate the blessings of a just and sympathetic Government.

SPECIAL MENTIONS.

29. I have been throughout most ably and loyally served by my subordinate commanders, staff and technical advisers, and take this opportunity of recording my most sincere thanks for all their good work.

In addition to the names already mentioned, I wish to bring to your notice those of—

Major-General G. F. MacMunn, K.C.B., C.S.I., D.S.O., Inspector-General of Communications.

Major-General W. Gillman, C.B., C.M.G., D.S.O., Chief of the General Staff.

Major-General the Honourable A. R. Montagu-Stuart-Wortley, K.C.M.G., C.B., D.S.O., Deputy Quartermaster-General.

Major-General F. R. Ready, C.B., C.M.G., D.S.O., Deputy Adjutant-General.

A further list of names of officers, ladies, non-commissioned officers, and men who have been deemed to have earned special distinction is being forwarded to you on a separate list.

30. This dispatch would not be complete without a reference to the valuable services rendered by Lieut.-Colonel A. T. Wilson, C.M.G., C.I.E., D.S.O., acting Civil Commissioner, and the political officers working under his direction. His advice has always been of the greatest value to me, and I tender him my warmest thanks for the whole-hearted and vigorous support which I have received from him throughout.

31. In addition to the foregoing, and in pursuance of the authority delegated to me as Commander-in-Chief, I have made the following immediate awards for gallantry and distinguished service in the field during the period covered by this dispatch : Distinguished Service Order, 8 ; Military Cross, 29 ; Bar to Military Cross, 4 ; Distinguished Conduct Medal, 10 ; Bar to Distinguished Conduct Medal, 1 ; Military Medal, 60 ; Indian Order of Merit, 3 ; Indian Distinguished Service Medal, 16.

I have the honour to be,

Sir,

Your obedient servant,

W. R. MARSHALL,

Lieut.-General, Commanding-in-Chief,

Mesopotamian Expeditionary Force.

APPENDIX III.

SIR G. F. MILNE'S SECOND DISPATCH.

THE FALL OF BULGARIA.

WAR OFFICE,
22nd January, 1919.

THE Secretary of State for War has received the following Dispatch from General Sir George F. Milne, K.C.B., D.S.O., Commanding-in-Chief, British Salonika Force :—

GENERAL HEADQUARTERS,
BRITISH SALONIKA FORCE.
1st December 1918.

MY LORD,

I have the honour to submit the following report on the operations of the British Army in Macedonia from October 1, 1917, to the present date.

During the greater part of this period I continued to be responsible for the eastern sector of the Balkan front. This part of the Allied line ran north-westward from the mouth of the Struma River, past Lake Tahinos and its marshes, up the broad valley to the junction of the Butkova and Struma Rivers. Here it turned westward, along the slopes of the Krusha Balkans, to Lake Doiran, and then near Doiran town swept south-east to the Vardar Valley. The whole sector was some 100 miles long and distant between 50 and 60 miles from the town of Salonika. On the north-east it barred the way against an advance from Serres and the Rupel Pass ; on the north-west it both guarded and threatened the Vardar Valley, the enemy's main line of communication and his shortest and easiest road to Salonika.

In view of the diminution in the strength of the Army caused by the transfer of two divisions and two cavalry brigades to another theatre, the question of the construction of communications, in order that troops might be moved rapidly from one point to another, and of the preparation of retired positions, became of primary importance. This work was methodically carried out. At the beginning of 1916 the rough and broken Serres Road had been, apart from the railway, which fed the Doiran front, the only line of communication. Now good metalled roads run to Serres, to Doiran and to Karasuli on the Vardar River. Neohori on the mouth of the Struma River, and Snevce and Rajanova at the foot of the Krucha Balkans can be reached by road and light railway; circular routes by road and rail give lateral communications behind both the first and second zones of defence. In the beginning of September 1917 an entrenched position was commenced running from Berovo on the east *via* Lahana, the high ground to the east of Kurkut, and the hills round Janes to the Vardar River at Vardino. This position, which was practically finished in September 1918, formed a strong and shorter line of defence, at a distance varying from 5 to 15 miles behind the front line, and covering all lines of advance from the north-east and north.

On the approach of autumn I decided that the troops which had been withdrawn from the valleys of the Rivers Struma and Butkova at the commencement of the summer should again be moved forward to the lower ground. During the month of October this movement, combined with minor operations against the villages in the valley, was successfully carried out by the troops of the 16th Corps. As a result, over 250 prisoners and several machine guns were captured, and severe casualties inflicted on the enemy.

Meanwhile, among the broken hills of the 12th Corps front,

between Doiran Lake and the Vardar, our raiding parties incessantly harassed the enemy and returned with prisoners. The most conspicuous of these raids, all of which were carried out with determination and skill, was against Boyau Hill, near Macukovo. Here the 12th Battalion, Argyll and Sutherland Highlanders, broke through the strong hostile outpost position, 500 yards in front of their main objective, entered the enemy trenches, and, having destroyed three machine guns and inflicted heavy casualties, returned bringing all their wounded with them.

In the middle of October the Allied Commander-in-Chief decided to extend the French front to the left bank of the Vardar, thus permitting me to withdraw another infantry brigade into reserve—a matter of no small value to troops who had been for over one year continuously in the front line.

The winter season had now fully set in, and the heavy rains, followed by snow and frost, considerably hampered operations on all fronts. Local raids continued to be of almost daily occurrence, resulting in a steady loss to the enemy both in killed and prisoners, and at the same time maintaining the offensive spirit of the troops, and training both infantry and artillery for the operations which they were called upon to carry out at a later date.

Towards the end of December General Sarrail was succeeded in the command of the Allied Armies by General Guillaumat, on whose initiative considerable attention was paid, during the winter and spring, to the amplification and improvement of the existing defences of the town and district of Salonika, which were constituted into a third line of defence.

In the beginning of March 1918 the 1st Hellenic (Larissa) Division was placed under my command, and was attached to the 16th Army Corps on the Struma River front, where it took over a sector of the line to the north of Lake Tahinos. With the unhealthy season approaching, this was a welcome reinforcement to my effectives. But almost immediately the gain in numbers was counter-balanced by an extension of front.

The Russian troops under General Guillaumat's command had failed him, and he found it necessary to ask me again to take over the line as far as the River Vardar in order to relieve French troops for employment elsewhere.

In the early days of this month there came a blizzard of extraordinary severity and deep snow, which hampered all movements both by land and in the air. But towards the end of the month fairer weather resulted in a marked increase in aerial activity. Almost every day the Royal Air Force raided the enemy's country, bombed his camps, dumps and railway stations, and attacked his troops with machine-gun fire from low altitudes. In the fighting that these raids entailed our airmen more than held their own.

During April it became necessary, owing to the likelihood of an offensive on the part of the enemy, to do everything possible to disturb his plans and obtain reliable information as to his intentions. Accordingly, on both the Struma and Doiran fronts local operations on our side were intensified.

On the night of the 14th–15th April strong detachments from the 1st Hellenic Division and the 27th and 28th Divisions, supported by artillery, were pushed forward to occupy the villages of Beglik-Mahale, Kakaraska, Salmahale, Kispeki, Homondos, Kalendra, Prosenik, and Kjupri in the Struma Valley. On the following day violent counter-attacks developed against our advanced troops holding the villages of Prosenik and Kumli. Severe fighting took place at close quarters, during which heavy casualties were inflicted on the enemy. In the course of the next few days these advanced detachments gradually withdrew to their former positions, having obtained sufficient information to verify the position of all the enemy's units opposed to them.

On the Doiran front, where the enemy held strongly entrenched and continuous positions in mountainous and rocky country, operations were necessarily restricted to small raids and artillery bombardment. In all these, casualties were inflicted on the enemy at slight loss to ourselves. One raid, novel in its plan and bold in its execution, is worthy of special notice. Shortly after midnight on the 15th–16th April, in bright moonlight, a mixed naval and military party left the shore of the lake by Doiran Station in four boats, silently driven by electric motors, which had been brought up from Salonika and assembled under the eyes of the enemy. From Doiran Station to Doiran Town by water is two miles, but the party landed well within the enemy lines unchallenged. Sentries were left to guard the boats, the town was searched and the lakeside road patrolled. Not a Bulgar was seen, and so, as the main purpose of the raid, the capture of prisoners, could not be achieved, the party embarked, recrossed the lake in safety and apparently unobserved, and landed again on our shore at four o'clock. This daring operation stands out as a striking testimony to the enterprise of the troops, and its skilful execution was undoubtedly due to the energy and care displayed by Captain R. S. Olivier, R.N., Senior Naval Officer at Salonika, and the officers and men of H.M.S. *St. George*, who not only trained the detachment on this occasion, but have at all times cordially assisted the Army.

During May and June the two remaining divisions of the 1st Hellenic Corps were placed under my orders, and General Paraskevopoulos took over the command in the Struma Valley. With a portion of the British troops thus relieved, I was enabled to extend my front to the right bank of the Vardar River in relief of a French Division.

About this time orders were received for the reduction of the infantry of the divisions from thirteen to ten battalions. As a result, one-quarter of the infantry of the Army was transferred to France.

It was during the month of June that the first indications of a lowering in moral of the Bulgarian Army became noticeable. The number of deserters largely increased, and from their statements it appeared that the Bulgarian Higher Command was meditating an attack on a large scale on the British front from the sea to Lake Doiran. Later information showed that certain enemy units were, however, in a state bordering on mutiny and refused to obey orders.

On 8th June I bade farewell to General Guillaumat, who vacated the post of Commander-in-Chief of the Allied Armies in order to take up an important appointment in France. During his short period of command he had gained, by his tact, courtesy, and soldierly qualities, the respect and admiration of all those with whom he came into contact, and I am deeply grateful to him for his cordial and sympathetic assistance. A few days later his distinguished successor, General Franchet d'Esperey, who was so shortly to bring about a sudden change in the whole situation in the Balkans, assumed command of the Allied Forces.

Towards the end of July I received instructions from the Allied Commander-in-Chief to prepare for my share in a general offensive of the Allied Armies, which was timed to take place during the first fortnight of September. In this the British troops—provided the Allies on the front held by the Royal Serbian Army succeeded in piercing the enemy's centre—were to attack and take the heights to the west and north-east of Lake Doiran. To reinforce my three divisions in this sector General Franchet d'Esperey placed at my disposal two divisions of the Corps of National Defence of the Hellenic Army, a regiment of Hellenic cavalry, and a group of Hellenic heavy artillery. The infantry intended for the attack were gradually withdrawn from the line, and during the latter part of August they were carefully trained for the *rôle* they were to fill. Meanwhile an offensive spirit was maintained, and the enemy harassed by constant raids, in which prisoners were secured for purposes of identification. In the air our machines were more active day by day, and our artillery fire steadily increased, especially on the right bank of the Vardar, cutting wire and drawing the enemy's batteries.

By now it was clear that the enemy suspected an impending attack, but did not know where the blow was to fall. His reserves were reported to be in the Vardar Valley. To prevent their withdrawal, and to deceive him as to the sector chosen for the main Allied attack, operations were begun on the afternoon of the 1st September, after heavy artillery preparation, against the rocky and strongly fortified salient north of Alcak Mahale, on the right bank of the Vardar. The troops engaged were the 2nd Battalion Gloucestershire Regiment and the 10th Battalion Hampshire Regiment of the 27th Division. The undertaking proved an entire success. Not only were determined counter-attacks launched fruitlessly against our new trenches, but on the right the Division was able to occupy the enemy's outpost line, thus gaining suitable positions for a further advance. With this operation and with the unhindered advance of the posts of the 1st Hellenic Corps in the Struma Valley about a week later, the preliminaries on the right section of the general offensive were completed.

On the morning of the 14th September the general attack began. All along the 80-mile front, from Lake Doiran to Monastir, the artillery bombardment of the hostile positions became intense. Twenty-four hours later the Franco-Serbian troops, under the command of Voivode Mischitch, stormed the Bulgar trenches on the mountain heights from Sokol to Vetrenik. Before noon the enemy's first and second line were in the possession of Allied troops. This initial victory forced a withdrawal on the flanks. The gap of 12 kilometres was enlarged to one of 25 kilometres. The way was opened for advance to the heights of Kozyak.

The success on which an assault on the Doiran sector was conditional had been attained. Early on the 15th September I received orders from General Franchet d'Esperey that the troops under my command were to attack on the morning of the 18th.

In the general instructions, which I had previously received, it was indicated that the main operations should be directed against the " P " Ridge and the neighbouring heights west of Lake Doiran, the scene of the battles in the spring of 1917. I had decided to reinforce the British troops here by one of the Hellenic Divisions of the Corps of National Defence, which, as I have previously stated, had been placed at my disposal, and had selected the Serres Division for this purpose. In addition, between Doiran Lake and the Vardar were the 22nd and 26th British Divisions, under Major-General J. Duncan, C.B., C.M.G., D.S.O., and Major-General A. W. Gay, C.B., C.M.G., D.S.O., respectively, and on the west of the Vardar the 27th Division under Major-General G. T. Forestier-Walker, C.B. This force was supported by the whole of the available heavy artillery, which included a brigade of Hellenic heavy guns.

The effective strength of the British troops at this most trying period of the year in Macedonia had, owing to climatic disease and a sudden and severe epidemic of influenza, fallen below one-half of the normal establishment. The Allied Commander-in-Chief, therefore, further reinforced my command by a regiment of French infantry. The whole of this composite force of British, Hellenic and French troops I entrusted to the command of Lieutenant-General Sir H. F. M. Wilson, K.C.B., K.C.M.G.

Simultaneously with the main attack, a secondary and surprise attack was to be made round the east and northern sides of the lake against the Bulgar trenches on the slopes of the Beles Range. If successful, the action would turn the Doiran-Vardar front on its left, and in any case would prevent reinforcements moving to the west. The operation was a difficult one, involving a large concentration by night and an advance without artillery preparation across the plain between the Krusha Balkans and the Beles. I therefore decided to support with troops of the 28th Division, commanded by Major-General H. L. Croker, C.B., C.M.G., the Cretan Division of the Corps of National Defence, to whom this movement had been assigned, and placed this sector under the orders of Lieutenant-General Sir C. J. Briggs, K.C.B., K.C.M.G.

The Bulgarian front between Doiran Lake and the Vardar was one of exceptional strength. To an observer from the centre of the line from which the Allied attack was to take place, the medley of broken hills forming his position baffles detailed description except at great length. There are steep hillsides and rounded hills. There is little soil. The hard rocky ground makes consolidation of a newly won position difficult, and gives overwhelming advantage to the defender, well dug into trenches that have been the careful work of three years. Deep cut ravines divert progress and afford unlimited opportunity for enfilading fire. But in all the complexity of natural features the " P " Ridge and Grand Couronne stand out in conspicuous domination. The former, from a height of over 2,000 feet, slopes southward towards our lines, overlooking our trenches and the whole country south to Salonika. To its right the country dips and rises to a less sharp, but no less intricate maze of hills, that mount, tier upon tier, from Petit Couronne with its steep and rugged sides, above Doiran Lake to Grand Couronne, itself little lower than the summit of the " P " Ridge. The enemy had taken full advantage of his ground. He was strongly entrenched in three successive lines, with communication trenches deeply cut into the rock and roomy well-timbered dug-outs, with concrete machine-gun emplacements, and, on the crest between " P " Ridge and Grand Couronne, with concrete gunpits. It was the key position of the Vardar-Doiran defences, and he held it with his best troops.

Shortly before dawn on the 18th September the bombardment of the last four days was intensified, and west of the lake the attack was launched. Soon after 6 o'clock the two regiments of the Hellenic Division on the right had stormed the enemy position up to the neighbourhood of Doiran Hill, which rises above the ruins of the town, and had taken a large number of prisoners. On the left the 66th Infantry Brigade, which had been detailed to lead the attack on the " P " Ridge, advanced with consummate self-sacrifice and gallantry. Here the enemy had established three strong lines of defence, teeming with concrete machine-gun emplacements from which they could sweep and enfilade the whole front. After severe fighting the 12th Battalion, Cheshire Regiment, and the 9th Battalion, South Lancashire Regiment, supported by the 8th Battalion, King's Shropshire Light Infantry, succeeded in reaching the third line of trenches. At this point they came under devastating machine-gun fire, and, unable to make further progress, were eventually compelled to fall back to their original position. In their heroic attempt they had lost about 65 per cent. of their strength, including Lieutenant-Colonel Hon. A. R. Clegg Hill, D.S.O., and Lieutenant-Colonel B. F. Bishop, M.C., who fell at the head of their battalions. In the centre, Hellenic and Welsh troops together assaulted the network of hills and trenches between the " P " Ridge and Grand Couronne and penetrated to a depth of about one mile. Severe loss was inflicted on the enemy, who offered a desperate resistance, supported by a heavy machine-gun fire from immensely strong emplacements blasted in the solid rock. In spite of this the lower slopes of Grand Couronne were reached. But the lack of success on the " P " Ridge made it impossible to retain the ground so hardly won, and the battalions gradually fell back to their former lines, the last to leave being the survivors of the 7th Battalion, South Wales Borderers—19 unwounded men and 1 wounded officer.

Meanwhile, on the east of the lake the Cretan Division, supported by troops of the 28th Division, had advanced across the gradually narrowing plain to attack the enemy's positions on the Blaga Planina, to the north of the lake. In difficult country they had assembled during the night behind the dismantled railway embankment. At dawn they carried the enemy's outpost line and pressed forward to his main line. This they penetrated in two places on a narrow front, but a permanent hold could not be maintained. Nothing was now to be gained by pressing this attack, and I therefore authorized a return to the line of the railway.

Apart from the prospect of a local advance it was essential to the progress of the Royal Serbian Army that none of the enemy reserves which had been attracted to the Doiran-Vardar front should be diverted elsewhere. I therefore gave orders that all the ground won should be held, and that the attack west of the lake should be renewed next morning with all available troops. To afford me a reserve, the Allied Commander-in-Chief placed at my disposal a regiment of the 14th Hellenic Division, then in training at Naresh, some 25 miles in rear.

During the night of the 18th–19th a heavy bombardment was maintained. At 5 a.m. Greek and Scottish troops moved forward against the enemy's positions on the lower slopes of Grand Couronne. Again, in spite of the intense machine-gun fire, they succeeded in reaching their objective at many points. Several of the intermediate works were captured and held against determined counter-attacks. Unfortunately, on the left the Allied troops at their position of assembly had come under heavy barrage, and could make no further progress. In spite of this the 65th Infantry Brigade, which had moved up rapidly during the night from an influenza observation camp, twice gallantly tried alone to capture the " P " Ridge, but were driven back by overwhelming fire from the enemy's machine guns. The effect was that the troops in the centre found their left flank exposed. Their right was also threatened, and they were compelled to fall back, stubbornly fighting the whole way. The 12th Battalion, Argyll and Sutherland Highlanders, the 8th Battalion, Royal Scots Fusiliers, and the 11th Battalion, Scottish Rifles, covered the retirement in spite of severe casualties, including loss of all their commanding officers, killed or wounded.

Accordingly, at midday on the 19th, I decided to hold and consolidate the ground won. This included Petit Couronne, Teton Hill, and Doiran town. " P " Ridge and Grand Couronne had not been taken, but the enemy was severely shaken ; he had suffered very heavy casualties, losing over 1,200 in prisoners alone. What was even more important, the whole of his reserves, which might have been employed effectively elsewhere, had been pinned down to this front, and had suffered so severely that they were now ineffective.

The results of these stubbornly contested operations were to be seen in the course of the next few days.

By the morning of the 21st the Franco-Serbian Army had reached the line Gradista-Bosava-Dragosil and the heights of Porca dominating the Vardar, thus turning the flank of the enemy in my front and cutting his communications down the Vardar Valley. By noon it was plain that a hurried retirement on the Doiran front had begun. The depôts at Hudova, Cestova, and other places behind the lines were observed to be in flames, and numerous explosions showed that ammunition depôts were being everywhere blown up. The observers of the Royal Air Force reported that the Kosturino Pass on the Strumica road, the only good line of retreat now open to the enemy, was blocked by masses of men and transport moving northwards. The pilots of the Royal Air Force, flying low, took full advantage of this opportunity. They bombed the Bulgar columns and shot down men and animals with their machine guns, causing heavy casualties and a confusion that bordered on panic.

During the evening patrols reported that the advanced trenches of the enemy were empty. Before dawn on the 22nd the whole of the Army was on the move. By nightfall the foremost troops had reached the line Kara Ogular-Hamzali-Bogdanci. Close touch was kept with the hostile rearguards which, well supplied with mountain and machine guns, did' all they could to delay our pursuit. West of the Vardar the 27th Division advanced with the Archipelago Division of the Franco-Hellenic Corps on their immediate left.

In the next few days the pursuit was pressed by all the Allied Armies from Doiran to Monastir. By the 24th the Serbian infantry, moving forward at an extraordinary speed, had reached the line Hadzi-Seidli-Cesme Dere ; their cavalry were approaching Stip.

The first of the Allies to enter Bulgaria was the Derbyshire

Yeomanry, early on the morning of the 25th September. These were the leading troops of the 16th Corps, under Lieutenant-General C. J. Briggs, K.C.B., K.C.M.G., whom I had brought round from the right to the left of the Army. They were followed shortly after by the 14th Hellenic and 26th Divisions, the former having replaced the Serres Division in the Anglo-Hellenic Army.

Simultaneously the 22nd Division from the west and the Cretan Division from the east of Lake Doiran began to climb the steep slopes of the Belasica Range, on the north of the lake. In the centre the 28th Division, which had made forced marches across from the extreme right, reached the heights of Dzuma Obasi. On the 26th September the 16th Corps descended to the Strumica Valley and gained the Strumica-Petric road. During the night French, Hellenic, and British troops stormed and captured the towering summits of the Belasica. This range is over 4,000 feet above the lake ; the ascents are severe, there are practically no paths, and communication was necessarily most irregular. In this operation the 8th Battalion, South Wales Borderers, under Lieutenant-Colonel R. C. Dobbs, D.S.O., specially distinguished themselves.

Up to this date thirty guns, large quantities of ammunition, and three hospitals had been captured, while many of our wounded prisoners had been recovered ; considerable quantities of guns, motor cars, and stores had been found abandoned all along the line of retreat and in the mountains.

At 8 o'clock on the morning of 26th September a Bulgarian parliamentaire, under a white flag, bearing a proposal to conclude an armistice, approached the British lines, and was immediately conducted to my headquarters, and thence to the Allied Headquarters at Salonika.

Two days later the Bulgarian plenipotentiaries, Mr. Lyaptcheff, Minister of Finance, General Lukoff, Commander of the 2nd Bulgarian Army, and Mr. Radeff with their staff, passed through *en route* for Salonika.

In the meanwhile the advance continued. The Strumica Valley runs eastward towards the Upper Struma Valley, which it joins near Petric, 15 miles north of Rupel and Demirhissar. The defile of the Upper Struma, through the Kresna and the Rupel Passes, formed the main line of communication for the Bulgar forces on the Lower Struma. To strike at this the 16th Corps now swung eastwards, sending a flank guard by way of Berovo to Pechovo on their left, while on the right the Cretan Division, in conjunction with the 228th Infantry Brigade, swept along the crest of the Belasica and down the Butkova Valley against Rupel and Demirhissar.

It was at this time that the Royal Air Force found the Kresna Pass choked by the retreating enemy, whose Struma army was now in danger. Again, our pilots, as subsequent reports showed, did enormous execution.

Considerable resistance was encountered to the north-east of Yenikoj, in the Strumica Valley, and on the northern slopes of the Belasica Mountain, where the steep slopes and the absence of water made operations very difficult. The troops of the two Hellenic Divisions, supported by British cavalry and artillery, were slowly but surely fighting their way forward, when at 2 a.m. on the 30th, at the moment when only 15 miles separated my advanced troops from the Rupel Pass and the lines of communication of the Bulgarian Army in the Struma Valley, I was informed that a military convention had been signed at the Allied Headquarters and that operations would cease at noon.

The orders now received were to the effect that the British Army should move by Petric and Radomir through Bulgaria to the Danube, in the vicinity of Vidin, in order to co-operate with the French and Serbian Armies in their operations against Austro-Hungary. This advance had begun when, on 10th October, I received instructions to assume the command of the Allied troops operating against Turkey in Europe, and to transfer the Army under my command to that theatre of operations.

In spite of the fact that the railway had been totally destroyed between Doiran and Serres, and that practically no roads exist in Eastern Macedonia, on the night of the 30th-31st October, when I received the news of the conclusion of an armistice with Turkey, two British divisions and one French division were ready on the River Maritza to seize the northern bridges and to occupy the town of Adrianople, the bridge at Ipsala was in my possession, while in the rear, the 1st Hellenic Corps was echeloned between Kavala and Drama, ready to take part in the general advance on Constantinople.

This rapid move of about 250 miles, including the re-basing of the troops on the small ports in the Ægean Sea, reflects the greatest credit on the staff and administrative services, but it would have been impossible of achievement without the hearty co-operation of the Royal Navy in clearing the mine-swept areas and ports, and in assisting in the transfer of troops and stores. My thanks are specially due to Vice-Admiral Hon. Sir S. A. Gough-Calthorpe, K.C.B., C.V.O., Commander-in-Chief in the Mediterranean ; Rear-Admiral M. Culme Seymour, C.B., M.V.O., Commanding the British Ægean Squadron ; Captain G. K. Chetwode, R.N., Commanding Destroyer Flotilla ; and to Commodore E. Unwin, V.C., C.M.G., the indefatigable Principal Naval Transport Officer in the Eastern Mediterranean, to whose energy was due the possibility of making any use of the open and unsuitable roadstead of Dedeagach as a base of supply.

I cannot speak too highly of the spirit and determination shown by all ranks during this short but arduous campaign. Malaria and influenza had taken a heavy toll, both in strength and in numbers, but rather than miss the opportunity for which they had waited three years, officers and men remained in the ranks till often they dropped from sheer exhaustion. The calls made on the infantry have been specially severe, but whether in the attacks on the almost impregnable positions between Doiran and the Vardar, in the operations in the unhealthy Struma Valley, or in surmounting the heights of the

Belasica Mountains, they have invariably met with the same ready response.

The Yeomanry have proved that the day of the mounted soldier is not yet over. Their only fault was their lack of numbers at the time when their services in the pursuit of the Bulgarian Army became invaluable.

The work of the Artillery, both Field and Heavy, desires special notice. The small amount available has necessitated their remaining in the line even on the few occasions when the infantry were placed in reserve. The organization of the counter-battery work has reached a very high standard, and I am glad to be able to record the active co-operation of the Hellenic Heavy Artillery, whose training was placed in the able hands of Major-General W. H. Onslow, C.B., C.M.G., Commanding the Artillery of the Army.

During the past year the Royal Engineers have done splendid service in the construction of the numerous communications and lines of defence over very difficult country, and in the final operations. The difficulties of road construction were rapidly and energetically overcome by their efforts, under the supervision of the Engineer-in-Chief, Major-General H. A. A. Livingstone, C.B., C.M.G.

I must again direct attention to the excellent work of the Royal Air Force. Throughout the whole year their duties of reconnaissance, artillery co-operation, photography, and bombing the hostile depôts have been continuously carried out. Once adequately provided with up-to-date aeroplanes, our pilots rapidly gained command of the air, and have succeeded in accounting for eight hostile machines for every one of our own missing. The present state of efficiency is largely due to the administrative energy of the late commander, Lieutenant-Colonel G. W. Dawes, D.S.O., while his successor, Lieutenant-Colonel G. E. Todd, has not only maintained the high standard of efficiency, but has handled his squadrons with marked ability during the late operations.

I desire to express my admiration for the gallantry and

determination of the Hellenic Army during the late operations, and my gratitude to the corps and divisional commanders for their ready co-operation at all times.

During the year special attention has been directed to the military education of both officers and other ranks. Continuous courses of instruction have been held at the various Army Schools, both infantry and artillery, and it is satisfactory to note that the results have fully justified my expectations. In addition, training camps were instituted for the instruction of men withdrawn from the Royal Army Service Corps and Royal Army Medical Corps for duty in infantry units. These men, who had for the most part voluntarily enlisted during the early stages of the war, showed great keenness to learn their new duties, and formed a valuable, and my only source of, reinforcement. The greatest credit is due to the instructional staff, including the Army Gymnastic Staff, for the energy and ability displayed, and the results attained.

In this unhealthy climate the efficient administration of the Medical Services is naturally of extreme importance, and in this respect a very high standard of efficiency has been attained. In an army saturated with malaria and passing through a severe outbreak of influenza, heavy calls were constantly made on the strength and devotion to duty of the Royal Army Medical Corps, of whose work I cannot speak too highly. I am much indebted to Major-General M. P. Holt, K.C.M.G., C.B., D.S.O., and his subordinates for the admirable manner in which their duties have been performed.

I should like to call attention to the indefatigable and devoted work of the personnel of the Nursing Services and Voluntary Aid Detachment during the past three years. In many instances they have sacrificed their own health for the sake of the soldiers in their charge.

The members of the General Service Voluntary Aid Detachment organization, although of comparatively recent arrival in this theatre of war, have proved their value.

To all these ladies the British Army in the Balkans, and many of our Allies, owes a deep debt of thanks.

Under the able direction of Hon. Lieutenant-Colonel H. L. Fitzpatrick the British Red Cross Society has been of the utmost service, not only to this Army, but to all our Allies. Its energies, like its resources, appear unlimited, and it merits the gratitude of all.

I desire to take this opportunity of expressing my admiration of the work of the Scottish Women's organizations serving with the Serbian Army.

The rapid movement of troops during the recent operations over a mountainous country, where roads are practically non-existent, has taxed the Signal Service to the utmost ; but despite all difficulties communication throughout the Army has never failed, thanks to the able management of Colonel A. H. Grubb, C.M.G., D.S.O., and to the hard work of his staff, as a result of which a complete telegraphic and telephonic system has been established over Macedonia reaching to Sofia and Constantinople.

The reconstruction of destroyed standard gauge and the construction of new light railways has naturally in a country so destitute of communications formed a most important task, rendered possible only by the continuous energy of the railway troops, of whose excellent spirit I cannot speak too highly. The Allied Railway Commission, under the tactful and able management of Colonel Delauney, of the French Army, and Colonel G. D. Rhodes, D.S.O., Director of Railways, has continued in the harmonious administration of the various railway lines in Macedonia, Bulgaria, and Turkey in Europe.

No very great strain has been placed on either the Royal Army Veterinary Department or the Remount Department, which have both proved equal to all demands made on them. The present uniformly good condition of the animals in the Force is largely due to the efforts of these two services to improve and simplify animal management, and to the efficient administration of Brigadier-General G. M. Dowell, C.M.G.,

Director of Remounts ; and Brigadier-General F. Eassie, C.M.G., D.S.O., Director of Veterinary Services, whose hospitals are models of their kind.

The work of all branches of the Royal Army Service Corps deserves special praise. Their responsibilities include not only supplying the British Army's requirements but those of the whole Greek Army and a very large proportion of the supplies for the other Armies in Macedonia. That, in spite of difficulties by sea and by land, the supply and transport services of forces extending from the Black Sea to the Adriatic has never failed for one day is a great tribute to the work done by all ranks serving both with the British and with the Serbian Army, and reflects great credit on the organizing ability of Brigadier-General A. Long, C.B., C.M.G., D.S.O., Director of Supplies and Transport, and his staff. Large areas of country have also been brought under cultivation in order to supply the troops from local resources, under the management of the Royal Army Service Corps.

The Ordnance Services, under Brigadier-General W. H. U. Smith, C.B., D.S.O., have continued to be well carried out, and have fulfilled all requirements. The workshop organization is excellent ; considerable ingenuity has been displayed in making full use of waste material.

Praise is due to Colonel A. G. Payne, C.M.G., Command Paymaster, and his staff, and to officers and men of the Third Echelon, General Headquarters, who have performed their irksome but necessary duties to my entire satisfaction. Graves registration has been carried out in an efficient manner ; attention is now being directed to the graves of those who fell on the Gallipoli Peninsula.

The results of the labours of all branches of the Field Survey Company, Royal Engineers, have proved invaluable, and full advantage has been taken of the opportunity for obtaining accurate maps of Macedonia, in close co-operation with the French and Siberian Topographical Sections. This task, undertaken in addition to the numerous trench maps, required on a front 100 miles long, has thrown a considerable strain on the personnel of one company.

The regularity with which the Army Postal Service has been conducted in spite of many difficulties is most gratifying, and is largely due to the energy of Lieutenant-Colonel J. S. Henderson, M.C., the Deputy Director of Postal Services, and to his excellent staff.

The religious welfare of the Army has been ministered to by a devoted band of Army Chaplains, who have received considerable assistance from that magnificent organization the Young Men's Christian Association, ever ready to establish its tents in the most inhospitable localities, and to whose devoted assistants I take this opportunity of offering our hearty thanks.

Another institution of incalculable value to the comfort of all ranks is the Expeditionary Force Canteen. Major E. V. Wellings and his staff have rendered yeoman service and shown great resource in establishing depôts and maintaining supplies in spite of great difficulties of transport.

The Meteorological Section has been of great assistance in a country subject to such sudden changes in the weather, and some valuable records have been obtained.

The conduct of the Military Police during our occupation has been a fine object lesson in organization and steady unruffled discipline under all conditions. By force of example they have gained the respect of the inhabitants of the occupied territories as well as that of all of our Allies, and this tact and forbearance have contributed greatly to the complete absence of all friction between the various nationalities. Crime is now practically unknown in Macedonia, where previously robbery by violence flourished. Lieutenant-Colonel C. W. Villiers, D.S.O., Deputy Provost Marshal, has shown tact and judgment in dealing with the difficult and delicate questions which naturally arise in an allied army.

The directorate of Inland Waterways and Docks, under the orders of Lieutenant-Colonel J. B. Parkhouse, has proved of the greatest value.

I am much indebted to Colonel A. B. Beavis, C.B.E., for his valuable advice and the general assistance he has rendered in relation to questions of finance.

My thanks are specially due to my two Corps Commanders, Lieutenant-General Sir H. F. M. Wilson, K.C.B., K.C.M.G., and Lieutenant-General C. J. Briggs, K.C.B., K.C.M.G., from whom I have always received the greatest assistance; and to Major-General G. N. Cory, C.B., D.S.O., Major-General, General Staff; Major-General H. J. Everett, C.B., C.M.G., Deputy Adjutant-General; and Major-General Sir W. H. Rycroft, K.C.M.G., C.B., Deputy Quartermaster-General, whose experience and tact in dealing with the many Allied administrative questions have proved invaluable.

I am glad to be in a position to report that our relations with our numerous Allies have been of a most cordial and intimate character, and that during the two-and-a-half years of my command I have received no complaint of serious injury to person or property against any one in the Army, the discipline of which is of the highest.

I desire to place on record the consideration I have always received from the Allied Commanders-in-Chief, General Guillaumat and General Franchet d'Esperey, and the complete harmony which has existed between the Allied staffs.

I cannot close this report without expressing my high appreciation of the splendid spirit and devotion to the service of their country shown by all ranks of this Army, the majority of whom will return to their homes with constitutions shattered by a prolonged stay in this malarious and inhospitable country.

I have the honour to be,

My Lord,

Your Lordship's obedient Servant,

G. F. MILNE,

General, Commanding-in-Chief,

British Salonika Force.

APPENDIX IV.

THE ARMISTICE CONVENTION WITH BULGARIA, SIGNED SEPTEMBER 29, 1918.

(Translation.)

1. Évacuation immédiate conformément à un arrangement à intervenir des territoires encore occupés en Grèce et en Serbie. Il ne sera enlevé de ces territoires ni bétail, ni grain, ni approvisionnement quelconque. Aucun dégât ne sera fait au départ. L'Administration bulgare continuera à fonctionner dans les parties de Bulgarie actuellement occupées par les Alliés.

2. Démobilisation immédiate de toutes les armées bulgares, sauf en ce qui concerne le maintien en état de combattre d'un groupe de toutes armes comprenant trois divisions de seize bataillons chacune, quatre régiments de

1. Immediate evacuation of the territories still occupied in Greece and Serbia in conformity with an arrangement to be concluded. No cattle, grain, or stores of any kind are to be removed from these territories. No destruction shall be caused by the Bulgarian troops on their departure. The Bulgarian Administration shall continue to carry on its functions in the parts of Bulgaria at present occupied by the Allies.

2. Immediate demobilization of all the Bulgarian armies, with the exception that a group of all arms, comprising three divisions of sixteen battalions each and four regiments of cavalry, shall be maintained on a war-footing,

cavalerie qui seront affectés, deux divisions à la défense de la frontière est de la Bulgarie et de la Dobroudja, 148ᵉ Division pour la garde des voies ferrées.

3. Dépôt en des points à désigner par le Haut Commandement des Armées d'Orient des armes, des munitions, véhicules militaires, appartenant aux éléments démobilisés, qui seront ensuite emmagasinés par les soins des autorités bulgares et sous le contrôle des Alliés.

Les chevaux seront également remis aux Alliés.

4. Remise à la Grèce du matériel du IVᵉ Corps d'Armée grec pris à l'armée grecque au moment de l'occupation de la Macédoine orientale, en tant qu'il n'a pas été envoyé en Allemagne.

5. Les éléments de troupes bulgares actuellement à l'ouest du méridien d'Uskub et appartenant à la XIᵉ Armée allemande déposeront les armes et seront considérés jusqu'à nouvel ordre comme prisonniers de guerre ; les officiers conserveront leurs armes.

of which two divisions shall be allocated to the defence of the Eastern frontier of Bulgaria and of the Dobrudja, and the 148th Division to the protection of the railways.

3. The arms, ammunition, and military transport belonging to the demobilized units shall be deposited at points to be indicated by the Supreme Command of the " Armées d'Orient." They will then be stored by the Bulgarian authorities, and under the control of the Allies.

The horses will likewise be handed over to the Allies.

4. The material belonging to the IVth Greek Army Corps, which was taken from the Greek army at the time of the occupation of Eastern Macedonia, shall be handed over to Greece, in so far as it has not been sent to Germany.

5. Those portions of the Bulgarian troops at the present time west of the meridian of Uskub, and belonging to the XIth German army, shall lay down their arms and shall be considered until further notice to be prisoners of war. The officers will retain their arms.

6. Emploi jusqu'à la paix par les Armées alliées des prisonniers bulgares en Orient sans réciprocité en ce qui concerne les prisonniers de guerre alliés. Ceux-ci seront remis sans délai aux autorités alliées et les déportés civils seront complètement libres de rentrer dans leurs foyers.

7. L'Allemagne et l'Autriche-Hongrie auront un délai de quatre semaines pour retirer leurs troupes et leurs organes militaires. Dans le même délai, devront quitter le territoire du Royaume les représentants diplomatiques et consulaires des Puissances centrales ainsi que leurs nationaux. Les ordres pour la cessation des hostilités seront donnés par les signataires de la présente convention.

(Signé) Général FRANCHET
D'ESPEREY.
ANDRÉ LIAPCHEF.
E. T. LOUKOF.

Grand Quartier général,
le 29 septembre, 1918,
22 heures 50.

6. Bulgarian prisoners of war in the East shall be employed by the Allied armies until the conclusion of peace, without reciprocity as regards Allied prisoners of war in Bulgarian hands. These latter shall be handed over without delay to the Allied authorities, and deported civilians shall be entirely free to return to their homes.

7. Germany and Austria-Hungary shall have a period of four weeks to withdraw their troops and military organizations. The diplomatic and consular representatives of the Central Powers, as well as their nationals, must leave Bulgarian territory within the same period. The orders for the cessation of hostilities will be given by the signatories of the present convention.

(Signed)   General FRANCHET
D'ESPEREY.
ANDRÉ LIAPCHEF.
E. T. LOUKOF.

General Headquarters,
September 29, 1918, 10.50 P.M.

APPENDIX V.

SIR EDMUND ALLENBY'S SECOND DISPATCH.

THE PALESTINE CAMPAIGN, FROM THE FALL OF JERUSALEM TO THE SUMMER OF 1918.

WAR OFFICE,
6th November 1918.

THE Secretary of State for War has received the following Dispatch from General Sir Edmund Allenby, G.C.M.G., K.C.B., Commanding-in-Chief, Egyptian Expeditionary Force :—

GENERAL HEADQUARTERS,
EGYPTIAN EXPEDITIONARY FORCE,
18th September 1918.

MY LORD,

I have the honour to submit a report on the operations undertaken since December 11, 1917, by the Force serving in Egypt and Palestine.

1. The operations described in my Dispatch of December 16, 1917, had resulted in the enemy's army being broken into two separate parts. One part had retired northwards, and had come to a halt on the hills overlooking the plain which lies to the north of Jaffa and Ramleh. This Force consisted of five divisions, four of which had been badly shaken in the recent retreat. Opposite it the 21st Corps held a line which,

starting at the mouth of the Nahr El Auja, three miles north of Jaffa, crossed the Turkish railway from Ludd to Jiljulieh at a point five miles north of Ludd, and thence ran in a south-easterly direction to Midieh.

The other part of the enemy's army had retired in an easterly direction towards Jerusalem. Here the remains of six divisions had been concentrated. The 20th Corps, after it had compelled the enemy to evacuate Jerusalem, held a line across the roads leading from Jerusalem to Jericho and Nablus, four miles east and north of the city, and thence westwards through the hills past Beit Ur El Foka to Suffa.

The two wings of the Turkish Army were separated by a roadless tract of country, the chief features of which consist of a series of spurs running west. The spurs are bare and rocky, the valleys between them are deep. No operations on a large scale are possible in this country until the tracks have been improved sufficiently to admit of the passage of guns and of wheeled transport. The only lateral communication possible to the Turks lay some 30 miles to the north of the line Tul Keram-Nablus.

2. In order to provide more effectively for the security of Jerusalem and Jaffa, it was essential that the line should be advanced. I therefore ordered the 20th Corps to advance to the line Beitin-Nalin. This involved an advance on a 12-mile front to a depth of 6 miles immediately north of Jerusalem. The 21st Corps on the left I ordered to advance to the line Kibbieh-Rantieh-Mulebbis-Sheikh El Ballutah-El Jelil. When this advance had been carried out the distance between the enemy and Jaffa would be increased to 8 miles.

3. Before either of these advances could take place a considerable amount of labour was necessary on the construction of roads and the improvement of communications. Supplies and ammunition had to be brought up, a task which was rendered more difficult by the weather. Heavy rains interfered with the progress of railway construction, and in some places washed away the existing line, while the roads became

deep in mud, rendering the use of mechanical transport and camels impossible, and that of horse transport slow and difficult.

4. The operation on the left was the first to be carried out. The chief obstacle lay in the crossing of the Nahr El Auja. This river is only fordable in places, and all approaches to it are overlooked from Sheikh Muannis and Khurbet Hadrah. At these places two spurs running from north to south terminate abruptly in steep slopes some 500 yards from the river.

Before the 21st Corps could reach its final objectives, it was necessary that the guns should move forward with the infantry. Consequently Sheikh Muannis, Khurbet Hadrah, and the high ground overlooking the river had to be captured as a preliminary to the general advance in order that bridges might be built.

The chief difficulty lay in concealing the collection and preparation of rafts and bridging material. All preparations were completed, however, without attracting the enemy's attention, and on the night of December 20th–21st the 52nd Division crossed the river in three columns. The enemy was taken completely by surprise. The left column, fording the river near its mouth, at this point 4 feet deep, captured Tell Er Rekkeit, 4,000 yards north of the river's mouth ; the centre and right columns, crossing on rafts, rushed Sheikh Muannis and Khurbet Hadrah at the point of the bayonet. By dawn a line from Khurbet Hadrah to Tell Er Rekkeit had been consolidated, and the enemy deprived of all observation from the north over the valley of the Nahr El Auja.

The successful crossing of the Nahr El Auja reflects great credit on the 52nd (Lowland) Division. It involved considerable preparation, the details of which were thought out with care and precision. The sodden state of the ground, and, on the night of the crossing, the swollen state of the river, added to the difficulties, yet by dawn the whole of the infantry had crossed. The fact that the enemy were taken by surprise, and that all resistance was overcome with the bayonet without a shot being fired, bears testimony to the discipline of this division. Eleven officers, including two battalion commanders, and 305 other ranks, and ten machine guns were captured in this operation.

The 21st of December was spent in building bridges. Considerable hostile shell fire was experienced during the day, chiefly from the right flank. From Mulebbis the enemy could observe the valley of the Auja. Despite this the bridges were completed, and by dusk the whole of the Divisional Artillery of the 52nd Division had crossed to the right bank, ready to support the advance to the final objectives.

On the morning of 22nd December, the 54th Division on the right drove the enemy from the orchards which surround Mulebbis, and captured the villages of Rantieh and Fejja. On the left the 52nd Division reached all their objectives and consolidated the line Tel el Mukhmar-Arsuf, the latter place, although two miles beyond the allotted objective, being occupied to deny direct observation on Jaffa Harbour to the enemy.

During the day the Royal Flying Corps attacked the enemy with bombs and machine-gun fire as he withdrew, inflicting numerous casualties.

Throughout these operations the 21st Corps received most effective support from the Royal Navy.

This operation, by increasing the distance between the enemy and Jaffa from three to eight miles, rendered Jaffa and its harbour secure, and gained elbow room for the troops covering Ludd and Ramleh and the main Jaffa-Jerusalem road.

5. In the meantime, on 20th Corps front, only minor operations had taken place, resulting in the capture of various points of local tactical importance.

The preparations for the advance to the Beitin-Nalin line were hindered by the weather, heavy rain falling during the week before Christmas. As they were nearing completion, various movements and concentrations of troops on the part of the enemy indicated that he intended to attack, with the object of recovering Jerusalem.

This proved to be the case. On the night of 26th–27th December, the enemy attacked with great determination astride the Jerusalem-Nablus road. A counter-attack against the right of his attack was carried out immediately by two divisions. As the result of three days' fighting, not only did the enemy's attempt to recapture Jerusalem fail, but by the end of the third day he found himself seven miles further from Jerusalem than when his attack started.

The enemy's attack was launched at 11.30 p.m. on 26th December, the advanced posts of the 60th Division, east of the Jerusalem road, being driven in. By 1.30 a.m. on 27th December the 60th Division was engaged along its whole front.

Between 1.30 a.m. and 8 a.m. the outposts of the 60th Division on the ridge north of Beit Hanninah repelled four determined attacks, but the heaviest fighting took place to the east of the Jerusalem-Nablus road. Repeated attacks were made against Tel el Ful, a conspicuous hill from which Jerusalem and the intervening ground can be overlooked. The attacks were made by picked bodies of troops, and were pressed with great determination. At only one point did the enemy succeed in reaching the main line of defence. He was driven out at once by the local reserves. In all these attacks he lost heavily.

In the meantime the enemy had delivered attacks against various points held by the 53rd Division east of Jerusalem. On the extreme right at Kh. Deir Ibn Obeid a company of Middlesex troops was surrounded by 700 Turks, supported by mountain artillery. Although without artillery support, it offered a most gallant resistance, holding out till relief came on the morning of the 28th. None of the other attacks on this division's front were any more successful.

On the 60th Division front north of Jerusalem a lull in the fighting occurred after 8 a.m. This lasted till 12.55 p.m., when the enemy launched an attack of unexpected strength against the whole front. In places this attack reached our main line of defence; but these small successes were short-lived, for in each case local counter-attacks, carried out immediately, were successful in restoring the line. This proved to be the final effort.

At noon the counter-attack by the 74th and 10th Divisions, which had been launched at 6.30 a.m., against the right of the enemy's attack, had made itself felt.

The 74th Division, climbing the western slopes of the Zeitun Ridge, advanced along it in an easterly direction. On their left a brigade of the 10th Division advanced along the neighbouring ridge, the left of the 10th Division advancing in a northerly direction to form a defensive flank.

These divisions met with a determined and stubborn resistance. The ground over which the advance took place was sufficiently rough and broken to render the advance slow and difficult, quite apart from any action of the enemy. In addition, the boulders on the hills rendered it ideal ground in which to fight a delaying action, providing positions for machine guns, which are difficult to locate.

Nevertheless, when night fell the 74th Division had reached the east end of the Zeitun Ridge, opposite Beitunia. On their left the 10th Division overlooked Ain Arik, and further to the left were in possession of Deir Ibzia.

The counter-attack of these two divisions had thus not only resulted in an advance of 4,000 yards on a six-mile front, but, by attracting the enemy's reserves, had prevented the enemy from repeating his attacks on the 60th Division, and, depriving him of the initiative, had forced him to abandon his attempt to capture Jerusalem.

Seeing that the Turkish attack was spent I ordered the 20th Corps to make a general advance northwards on 28th December.

The enemy, after the failure of his attack on 27th December, was still holding his original position in front of the 60th Division. This position was of considerable strength, and included Khurbet Adaseh, a high ridge overlooking the approaches from Beit Hanninah, while further west it included the villages of Bir Nebala and El Jib, the scene of heavy fighting at the end of November.

El Jib and Bir Nebala were captured by 1 p.m. Khurbet Adaseh was then attacked and captured by 5.30 p.m.

At 6.30 p.m. the advance was resumed, and by 9.15 p.m. the 60th Division had reached the line Er Ram-Rafat. Considerable resistance was met with at Er Ram. The right of this advance was protected by the 53rd Division, which extended its left northwards, capturing the villages of Anata and Kh. Almit.

On the left the 74th Division, advancing from the east end of the Zeitun Ridge, captured Beitunia, which was defended with obstinacy, and seized the high ridge east and north of it. Further to the left, the right of the 10th Division, descending into the valley of the Ain Arik, climbed the opposite slopes and captured Kefr Shiyan Hill, one mile east of Ain Arik, and the ridge between this hill and Kh. Rubin. Considerable opposition was encountered, and great difficulty was experienced in locating the enemy's machine guns.

The 60th Division continued its advance on 29th December. At the start no opposition was met with, the enemy having withdrawn to Bireh and the Et Tahuneh Ridge just north of the village, leaving a garrison at Shab Salah, a precipitous hill 1,000 yards south of Bireh overlooking the Jerusalem-Nablus road. As soon as the leading troops came within range of Bireh they were met with heavy rifle and machine-gun fire. Some delay was caused owing to the difficulty experienced in bringing the guns forward.

By 4.15 p.m. the left of the attack reached the Bireh-Ram Allah road, and then stormed the Tahuneh ridge, the last position from which the enemy could observe the approaches to Bireh.

Simultaneously with this attack the right of the 60th Division had stormed Shab Saleh in face of heavy machine-gun fire, subsequently capturing the ridge east of Bireh.

At 9 p.m. the advance was continued to the line Beitin-

El Balua-Kh. El Burj. Little opposition was encountered. On this day the 53rd Division extended its line northwards to protect the right of the 60th Division, occupying Hizmeh Jeba and the high ground north of it overlooking the Wadi El Medineh, with little opposition.

On the left the 74th Division occupied Ram Allah, and the 10th Division advanced without opposition to the line Khurbet Rubin-Ras Kerker-Deir El Kuddis.

The final line occupied by the 20th Corps thus ran from Deir Ibn Obeid, south-east of Jerusalem, northwards past Hizmeh and Jeba to Beitin, and thence westwards through El Burj, Ras Kerker to Deir El Kuddis.

During these days the Royal Air Force not only gained valuable and timely information, but repeatedly attacked the enemy's troops and transport with bombs and machine-gun fire from low altitudes, inflicting considerable losses.

The Turkish attempt to recapture Jerusalem had thus ended in crushing defeat. He had employed fresh troops who had not participated in the recent retreat of his army from Beersheba and Gaza and had escaped its demoralizing effects. The determination and gallantry with which his attack was carried out only served to increase his losses. The attack had commenced on the night December 26th–27th. By the evening of 30th December the 20th Corps had advanced on a front of 12 miles to a depth varying from 6 miles on the right to 3 miles on the left. This advance had to overcome not only a determined and obstinate resistance, but great natural difficulties as well, which had to be overcome before guns could be brought up to support the infantry.

Seven hundred and fifty prisoners, twenty-four machine guns, and three automatic rifles were captured during these operations, and over 1,000 Turkish dead were buried by us. Our own casualties were considerably less than this number.

As a result of this advance and of that of the 21st Corps, my force was in a far better position to cover Jerusalem and the towns of Ramleh and Jaffa, and the road which, running from Jaffa to Jerusalem, formed the chief artery of lateral communication behind my line.

6. Any further advance northwards on my part was out of the question for the time being. Besides the construction of roads and the improvement of communications in the forward areas, stores of supplies and ammunition had to be accumulated. Until the railway had reached a point considerably nearer my front, this was of necessity a difficult task, and one rendered still more difficult by frequent spells of wet weather. Moreover, before a further advance could be made, it was necessary to drive the enemy across the River Jordan to render my right flank secure. The possession of the crossings over the Jordan offered other advantages. These were :—

(a) The enemy would be prevented from raiding the tract of country to the west of the Dead Sea.

(b) Control of the Dead Sea would be obtained.

(c) A point of departure would be gained for operations eastwards, with a view to interrupting the enemy's line of communication to the Hedjaz, in conjunction with the Arab forces based on Akaba.

7. Before the country around Jericho could be used as a base for operations against Amman, a further advance northwards was necessary to gain sufficient space to the north to render any interruption from that direction impossible.

I had intended to carry out this advance to the north simultaneously with the advance eastwards to the River Jordan. It, however, became apparent that, if this was to be carried into effect, the operations against Jericho would have to be postponed for a considerable time to enable preparations for the advance northwards to be completed. I, therefore, decided to carry out the advance to the Jordan as a separate enterprise, the limits of the advance being the Jordan on the east and the Wadi el Auja on the north. This Wadi joins the Jordan eight miles north of the point where the Jordan enters the Dead Sea.

For this operation the Australian and New Zealand Mounted Division, less one Mounted Brigade and the Divisional Artillery, was attached to the 20th Corps.

The 60th Division had taken over the line east of Jerusalem some time previously. Opposed to it were some 5,000 rifles, while to the north another 2,000 rifles were in a position from which to act against the left flank of the 60th Division as it advanced.

The chief obstacle to the advance lay in the difficulties of the ground rather than any opposition the enemy might offer.

The descent from the vicinity of Jerusalem to the valley of the Jordan is very steep. The beds of the main wadis run from west to east. Their banks are often precipitous, rendering any crossing from one bank to the other impossible. Numerous tributaries join the main wadis from all directions, breaking up the ridges into a tumbled mass of hills.

The descent to the Jordan Valley from the line then held by the 60th Division is not, however, continuous. It is interrupted by a series of ridges which afforded the enemy strong defensive positions.

Opposite the right of the 60th Division's line El Muntar formed a conspicuous landmark, overlooking all the country in the vicinity : opposite the centre the high ground about Ras Umm Deisis and Arak Ibrahim afforded the enemy a strong position, while further north, on the left bank of the Wadi es Suweinit, Ras el Tawil formed a dominating feature. After a further fall the ground rose again at Talaat ed Dumm. This rise continued in a south-easterly direction to Jebel Ekteif, thence eastwards to Neby Musa, descending from there to the Jordan Valley, five miles south of Jericho.

To the west of Jericho at Jebel Kuruntul the ground falls sharply in steep cliffs to the Jordan Valley.

The general plan consisted of a direct advance by the 60th Division to the cliffs overlooking Jericho. The Australian and New Zealand Mounted Division was to co-operate on the right flank with a view to entering the Jordan Valley near Neby Musa, thus cutting off the enemy's retreat from Jericho.

The first step of the operation was carried out on 19th February. By 9 a.m. the 60th Division had captured El Muntar, Arak Ibrahim and Ras et Tawil, the 53rd Division extending its right to include Rummon, thence along the right bank of the Wadi el Asa, in touch with the left of the 60th Division. The greatest opposition was encountered on the left at Rummon by the 53rd Division, and in the vicinity of Ras et Tawil by the 60th Division.

The capture of El Muntar enabled the mounted troops to concentrate behind it, preparatory to operating against the enemy's left on the 20th.

On the left the 53rd Division was now in a position to command the Et Taiyibeh-Jericho road, along which any troops intended to act against the left of the 60th Division would move.

During the day further ground was secured by the 60th Division in face of considerable opposition, to cover the deployment for the attack on 20th February.

During the night of 19th–20th February the 60th Division moved into positions of deployment in the Wadi Es Sidr. The covering troops of the centre brigade were attacked during the night, but the enemy was repulsed after a sharp struggle. On the morning of the 20th the centre brigade captured Talat Ed Dumm at 7.15 a.m., the enemy resisting with stubbornness. After a pause to enable guns to be brought forward, a further advance of 2,000 yards was made.

The right brigade, advancing on Jebel Ekteif, met with great opposition. Moreover, the ground over which the attack had to take place proved the most rugged and difficult yet met with in this country. Only one approach existed by which the assaulting waves could climb Jebel Ekteif, but by midday it had been stormed.

The left brigade, on the north of the Wadi Farah, advanced

four miles, over difficult country, the enemy fighting a rear-guard action from ridge to ridge.

Thus by the evening the 60th Division had reached a line running north from Jebel Ekteif, four miles west of the cliffs overlooking Jericho.

In the meantime the mounted troops on the right had encountered considerable opposition, and had been much hampered by the difficulties of the ground.

Two miles south of Neby Musa the enemy held the high ground at Jebel el Kalimum and Tubk el Kaneiterah. Compelled to move in single file over tracks which were exposed to machine-gun fire from the enemy's position, and which had been registered accurately by the enemy's guns at Neby Musa, the progress of the mounted troops was necessarily slow. By 2 p.m., however, the enemy was driven from his position at Jebel el Kalimum and Tubk el Kaneiterah. The further advance of the New Zealand Brigade on Neby Musa was hampered by the ground, and was finally checked at the Wadi Mukelik, the only possible crossing over which was subjected to a heavy fire from Neby Musa. On the right of the New Zealanders an Australian mounted brigade discovered a crossing over the Wadi Kumran, and entering the Jordan plain reached the Wadi Jufet Zeben by dusk.

The chief feature of the enemy's resistance was the volume of machine-gun fire.

By 6 a.m. the New Zealanders and a battalion of the 60th Division reached Neby Musa, meeting with no opposition.

The Australian Mounted Brigade, advancing along the plain, entered Jericho at 8.20 a.m., the enemy having withdrawn during the night.

The 60th Division advanced to the line Rujm es Shema-Liyeh-Kh. Kakun-Jebel Karuntul, overlooking Jericho.

Meanwhile, patrols from the Australian Mounted Brigade reconnoitred as far as the Wadi el Aujah to the north and the El Ghoraniyeh Bridge. The enemy was found to be holding the high ground north of the Aujah, and a bridgehead covering the El Ghoraniyeh Bridge with guns on the left bank.

As a direct attack on the bridgehead would have involved heavy losses, without compensating advantages, it was not attempted. On the 22nd the 60th Division withdrew to the line Jebel Ekteif-Talat ed Dumm-Ras et Tawil, leaving outposts on the cliffs overlooking Jericho. The Mounted Division, leaving one regiment to patrol the Jordan Valley, returned to Bethlehem.

During these operations four officers, 140 other ranks, and six machine guns were captured from the enemy.

On no previous occasions had such difficulties of ground been encountered. As an instance of this, a Field Artillery battery took thirty-six hours to reach Neby Musa, the distance covered, as the crow flies, being only eight miles.

The Royal Air Force rendered valuable service, but mist and low-lying clouds interrupted their work to a great extent.

8. This operation, by driving the enemy across the Jordan, had rendered my right flank secure, but the base thus obtained was not sufficiently broad to permit of operations being carried out east of the Jordan against the Hedjaz Railway.

Before any such operation could be undertaken it was essential in the first place to cross the Wadi Aujah and secure the high ground on the north bank covering the approaches to the Jordan Valley by the Beisan-Jericho road, and, secondly, by advancing sufficiently far northwards on either side of the Jerusalem-Nablus road, to deny to the enemy the use of all tracks and roads leading to the lower Jordan Valley. This accomplished, any troops he might determine to transfer from the west to the east bank of the Jordan would have to make a considerable detour to the north.

I therefore ordered the 20th Corps to secure Kh. el Beiyudat and Abu Tellul, in the Jordan Valley, north of the Wadi el Aujah, and further to the west the line Kefr Malik-Kh. Abu Felah, the high ground south of Sinjil, and the ridge north of the Wadi el Jib running through Kh. Aliuta-Jiljilia-Abwein-Arura, thence to Deir es Sudan and Nebi Saleh.

The watershed from which the wadis run, in the one direction to the River Jordan, in the other through the hills to the plain north of Ludd and thence to the sea, runs parallel to and some two miles east of the Jerusalem-Nablus road. The fall to the Jordan Valley is short and sharp, with the result that the beds of the wadis are deep and their sides almost precipitous. The country is so intricate that it cannot be crossed by large bodies of troops. Consequently, there was no danger in leaving a gap between the right of the 20th Corps at Kefr Malik and the detachment in the Jordan Valley at Abu Tellul.

To conform to the advance of the 20th Corps, I ordered the 21st Corps to advance its right to include the ridge north of the Wadi Ballut, the village of Mejdel Yaba, a conspicuous landmark on a foothill overlooking the plain north of Ludd, Ras el Ain, an old Crusader stronghold on the railway from Ludd to Tul Keram, and El Mirr.

As a result of this advance the 21st Corps would be placed in a better position for a further advance, should it be decided to attack the defensive system constructed by the enemy from Jiljulieh westwards through Tabsor to the sea.

The two Corps were thus advancing on a front, from Kefr Malik to El Mirr, of 26 miles—to a maximum depth of 7 miles.

The ground over which the advance was to take place is rugged and difficult. A succession of high and rocky ridges, separated by deep valleys, afforded the enemy a series of positions of great natural strength. The slopes of the ridges are in many places precipitous. Ledges of rock confine the descent to definite places, on which the enemy could concentrate his fire. In places the slopes are terraced, and men had to pull or hoist each other up.

It was necessary to reconnoitre each successive position held by the enemy, and the subsequent movement of troops into positions of assembly was of necessity a slow process.

Under these conditions no rapid advance could be looked for.

As soon as supplies and ammunition had been collected and preparations were complete, both Corps made a preliminary advance to enable a closer reconnaissance of the enemy's main positions to be made, and to allow of the construction of roads for the movement of guns and supplies.

By 8th March the 20th Corps had reached the line En Nejmeh-Et Taiyibeh-Ain Sinia, on the Jerusalem-Nablus road, Hill 2665 overlooking Bir ez Zeit-Beit Ello, the 53rd Division being on the right, the 74th Division in the centre astride the Jerusalem-Nablus road, and the 10th Division on the left.

On the right of the 21st Corps the 75th Division had captured Abud and the ridge between the wadis Barbara and Abud.

In neither case was any serious opposition encountered.

When the subsequent advance began, the opposition stiffened considerably on the front of both Corps.

On 9th and 10th March the 20th Corps had to drive the enemy from ridge after ridge before the final objectives were reached.

During the night of 8–9th March the brigades of the 20th Corps moved forward to their positions of assembly. On the extreme right, in the Jordan Valley, the brigade of the 60th Division entrusted with the task of capturing Kh. el Beiyudat and Abu Tellul experienced some difficulty in crossing the Wadi el Auja in the dark, and subsequently met with determined resistance. By 3 p.m., however, Kh. el Beiyudat and Abu Tellul had been captured. The occupation of a position astride the Beisan-Jericho road completed this operation. Further west the 53rd, 74th, and 10th Divisions had advanced by the evening to a depth varying between 3,000 and 7,000 yards, and had reached a line running east and west through Tell Asur, thence along the ridges overlooking the wadis En Nimr and El Jib. The 53rd Division on the right had met with considerable opposition and great natural difficulties, especially on the extreme right and at Tell Asur, a conspicuous landmark among a mass of high hills. The importance attached to Tell Asur by the enemy was shown by the number of determined efforts he made to recapture it, all of which were repulsed.

On 10th March both the enemy's resistance and the difficulties of the ground increased, but during the day and the early hours of the night of 10–11th March an advance of 3,000 yards was made on a front of 12 miles. The line reached ran from Kefr Malik, along the ridge overlooking the Wadi el Kola and the Burj el Lisaneh ridge, past Kh. el Sahlat, Kh. Aliuta, Jiljilia, Abwein, and Arura to its former position at Deir es Sudan and Naby Saleh.

The enemy contested the ridges north of the wadis En Nimr and El Jib with great obstinacy, while on the extreme left near Neby Saleh he counter-attacked the left of the 10th Division on several occasions. The descent of the slopes leading down to the wadis En Nimr and El Jib and the ascent on the far side presented great difficulties. The downward slopes were exceptionally steep, almost precipitous in places. It was impossible for companies and platoons to move on a wide front. The slopes were swept by machine-gun and rifle fire, and the bottom of the wadis by enfilade fire. The ascent on the far side was steeply terraced. Men had alternatively to hoist and pull each other up, under fire, and finally to expel the enemy from the summits in hand-to-hand fighting.

On 11th March the operation of the 20th Corps was completed by the occupation of Kh. Abu Felah and the heights overlooking Sinjil and the comparatively low-lying country to the north-east. The result of this operation was the capture of a line with great natural facilities for defence, and of 11 officers, 160 other ranks, 11 machine guns, and considerable amounts of ammunition and other booty.

The second phase of the operation by the 21st Corps, the preliminary phase having taken place on 7th March, was carried out on 12th March.

At first the opposition encountered was not serious, but from the time the 75th Division reached the ridge overlooking the Wadi Ballut it stiffened, the enemy contesting the ridge on the far side of the wadi stubbornly, and when driven off making several counter-attacks to regain it. At Benat Burry, a razor-edged ridge north of Kh. Balatah, the top of the ridge is honeycombed with caves with entrances on both sides. Considerable difficulty was experienced in overcoming the enemy's resistance here. Eventually, however, a platoon of Gurkhas worked round to the rear of the ridge. A Lewis gun was brought to bear on the exits. The garrison of the caves, numbering 5 officers and 50 other ranks, then surrendered.

On the left of the 75th Division the 54th Division captured the villages of El Mezeireh, Kh. Dikerin, and Mejdel Yaba in the foothills, and Ras El Ain and El Mirr in the plain. Seven officers, 105 other ranks, and 2 machine guns were taken by these two divisions.

9. The Jordan Valley had now been sufficiently cleared of the enemy to enable operations to be carried out against the Turkish line of communication to the Hedjaz, in conjunction with the Arab forces under Sherif Feisal, which were operating in the country to the south-east of the Dead Sea, and were under my control.

Sherif Feisal's forces were based on Akaba. In January 1918 he had captured the high ground about Uheida, within 7 miles of Maan, his main objective. At the same time a force under Sherif Abdul Magin had occupied the whole of the Hish Forest up to and including Shobek, 20 miles north by west of Maan, destroying 35 kilometres of the enemy's light railway, which left the main line at Kalaat Aneiza and was used to transport wood as fuel for locomotives. After the capture of Shobek a force under Sherif Nazir raided Jauf Ed Derwish, a station on the main line, 30 miles north of Maan. This they held for three days, burning the station buildings and destroying two locomotives and some rolling stock. In this successful raid the Turkish losses amounted to over 100 killed,

over 200 prisoners, a mountain gun, and 2 machine guns.
Further north a separate force of Arab tribesmen, under Sherif
Nazir, captured Tafile, 15 miles south-east of the south end
of the Dead Sea, on 16th January. The garrison, which consisted of 100 Turks and the officials of the place, surrendered
after a short resistance. Ten days later a Turkish force,
consisting of three battalions, with two mountain guns and
27 machine guns, advanced from Karak to recapture Tafile.
An engagement took place on 26th January in which the enemy
suffered a crushing defeat. His losses amounted to over 450
in killed and 250 in prisoners. In addition, the whole of his
artillery and machine guns fell into the hands of the Arabs.
In March the Turks concentrated a considerable force, including a battalion of German infantry, and, advancing from
Katrani and Jauf Ed Derwish, reoccupied Tafile, the Arab
tribesmen, in face of superior numbers, withdrawing to positions north of Shobek.

The situation to the east of the Jordan thus presented a
favourable opportunity for a raid on the enemy's communications with the Hedjaz.

Its immediate effect would be to compel the enemy to
recall the force which had recently occupied Tafile. It might,
in addition, compel the enemy to call on the garrison of Maan
for support. If this should prove to be the case, Sherif Feisal
would be afforded his opportunity to attack Maan with some
prospects of success. The extent of this opportunity would
depend on the amount of damage done to the Hedjaz Railway.
Near Amman, the railway crosses a viaduct and passes through
a tunnel. If these could be destroyed it would be some weeks
before traffic could be resumed. I determined therefore to
carry out a raid on Amman, with the object of destroying the
viaduct and tunnel, and, if this should be found impossible, to
damage the railway as much as possible. Even if traffic was
only interrupted for a short time, the mere threat of a repeti-
tion of this raid would compel the enemy to maintain a considerable force to cover Amman. The troops available to

operate against the Arabs would be reduced, and possibly the enemy might transfer a portion of his reserves from the west to the east of the Jordan, thereby weakening his power to make or meet any attack on the main front.

Amman is 30 miles east by north of Jericho as the crow flies. The nature of the intervening country varies to a marked degree. From the banks of the Jordan to the clay ridges, a mile east of the river, the ground is flat, and after rain becomes marshy. Beyond the ridges the country is covered with scrub and intersected by numerous wadis. For the first 5 miles the total rise is only 500 feet. In the next 12 miles the ground rises some 3,500 feet till the edge of the plateau of Moab is reached. The hills are rugged and steep. The main wadis descend from the plateau to the Jordan in deep valleys. The plateau itself is undulating, the lower portions of it marshy after rain. The hills which rise from it are rocky and covered with scrub. They are isolated features, and only form continuous ridges immediately west of Amman, which lies in a cultivated plain, extending some 2 miles west and 4 miles north-west of the town. This plain, which is the site of many ruins, is intersected by numerous deep wadis difficult to cross—especially the Wadi Amman, which runs from south to north, leaving the town of Amman on its right.

The Turks had constructed a metalled road from Ghoraniyeh bridge to Es Salt and Amman. Following the Wadi Nimrin, it enters the hills at Shunet Nimrin and winds round the slopes of the valley of the Wadi Shaib, supported by embankments, in places 20 feet high. At Es Salt, a town of some 15,000 inhabitants, 18 miles from Ghoraniyeh by road, it is joined by tracks leading from the fords over the Jordan at Umm es Shert and Jisr ed Damieh and from Jerash to the north. On leaving Es Salt the road runs in a northerly direction for two miles, and then turns east, reaching the edge of the plateau five miles further on. This is the only road, and is in bad repair. Various tracks follow the wadis to the plateau, but are unfit for wheeled transport. One leaves the main road at Shunet Nimrin, and follows the wadis Jeria and Sir, passing the village of Ain es Sir. Another leads from Ghoraniyeh and Makhadet Hajlah up the Wadi el Kefrein to Naaur, where it joins the main route from Madeba to Amman.

11. The force detailed to carry out the raid consisted of the 60th (London) Division, the Australian and New Zealand Mounted Division, the Imperial Camel Brigade, a Mountain Artillery Brigade, the Light Armoured Car Brigade, and a heavy battery. This force was placed under the command of the General Officer Commanding 60th Division. The 60th Division was to force the crossings over the Jordan and advance astride the metalled road to Es Salt, which it was to hold, its left flank being protected by a mounted brigade. The mounted troops and the Camel Brigade, following the 60th Division across the Jordan, were to move direct on Amman by the tracks passing through Ain es Sir and Naaur. On reaching Amman the railway was to be destroyed and the viaduct and tunnel demolished. This having been accomplished, the mounted troops were to withdraw on the 60th Division, the whole force then withdrawing to bridgeheads at the Jordan.

The operations, which started during the night of 21st–22nd March, were hampered considerably by rain, which fell during the days preceding the raid and on 27th March and the three following days. The Jordan is unfordable at this time of the year. The current is at all times rapid, and is liable to sudden floods which render the banks boggy and difficult of approach for transport. On 28th March it rose 9 feet. The rain which fell during the operations rendered the tracks in the hills slippery and the movement of horses, and especially of camels, slow and difficult. The delay thus caused enabled the enemy to bring up reinforcements. Before Amman could be attacked in strength some 4,000 Turks supported by 15 guns were in position near Amman, covering the viaduct and tunnel, while another 2,000 were moving on Es Salt from the north. To have driven the enemy from his position, without adequate artillery support, would have entailed very heavy losses. Owing to the marshy nature of the country it was only possible to bring up mountain artillery, and I therefore ordered a withdrawal, which was carried out without serious interruption. Although it had not been possible to effect any permanent demolitions, five miles of railway line, including several large culverts, and the points and crossings at Alanda station, were destroyed to the south of Amman, while to the north of the town a two-arch bridge was blown up.

Considerable losses were inflicted on the enemy, and in addition 53 officers and over 900 other ranks were taken prisoner, including several Germans.

The raid also enabled a considerable number of Armenians to escape and find a refuge west of the Jordan.

12. The crossing of the Jordan took place during the night of 21st–22nd March.

The crossing was to have been effected by a brigade of the 60th Division at Ghoraniyeh and Makhadet Hajlah. This brigade was then to cover the construction of bridges, the 60th Division crossing at the former, the mounted troops at the latter place. The attempt to cross at Ghoraniyeh failed owing to the strength of the current, which prevented all attempts to cross both by swimming and by means of rafts and pontoons.

At Hajlah, however, the swimmers succeeded in reaching the opposite bank at 1.20 a.m., and by 7.45 a.m. the leading battalion was across. Till dawn this crossing was unperceived by the enemy, but subsequently the troops had to be ferried across, and a bridge constructed, under fire. The bridge was completed by 8.30 a.m. Further troops crossed, but it was found impossible to enlarge the bridgehead till dark, owing to the enemy's fire and the thickness of the scrub.

A further attempt to cross at Ghoraniyeh during the night of the 22nd–23rd was again frustrated by the current and the enemy's fire. Early in the morning, however, a New Zealand regiment crossed at Hajlah, and, galloping northwards, drove back the enemy and formed a bridgehead at Ghoraniyeh. The current having diminished, three bridges were constructed during the day, and by 10 p.m. the whole of the infantry of the 60th Division and the greater part of the mounted troops were east of the Jordan, but owing to the swollen state of the river much valuable time had been lost.

On 24th March the 60th Division attacked the enemy and drove him from his position at El Haud and Shunet Nimrin, covering the entrance to the pass leading to Es Salt. Three guns were captured by a battalion of the London Regiment, the teams being shot down by the fire of the Lewis guns. Following on the heels of the retreating enemy, the 60th Division advanced four miles along the road to Es Salt, which was occupied the following evening without opposition.

In the meantime the mounted troops, followed by the Camel Brigade, made their way along the tracks towards Ain es Sir and Naaur. Early in the day all wheeled transport had to be sent back. Even so, the tracks had been rendered so slippery by rain, which fell continuously on the 25th, that progress was slow. In many places horses had to move in single file, and had to be pulled or pushed up the slippery slopes.

Naaur was reached late in the evening of 25th March.

The rain continued to fall on 26th March. At 5 a.m. the New Zealand and Australian Brigades met at Ain es Sir. The Australians moved on to Suweileh, north of the Es Salt-Amman road, capturing 170 Turks there. Both men and horses were, however, too exhausted by their exertions to admit of more than demolition parties being sent on to the railway.

On 27th March the advance was resumed. The ground favoured the enemy, the rocks and scrub on the hills affording excellent cover to his riflemen. The wadis could only be crossed at a few places, and then only in single file.

By evening the New Zealanders had reached the railway south of Amman, their demolition parties working southwards. In the centre the Camel Brigade advanced direct on Amman, but were checked some 1,500 yards west of Amman village. On the left the Australians were unable to reach the railway north of Amman, being heavily counter-attacked ; but during the night a demolition party succeeded in blowing up a small bridge seven miles north of Amman.

On 28th March a brigade of the 60th Division arrived from Es Salt accompanied by mountain artillery. The road was too soft to admit of field guns being brought. In fact, twenty-two Turkish motor lorries and other vehicles found along the road were so embedded in the mud that they had to be destroyed. On its arrival this brigade attacked along the Es Salt-Amman road, the Australians attacking on its left, the Camel Brigade on its right, while the New Zealanders attacked Hill 3039 just south of Amman.

Little progress was made. The enemy made several counter-attacks, especially against the Australians, who were forced back a short distance.

On 29th March Turkish reinforcements arrived, and the counter-attacks were renewed, but without success.

During the afternoon two more battalions of the 60th Division and a battery of Royal Horse Artillery arrived after a long and arduous march.

The attack on Amman was renewed at 2 a.m. on 30th March. The New Zealanders captured a portion of Hill 3039, but were unable to drive the enemy from the northern and eastern ends. Parties of New Zealanders entered the village, but were fired on from the houses. Elsewhere the attack met with only slight success. It was apparent that without greater artillery support further attacks could only succeed at the cost of heavy losses. Moreover, Turkish troops from Jisr ed Damieh and from the north had begun to make their presence felt at Es Salt. Orders were therefore issued for a withdrawal to take place during the night. This was carried out without interruption, after all the wounded had been evacuated.

By the evening of the 2nd April the whole force had re-crossed the Jordan, with the exception of the troops left to hold the bridgehead on the east bank.

Although no permanent damage had been done to the Hedjaz Railway, the raid had succeeded in drawing northwards and retaining not only the Turkish troops which had been operating against the Arabs, but in addition a portion of the garrison of Maan and the stations further south.

Before the raid was carried out the enemy's strength in the Amman-Es Salt-Shunet Nimrin area was approximately 4,000. By the middle of April it had increased to over 8,000.

13. Taking advantage of this opportunity Sherif Feisal commenced operations against Maan. The railway was first cut both north and south of Maan at Ghadir el Haj and Jerdun. At these places 270 Turks and 3 machine guns were captured. On 13th April, Senna, a Turkish post 4,000 yards south-west of Maan Station, was captured, and on 17th April the station was entered and 100 prisoners made, but the attack was unable to make any impression on the strong Turkish position 400 yards north of the station. This position was of considerable strength, and was provided with concrete machine-gun emplacements. The Arabs then withdrew to a strong position at Senna to await the arrival of further ammunition for the artillery.

In the meantime another column attacked the line between Batn el Ghul and Kalaat et Mudawara, 70 kilometres south of Maan, and destroyed 100 kilometres of line so effectively that at least a month's uninterrupted work will be required to repair it, and then only if large gangs of labourers are available. The damage to the railway north of Maan was not so thorough, but was sufficient to prevent through traffic for several days.

14. After the troops employed in the last raid had been withdrawn to the west bank of the Jordan, the enemy reoccupied the Shunet Nimrin position, which he held with some 5,000 rifles.

On 11th April he made simultaneous attacks on the Ghoraniyeh bridgehead and on El Musallabeh, which covers the Beisan-Jericho road west of the Jordan. Both attacks were pressed with considerable determination, but brought him no success, and during the night 11–12th April he withdrew to his positions at Shunet Nimrin, which he commenced to strengthen. His losses in these attacks were heavy. He left 3 officers and 113 other ranks in our hands as prisoners, while some 500 dead were buried by us or seen to be buried by the enemy.

I determined to seize the first opportunity to cut off and destroy the enemy's force at Shunet Nimrin, and, if successful, to hold Es Salt till the Arabs could advance and relieve my troops. This would have denied the enemy the use of the harvest. I had intended to carry out this operation about the middle of May, when the reorganization of the 1st Mounted Division had been completed. In the meantime, however, a deputation from the Beni Sakhr tribe arrived stating that the tribe was concentrated near Madeba, ready to co-operate with any advance I might make, provided it took place before 4th May, after which date their supplies would be finished, and the tribe would have to disperse.

The troops available to carry out this raid were the Desert Mounted Corps, less the 1st Mounted Division, the 60th Division, less one brigade, and the Imperial Service Cavalry and Infantry Brigades.

The 60th Division was to attack the enemy's position at Shunet Nimrin, whilst the Mounted Troops, moving northwards from Ghoraniyeh, were to turn east along the tracks leading from Umm es Shert and Jisr ed Damieh to Es Salt, after leaving a force to watch Jisr ed Damieh and protect the left flank.

In the former raid the only route found fit for wheeled transport between Amman and Shunet Nimrin had been the metalled road passing through Es Salt. The arrival of the mounted troops at Es Salt would thus sever the main line of communication of the force at Shunet Nimrin, who would be dependent for their supplies on the track further south through Ain es Sir. This track was exposed to attack by the Beni Sakhr tribe.

There appeared every chance therefore of the Turkish Force at Shunet Nimrin being compelled to retreat under very difficult conditions, and a fair chance of its being captured.

The operations were commenced early on the morning of 30th April, and proceeded according to plan.

The 60th Division captured the advanced works of the Shunet Nimrin position, but were unable to make further progress in face of the stubborn resistance offered by the enemy.

The mounted troops, moving northwards, rode round the right of the Shunet Nimrin position, and by 6 p.m. had captured Es Salt, leaving an Australian Brigade to watch the left flank.

This Brigade took up a position facing north-west astride the Jisr ed Damieh-Es Salt track, with patrols watching the Wadi Ez Zerka, and with a detachment on the high ground on the east bank of the Jordan, two miles north of Umm es Shert.

At 7.30 a.m. on 1st May this Brigade was attacked by the 3rd Turkish Cavalry Division, and a part of the 24th Division, which had crossed from the west bank of the Jordan during the night at Jisr ed Damieh. The enemy succeeded in penetrating between the left of the brigade and the detachment on the bank of the Jordan. The brigade was driven back through the foothills to the Wadi El Abyad. During its retirement through the hills nine guns and part of its transport had to be abandoned, being unable to traverse the intricate ground.

The Umm es Shert-Es Salt track was thus the only line of supply or retreat left to the mounted troops in Es Salt, till the main road and the Wadi Arseniyet track could be opened by the capture of the Shunet Nimrin position and El Haud.

Arrangements were made for a combined attack to take place on this position on 2nd May. The 60th Division was to attack from the west and the mounted troops at Es Salt from the north-east.

On 2nd May the mounted troops in Es Salt were attacked by two Turkish battalions which had arrived from Amman accompanied by heavy guns, as well as by cavalry from the north, and troops from Jisr ed Damieh. These attacks were driven off, but the force intended to attack Shunet Nimrin from the north-east had to be weakened, and was checked at El Howeij, five miles south of Es Salt. The 60th Division was also unable to make any substantial progress, in spite of determined efforts.

As the assistance of the Beni Sakhr tribe had not materialized, the Ain es Sir track was still open to the garrison of Shunet Nimrin. Further Turkish reinforcements were known to be on their way. It was evident that the Shunet Nimrin position could not be captured without losses, which I was not in a position to afford. In these circumstances, I ordered the mounted troops to withdraw from Es Salt. Their retirement was accomplished successfully. The enemy, who followed up closely, was held off without difficulty. By the evening of 4th May all the troops had recrossed the Jordan, bridgeheads being left to cover the bridges at Ghoraniyeh and the crossing at El Auja.

Although the destruction of the Turkish force at Shunet Nimrin had not been effected, the enemy's losses were considerable, the prisoners brought in amounting to 50 officers and 892 other ranks ; 29 machine guns and several motor cars and lorries were destroyed by the mounted troops before they left Es Salt.

The raid has undoubtedly rendered the enemy apprehensive of further operations east of the Jordan, and has compelled him to maintain considerable forces in the Amman-Shunet Nimrin area, reducing the forces available to meet the Arab menace.

15. The dispatch of troops to France, and the reorganization of the force, has prevented further operations, of any size, being undertaken, and has rendered the adoption of a policy of active defence necessary. During the first week in April the 52nd Division embarked for France, its place being taken by the 7th (Meerut) Division, which had arrived from Mesopotamia.

The departure of the 52nd Division was followed by that of the 74th Division, which left Palestine during the second week in April. The 3rd (Lahore) Division was sent from Mesopotamia to replace the 74th Division, but it was not till the middle of June that the last units disembarked. In addition to the 52nd and 74th Divisions, nine Yeomanry Regiments, five and a half siege batteries, ten British battalions, and five machine-gun companies were withdrawn from the line, preparatory to embarkation for France.

By the end of April the Yeomanry Regiments had been replaced by Indian Cavalry Regiments, which had arrived from France, and the British battalions by Indian battalions dispatched from India. These Indian battalions had not, however, seen service during the present war ; and, naturally, had not the experience of the battalions they replaced.

Thus in April the strength of the force had been reduced by one division, five and a half siege batteries, and five machine-gun companies ; while one mounted division was in process of being reorganized, and was not available for operations.

In May a further 14 battalions of British infantry were withdrawn and dispatched to France. Only two Indian battalions were available to replace them. Thus at the end of May the force had been further reduced by 12 battalions, while the loss of the 74th Division had not yet been fully made good. On the other hand, the reorganization of the mounted division had been completed.

In June the places of the British battalions which had been dispatched to France were filled by Indian battalions. Six of the Indian battalions had, however, been formed by withdrawing a company from 24 of the Indian battalions already in the Force. As few reinforcements were available for the battalions thus depleted, the Force had been completed in name only.

During July and the first week in August a further 10 British battalions were replaced by 10 Indian battalions, the personnel of the British battalions being used as reinforcements.

16. During these months of reorganization various minor operations and a number of raids have been carried out.

Between the 9th and 11th of April the right of the line held by the 21st Corps was advanced on a front of 12 miles, to a maximum depth of 3 miles ; the villages of Kefr Ain, Berukin, El Kefr and Rafat being captured. Considerable resistance was met with, the Turkish troops being stiffened by a German battalion. The enemy made several attempts to recapture Berukin and Rafat. His counter-attacks were broken up by the infantry, ably supported by the artillery, but, in some cases, only after sharp hand-to-hand fighting. The enemy's losses were considerable, over 300 of his dead being counted.

On 8th June an advance was made on the coast, at the extreme left of my line, with the object of depriving the enemy of observation. The enemy's positions were captured by two battalions—the Black Watch and the Guides. Two counter-attacks were made. In the first the enemy succeeded in reoccupying a portion of the position, but he was expelled. The second counter-attack broke down before it reached our new position. The enemy's losses were considerable, and 4 officers and 101 other ranks were captured. The capture of these positions not only prevented the enemy from overlooking a considerable length of our defences and the ground in rear, but secured observation of the approaches to the enemy's positions, with the result that his movements, by day, have been considerably restricted.

The Indian troops have carried out a number of minor raids with success. On 13th July a party of the Guides surprised the enemy in his trenches in the middle of the day, bringing back 15 prisoners and a machine gun. On 27th July a Pathan company of the 53rd Sikhs F.F. inflicted heavy casualties on the enemy, and brought in 33 prisoners and two machine guns.

A raid on a larger scale, carried out on 12th August by the Leinster Regiment, 54th Sikhs and 1st Battalion, 101st Grenadiers, was crowned with complete success. The objective was the enemy's defences on the El Burj-Ghurabeh ridge, north-west of Sinjil. This ridge is some 5,000 yards in length, and lies 2,000 yards in front of our line. It was held by 800 rifles and 36 machine guns. The defences consisted of strongly-built sangars, protected by thick wire entanglements. The approaches to it are rocky and broken, involving a climb of 900 feet. The position was attacked from both flanks. The enemy was surprised. His losses were heavy, and the raiders brought back 239 prisoners, including a battalion commander and 16 officers and 13 machine guns. Great dash was shown by all the troops taking part in it.

In the Jordan Valley the mounted troops have carried out successful raids, and have ambushed a number of hostile patrols. The Indian cavalry have used the lance with good effect on several occasions.

17. This activity on our part has not been imitated by the enemy, except in one instance. Then the brunt of the fighting fell on German troops. Early in July movements of troops, and increased artillery and aeroplane activity, foreshadowed an attack on our defences in the Jordan Valley.

On the right bank of the Jordan our defences form a marked salient. The eastern side of the salient faces the ford at Umm es Shert. The apex is at El Musallabeh, while the western face runs across the north-west slopes of Abu Tellul.

Early on the morning of 14th July the enemy was seen to be concentrating in the deep wadis north-west of Abu Tellul. At 3.30 a.m. the attack began. The enemy penetrated between the advanced posts and seized Abu Tellul, thus cutting off the posts further north at El Musallabeh. At 4.30 a.m. the 1st Australian Light Horse Brigade counter-attacked. By 5 a.m. Abu Tellul had been regained. The enemy, driven against our advanced posts, which, with one exception, had held their ground, suffered heavily. Two hundred and seventy-six Germans, including 12 officers, and 62 Turks were captured, in addition to 6 machine guns and 42 automatic rifles. One hundred wounded and many dead were left on the ground.

Great credit is due to the Australians for the quickness of their counter-attack and for the determination displayed by the garrisons of the advanced posts in holding out, although surrounded.

While this fighting was in progress a Turkish force of considerable strength was observed to be concentrating to the east of the Jordan, opposite El Henu Ford, which is midway between the El Ghoraniyeh bridgehead and the Dead Sea. A cavalry brigade moved out to counter-attack. Taking advantage of the ground, the cavalry arrived within charging distance before they were observed. In the charge that ensued some 90 Turks were speared ; and 91, including 6 officers, in addition to 4 machine guns, were captured. It was only by reaching ground impassable for cavalry that the remainder of the Turks effected their escape. The Jodhpur Lancers played a distinguished part in this charge.

The enemy's attack on both banks of the Jordan thus failed ignominiously. His losses, especially those of the German troops, were heavy, and it is probable that the German units which took part will need a long rest before being ready for active operations again. Our casualties were comparatively light.

18. Since April no events of any importance have taken place in the Hedjaz. The Turks have been unable to restore through railway communication between Maan and the north. South of Maan a detachment of the Imperial Camel Corps attacked and captured the station at Kalaat et Mudawara. destroying the water tower and pumps. Thirty-five Turks were killed, 6 officers and 146 other ranks, 2 guns and 3 machine guns were captured.

As a result of this operation, no water supply now exists on the railway for a distance of 150 kilometres south of Maan. Medina has thus been definitely cut off from the north.

19. The operations, which took place during the first half of the period covered by this dispatch, rendered secure the fruits of the fighting, which, commencing with the capture of Beersheba, culminated in the occupation of Jerusalem.

On 12th December the enemy still remained within 4 miles of Jerusalem. He is now 22 miles from the Holy City. To the east he has been driven across the Jordan, and his communications to the Hedjaz raided. His losses between December 12, 1917, and May 31, 1918, were considerable, the number of prisoners amounting to 331 officers and 6,088 other ranks. His one attempt on a large scale to assume the offensive and retake Jerusalem failed, and was turned into a defeat, accompanied by a considerable loss of territory.

In driving back the enemy my troops suffered considerable hardships. The rugged country in which the majority of the fighting took place not only favoured the defence, but demanded great physical exertion on the part of the attackers. In the early months of the year their task was often rendered more difficult by the cold and heavy rains which added greatly to their discomfort. They responded to every call made on them, and proved their superiority over the enemy on every occasion. The second half of the period under review has been spent in reorganization and in training. Although operations have been limited to raids, 69 officers and 1,614 other ranks have been taken from the enemy since 1st June.

20. Throughout the whole period, the work of the Royal Air Force has been of great value. Fifty-three hostile aeroplanes have been destroyed, in addition to twenty-three which have been driven down out of control. The enemy's troops, camps and railways have been bombed with good results, while very important photographic work has been carried out. Co-operation with the other arms has been excellent.

21. During the early months of the year, whilst the rainy season was still in progress, and before railhead had reached the troops, the supply situation presented great difficulties. The wadis came down in spate, overflowing their banks and flooding the surrounding country. Not only was railway construction hindered, but the country became almost impassable for motor, and extremely difficult for horse transport. Nevertheless, all difficulties were overcome.

22. I am indebted to His Excellency General Sir Francis Wingate, G.C.B., G.C.V.O., K.C.M.G., D.S.O., High Commissioner for Egypt, for the cordial assistance he has given me at all times.

Egypt has provided transport personnel, drivers for the Camel Transport Corps, and men for the Egyptian Labour Corps in large numbers, in addition to several units of the Egyptian Army. These have all done work which, though unostentatious, has been of great value. During the operations in the hills of Judæa and of Moab, the troops often depended for their supplies on the Camel Transport Corps. The drivers displayed steadiness under fire and devotion to duty in the face of cold and rain which they had never experienced previously. The Egyptian Labour Corps shared these hardships. The construction and maintenance of roads was a task of considerable importance and difficulty during the rainy season, and threw a great strain on the Egyptian Labour Corps. Its successful accomplishment reflects credit on the Corps. The Egyptian authorities have complied at once with all requests that I have made, and my thanks are due to them for their loyal support.

23. The Army Postal Service has carried out its work efficiently. During the early months of the year, when my troops were far in advance of railhead, the delivery and collection of mails was a matter of considerable difficulty, which was invariably overcome.

24. Throughout the period I have received every help from Rear-Admiral T. Jackson, C.B., M.V.O.

I have the honour to be,

Your Lordship's most obedient Servant,

E. H. H. ALLENBY, General,

Commanding-in-Chief,

Egyptian Expeditionary Force.

APPENDIX VI.

Sir Edmund Allenby's Third Dispatch.

THE OVERTHROW OF TURKEY.

GENERAL HEADQUARTERS,
31st October 1918.

My Lord,

I have the honour to forward a Dispatch describing the operations which, commencing on 19th September, resulted in the destruction of the enemy's army, the liberation of Palestine and Syria, and the occupation of Damascus and Aleppo.

1. The latter months of the period covered by my Dispatch of September 18, 1918, had been spent in the reorganization of my Force. The last Indian battalions to arrive had been incorporated in divisions early in August. Some of these battalions had only been formed a few months, and I should have liked to have given them further opportunities to accustom themselves to the conditions prevailing on this front before calling on them to play a part in arduous operations on a large scale. The rains, however, usually commence at the end of October, rendering the plains of Sharon and Esdraelon impassable for transport, except along the few existing roads. Consequently, operations could not be postponed beyond the middle of September.

2. At the beginning of September I estimated the strength

of the IVth, VIIth, and VIIIth Turkish Armies to be 23,000 rifles, 3,000 sabres, and 340 guns. The IVth Army, 6,000 rifles, 2,000 sabres, and 74 guns, faced my Forces in the Jordan Valley. The VIIth Army held a front of some 20 miles astride the Jerusalem Nablus road with 7,000 rifles and 111 guns, while the VIIIth Army front extended from Furkhah to the sea, and was held by 10,000 rifles and 157 guns.

In addition, the garrison of Maan and the posts on the Hejaz railway north of it consisted of some 6,000 rifles and 30 guns.

The enemy's general reserve, only 3,000 rifles in strength, with 30 guns, was distributed between Tiberias, Nazareth, and Haifa.

Thus his total strength amounted to some 4,000 sabres, 32,000 rifles, and 400 guns—representing a ration strength, south of the line Rayak-Beirut, of 104,000.

3. I had at my disposal two cavalry divisions, two mounted divisions, seven infantry divisions, an Indian infantry brigade, four unallotted battalions, and the French detachment (the equivalent of an infantry brigade, with other arms attached) —a total, in the fighting line, of some 12,000 sabres, 57,000 rifles, and 540 guns.

I had thus a considerable superiority in numbers over the enemy, especially in mounted troops.

Allenby's Plans.

4. I was anxious to gain touch with the Arab Forces east of the Dead Sea, but the experience gained in the raids which I had undertaken against Amman and Es Salt in March and May had proved that the communications of a force in the hills of Moab were liable to interruption as long as the enemy was able to transfer troops from the west to the east bank of the Jordan. This he was in a position to do, as he controlled the crossing at Jisr ed Damieh.

The defeat of the VIIth and VIIIth Turkish Armies west

of the Jordan would enable me to control this crossing. More-over, the destruction of these armies, which appeared to be within the bounds of possibility, would leave the IVth Army isolated, if it continued to occupy the country south and west of Amman. I determined, therefore, to strike my blow west of the Jordan.

5. With the exception of a small and scattered reserve, the whole of the Turkish Force west of the Jordan was enclosed in a rectangle 45 miles in length and only 12 miles in depth. The northern edge of this rectangle was a line from Jisr ed Damieh on the Jordan, through Nablus and Tul Keram, to the sea. All the enemy's communications to Damascus ran northwards from the eastern half of this line, converging on El Afule and Beisan, some 25 miles to the north. Thence, with the exception of the roads leading from El Afule along the western shore of the Sea of Galilee, his communications ran eastwards up the valley of the Yarmuk to Deraa, the junction of the Palestine and Hejaz Railways.

Thus El Afule, Beisan, and Deraa were the vital points on his communications. If they could be seized the enemy's retreat would be cut off. Deraa was beyond my reach, but not beyond that of mobile detachments of the Arab Army. It was not to be expected that these detachments could hold this railway junction, but it was within their power to dislocate all traffic.

El Afule, in the Plain of Esdraelon, and Beisan, in the Valley of Jezreel, were within reach of my cavalry, provided the infantry could break through the enemy's defensive systems and create a gap for the cavalry to pass through. It was essential that this gap should be made at the commence-ment of operations, so that the cavalry might reach their destinations, 45 and 60 miles distant, before the enemy could make his escape. Moreover, whichever route the cavalry followed, the hills of Samaria, or their extension towards Mount Carmel, had to be crossed before the plain of Esdraelon and the valley of Jezreel could be reached ; and it was most important that the enemy should not be given time to man the passes.

6. For this reason I decided to make my main attack in the coastal plain rather than through the hills north of Jerusalem. In the hills the ground afforded the enemy positions of great natural strength and taxed the physical energy of the attackers to the utmost. The operations in March, astride the Jerusalem-Nablus road, had proved that an advance of five miles in one day, in face of determined opposition, was the most that could be expected. A far more rapid and decisive advance than this was necessary. In addition, the route along the coast would enable the cavalry to pass through the hills of Samaria into the plain of Esdraelon at their narrowest point, thus ensuring greater speed and less likelihood of being checked. The supply of a large force of troops in the plain also presented fewer difficulties.

7. The coastal plain at Jiljulieh, the ancient Gilgal, is some 10 miles in width. The railway from Jiljulieh to Tul Keram skirts the foothills, running through a slight depression on the eastern edge of the plain. To the west of this depression the Turks had constructed two defensive systems. The first, 14,000 yards in length and 3,000 in depth, ran along a sandy ridge in a north-westerly direction from Bir Adas to the sea. It consisted of a series of works connected by continuous fire trenches. The second, or Et Tireh system, 3,000 yards in rear, ran from the village of that name to the mouth of the Nahr Falik. On the enemy's extreme right the ground, except for a narrow strip along the coast, is marshy, and could only be crossed in few places. The defence of the second system did not, therefore, require a large force.

The railway itself was protected by numerous works and by the fortified villages of Jiljulieh and Kalkilieh. The ground between our front line at Ras El Ain and these villages was open, and was overlooked from the enemy's works on the foothills round Kefr Kasim.

8. By reducing the strength of the troops in the Jordan

Valley to a minimum, and by withdrawing my reserves from the hills north of Jerusalem, I was able to concentrate five divisions and the French detachment, with a total of 383 guns, for the attack on these defences. Thus, on the front of the attack I was able to concentrate some 35,000 rifles against 8,000, and 383 guns against 130. In addition, two cavalry and one Australian mounted divisions were available for this front.

Commanders and Corps.

9. I entrusted the attack on the enemy's defences in the coastal plain to Lieutenant-General Sir Edward Bulfin, K.C.B., C.V.O., commanding the 21st Corps. In addition to the 3rd (Lahore), 7th (Meerut), 54th and 75th Divisions, which already formed part of the 21st Corps, I placed at his disposal the 60th Division, the French detachment, the 5th Australian Light Horse Brigade, two brigades of mountain artillery, and eighteen batteries of heavy and siege artillery.

I ordered him to break through the enemy's defences between the railway and the sea, to open a way for the cavalry, and at the same time to seize the foothills south-east of Jiljulieh. The 21st Corps was then to swing to the right, on the line Hableh-Tul Keram, and advance in a north-easterly direction through the hills, converging on Samaria and Attaro, so as to drive the enemy up the Messudie-Jenin road into the arms of the cavalry at El Afule.

I ordered Lieutenant-General Sir Harry Chauvel, K.C.B., K.C.M.G., commanding the Desert Mounted Corps, less the Australian and New Zealand Mounted Division, to advance along the coast, directly the infantry had broken through and had secured the crossings over the Nahr Falik. On reaching the line Jelameh-Hudeira he was to turn north-east, cross the hills of Samaria, and enter the plain of Esdraelon at El Lejjun and Abu Shusheh. Riding along the plain, the Desert Mounted Corps was to seize El Afule, sending a detachment to Nazareth, the site of the Yilderim General Headquarters. Sufficient troops were to be left at El Afule to intercept the Turkish retreat there. The remainder of the Corps was to ride down the Valley of Jezreel and seize Beisan.

I ordered Lieutenant-General Sir Philip Chetwode, Bart., K.C.B., K.C.M.G., D.S.O., commanding the 20th Corps, to advance his line, east of the Bireh-Nablus road, on the night preceding the main attack, so as to place the 53rd Division on his right flank, which was somewhat drawn back, in a more favourable position to advance and block the exits to the lower valley of the Jordan.

I ordered him to be prepared to carry out a further advance, with both the 53rd and 10th Divisions, on the evening of the day on which the attack in the coastal plain took place, or later, as circumstances demanded.

10. The main difficulties lay in concealing the withdrawal of two cavalry divisions from the Jordan Valley, and in concentrating, secretly, a large force in the coastal plain.

To prevent the decrease in strength in the Jordan Valley being discovered by the enemy, I ordered Major-General Sir Edward Chaytor, K.C.M.G., C.B., A.D.C., to carry out, with the Australian and New Zealand Mounted Division, the 20th Indian (Imperial Service) Infantry Brigade, the 38th and 39th Battalions Royal Fusiliers, and the 1st and 2nd Battalions British West Indies Regiment, a series of demonstrations with the object of inducing the enemy to believe that an attack east of the Jordan was intended, either in the direction of Madeba or Amman. The enemy was thought to be anticipating an attack in these directions, and every possible step was taken to strengthen his suspicions.

Arab Mobile Column.

At this time a mobile column of the Arab Army, accompanied by British armoured cars and a French mountain battery, was assembling at Kasr el Azrak, fifty miles east of Amman. The real objective of this column was the railway north, south, and west of Deraa. There was always the possibility, however, that this concentration might be observed.

Should this occur, it was hoped that the demonstrations by Chaytor's force would strengthen the enemy's belief that a concerted attack on Amman was intended.

The concentration in the coastal plain was carried out by night, and every precaution was taken to prevent any increased movement becoming apparent to the Turks. Full use of the many groves round Ramleh, Ludd, and Jaffa was made to conceal troops during the day. The chief factor in the secrecy maintained must be attributed, however, to the supremacy in the air which had been obtained by the Royal Air Force. The process of wearing down the enemy's aircraft had been going on all through the summer. During one week in June 100 hostile aeroplanes had crossed our lines. During the last week in August this number had decreased to eighteen. In the next few days a number were shot down, with the result that only four ventured to cross our lines during the period of concentration.

11. That the enemy expected an offensive on my part about this date is probable. That he remained in ignorance of my intention to attack in the coastal plain with over-whelming numbers is certain. On the morning of 19th September, when the attack in the coastal plain was launched, his dispositions were normal.

12. Whilst the concentration in the coastal plain was nearing completion the enemy's railway communications at Deraa were attacked by the Royal Air Force, and by the Mobile Column of the Arab Army, which, after concentrating at Kasr el Azrak, 50 miles east of Amman, had moved into the Hauran.

The railway line and station buildings at Deraa were damaged by the Royal Air Force on 16th and 17th September. On 16th September the Arab column, which had been joined by the Shalaan sections of the Roalla, Anazeh, and by a number of Druses, attacked the Hejaz Railway, fifteen miles south of Deraa, destroying a bridge and a section of the railway. On the following day the line was attacked both north and west of Deraa, extensive demolitions being carried out.

As the result of these demolitions all through traffic to Palestine ceased, and a considerable quantity of transport, which had been intended for the Hejaz, was diverted to bridge the break in the railway.

13. The concentration in the coastal plain had been completed by the morning of 18th September. During the night of 18th–19th September, the 20th Corps swung forward its right on the east of the Bireh-Nablus Road. The 53rd Division descended into the basin at the head of the Wadi Samieh, captured Kh. Jibeit, El Mugheir, and the ridge on the far side of the basin, and all its objectives with the exception of one hill, Kh. Abu Malul. Considerable opposition was encountered, and hand-to-hand fighting took place, in which over 400 prisoners were taken.

In the early hours of 19th September El Afule and the headquarters of the Turkish VIIth and VIIIth Armies at Nablus and Tulkeram were bombed by the Royal Air Force with a view to disorganizing their signal communications.

At 04.30 the artillery in the coastal plain opened an intense bombardment, lasting fifteen minutes, under cover of which the infantry left their positions of deployment. Two torpedo boat destroyers assisted, bringing fire on the coastal road to the north.

The Five Phases.

14. The operations which followed fall into five phases.

The first phase was of short duration. In 36 hours, between 04.30 on 19th September and 17.00 on 20th September, the greater part of the VIIIth Turkish Army had been overwhelmed, and the troops of the VIIth Army were in full retreat through the hills of Samaria, whose exits were already in the hands of my cavalry.

In the second phase the fruits of this success were reaped. The infantry, pressing relentlessly on the heels of the retreating enemy, drove him into the arms of my cavalry, with the result that practically the whole of the VIIth and VIIIth Turkish Armies were captured, with their guns and transport.

This phase also witnessed the capture of Haifa and Acre, and the occupation of Tiberias, and of the country to the south and west of the Sea of Galilee.

As the result of the rout of the VIIth and VIIIth Armies the IVth Turkish Army, east of the Jordan, retreated, and Maan was evacuated.

The third phase commenced with the pursuit of this army by Chaytor's Force, and closed with the capture of Amman, and the interception of the retreat of the garrison of Maan, which surrendered.

The fourth phase witnessed the advance by the Desert Mounted Corps to Damascus, the capture of the remnants of the IVth Turkish Army, and the advance by the 21st Corps along the coast from Haifa to Beirut.

In the fifth phase my troops reached Homs and Tripoli without opposition. My cavalry then advanced on Aleppo, and occupied that city on 26th October.

Enemy's Coast Force overwhelmed.

15. The attack in the coastal plain on the morning of 19th September was attended with complete success. On the right, in the foot-hills, the French Tirailleurs and the Armenians of the Légion d'Orient advanced with great dash, and, in spite of the difficulties of the ground, and the strength of the enemy's defences, had captured the Kh. Deir el Kussis ridge at an early hour. On their left the 54th Division stormed Kefr Kasim village and wood, and the foot-hills overlooking the railway from Ras el Ain to Jiljulieh. North of Kefr Kasim the advance was checked for a time at Sivri Tepe, but the enemy's resistance was quickly overcome, and the remaining hills, south of the Wadi Kanah, captured.

In the coastal plain the 3rd (Lahore) Division attacked the enemy's first system between Bir Adas and the Hadrah road. On its left the 75th Division attacked the Tabsor defences, the 7th (Meerut) Division the works west of Tabsor, while the 60th Division attacked along the coast. The enemy replied energetically to our bombardment, but in most cases his barrage fell behind the attacking infantry. The enemy was overwhelmed. After overrunning the first system, the three divisions on the left pressed on, without pausing, to the Et Tireh position. On the left the 6oth Division reached the Nahr Falik, and moved on Tul Keram, leaving the route along the coast clear for the Desert Mounted Corps. The 7th (Meerut) Division, after passing through the second system, swung to the right, and headed for Et Taiyibeh, leaving Et Tireh, where the 75th Division was still fighting, on its right.

By 11.0 the 75th Division had captured Et Tireh, a strongly fortified village standing on a sandy ridge, where the enemy offered a determined resistance. On the right the 3rd (Lahore) Division turned to the east, and attacked Jiljulieh, Railway Redoubt, Kefr Saba, and Kalkilieh, all of which were defended with stubbornness by the enemy. His resistance was, however, broken ; and the 3rd (Lahore) Division pressed on eastwards into the foothills near Hableh, joining hands with the 54th Division north of the Wadi Kanah.

Disorganized bodies of the enemy were now streaming across the plain towards Tul Keram, pursued by the 6oth Division and the 5th Australian Light Horse Brigade. This brigade, which had been attached to the 21st Corps, consisted of two Australian Light Horse Regiments, with a composite regiment of Chasseurs d'Afrique and Spahis attached. Great confusion reigned at Tul Keram. Bodies of troops, guns, motor lorries, and transport of every description were endeavouring to escape along the road leading to Messudie and Nablus. This road, which follows the railway up a narrow valley, was already crowded with troops and transport. The confusion was added to by the persistent attacks of the Royal Air Force, and Australian Flying Corps, from which there was no escape. Great havoc was caused, and in several places the road was blocked by overturned lorries and vehicles. Later in the evening an Australian regiment, having made a detour, succeeded in reaching a hill four miles east of Tul Keram, over-looking the road. As a result, a large amount of transport and many guns fell into our hands.

In the meantime the 7th (Meerut) Division and 3rd (Lahore) Division had entered the hills, and, in conjunction with the 54th Division, had pressed eastwards. By dusk the line Bidieh-Kh. Kefr Thilth-Jiyus-Felamieh-Taiyibeh had been reached. The 75th Division remained in the vicinity of Et Tireh in corps reserve.

Fierce Hill Fighting.

16. As soon as the success of the initial attack by the 21st Corps, on the morning of 19th September, had become apparent, I ordered the 20th Corps to advance that night on Nablus, and the high ground north-east of that town, in order to close the roads leading to the lower valley of the Jordan, and to drive the enemy from the triangle formed by the Kh. Fusail-Nablus road, our original front line, and the El Funduk-Nablus track, by which the 3rd (Lahore) Division was advancing.

The two divisions of the 20th Corps had been concentrated beforehand, in readiness to carry out this operation ; the 53rd Division to the east of the Bireh-Nablus road, the 10th Division on the extreme left of the Corps Area, in the vicinity of Berukin and Kefr Ain. The enemy had long anticipated an attack astride the Bireh-Nablus road, and had constructed defences of great strength on successive ridges. For this reason the 10th Division was ordered to attack in a north-easterly direction astride the Furkhah-Selfit and Berukin-Kefr Haris ridges, thus avoiding a direct attack. Even so, the task of the 20th Corps was a difficult one. The enemy in this portion of the field was not disorganized, and was able to oppose a stout resistance to the advance. The country is broken and rugged, demanding great physical exertion on the part of the troops, and preventing the artillery keeping pace with the infantry.

Nevertheless, good progress was made on the night of 19th September and during the following day. The 53rd Division captured Kh. Abu Malul, and advanced their line in the centre. On their right Khan Jibeit was heavily counter-attacked on the morning of 20th September. The Turks succeeded in regaining the hill, but were driven off again after a sharp fight. This incident, and the necessity of making a road to enable the guns to be brought forward, caused delay.

The 10th Division advanced in two columns, and by midday on 20th September the right column, after a hard fight at Furkhah, had reached Selfit and was approaching Iskaka, which was strongly held by the enemy. The left column reached Kefr Haris, which was only captured after heavy fighting. The 10th Division had already driven the enemy back seven miles. The artillery, however, had been unable to keep up with the infantry, and little progress was made during the afternoon.

On the left of the 10th Division the 21st Corps had continued its advance in three columns. On the right the 3rd Division advanced up the Wadi Azzun. In the centre the Meerut Division moved on Kefr Sur and Beit Lid. The 60th Division and the 5th Australian Light Horse Brigade advanced along the Tul Keram-Nablus road on Messudie Station. By evening the line Baka-Beit Lid-Messudie Station-Attara had been reached.

The 3rd (Lahore) and 7th (Meerut) Divisions encountered a determined and well-organized resistance, which stiffened as the Meerut Division approached Beit Lid. The enemy showed no signs of demoralization, and the country was very rugged and difficult.

Considerable confusion existed, however, behind the enemy's rearguards. All day his transport had been withdrawing. The Messudie-Jenin road was crowded. Its defiles had been bombed continuously by the Royal Air Force, as had long columns of troops and transport moving on Nablus in order to reach the Beisan road. It is probable that the enemy did not yet realize that my cavalry was already in Afule and Beisan, and had blocked his main lines of retreat.

17. Early on the morning of 19th September, before the infantry had advanced to the attack, the 4th and 5th Cavalry Divisions moved out of the groves round Sarona, and formed up in rear of the 7th (Meerut) and 60th Divisions. The Australian Mounted Division, less the 5th Light Horse Brigade, was on its way from Ludd.

Von Sanders's Flight from Nazareth.

Thanks to the rapidity with which the infantry broke through both Turkish systems of defence, the cavalry obtained a good start. By noon the leading troops of the Desert Mounted Corps had reached Jelameh, Tell ed Drurh, and Hudeira, eighteen miles north of the original front line. After a brief rest the advance was continued. The 5th Cavalry Division moved north to Ez Zerghaniyeh. It then turned north-east, and, riding through the hills of Samaria past Jarak, descended into the Plain of Esdraelon at Abu Shusheh. The 13th Cavalry Brigade was then directed on Nazareth, the 14th on El Afule.

The 4th Cavalry Division turned north-east at Kh. es Sumrah, and followed the valley of the Wadi Arah into the hills. The valley gradually narrows as the pass at Musmus is reached.

The enemy had sent a battalion from El Afule to hold this pass, but only its advanced guard arrived in time. Overcoming its resistance, the cavalry encountered the remainder of the battalion at El Lejjun. The 2nd Lancers charged, killed forty-six with the lance, and captured the remainder, some 470 in number.

The 4th Cavalry Division then marched to El Afule, which it reached at 08.00, half an hour after its capture by the 14th Cavalry Brigade.

In the meantime the 13th Cavalry Brigade of the 5th Cavalry Division, riding across the Plain of Esdraelon, had reached Nazareth, the site of the Yilderim General Head-quarters, at 05.30. Fighting took place in the streets, some 2,000 prisoners being captured. Liman von Sanders had already made good his escape, but his papers and some of his staff were taken. This brigade then marched to El Afule ; arriving there as the 4th Cavalry Division rode down the Plain of Jezreel to Beisan, which it reached at 16.30, having covered some eighty miles in thirty-four hours. The 4th Cavalry Division detached a regiment to seize the railway bridge over the Jordan at Jisr Mejamie.

The Australian Mounted Division, which had followed the 4th Cavalry Division into the Plain of Esdraelon, was directed on Jenin, where the road from Messudie to El Afule leaves the hills. Jenin was reached at 17.30, and was captured after a sharp fight, a large number of prisoners being taken.

Thus, within 36 hours of the commencement of the battle all the main outlets of escape remaining to the Turkish VIIth and VIIIth Armies had been closed. They could only avoid capture by using the tracks which run south-east from the vicinity of Nablus to the crossings over the Jordan at Jisr ed Damieh. These were being rapidly denied to them.

The first phase of the operations was over.

18. The enemy's resistance had been broken on 20th September. On 21st September the Turkish rearguards were driven in early in the morning. All organized resistance ceased. The 5th Australian Light Horse Brigade, with the French Cavalry leading, entered Nablus from the west ; the 10th Division from the south.

By the evening the 20th Corps had reached the line Neby Belan, on the high ground north-east of Nablus and Mount Ebal ; the 21st Corps the line Samaria, Attara, Belah.

Air Force blocks the Retreat.

Since the early hours of the morning great confusion had reigned in the Turkish rear. Camps and hospitals were being hurriedly evacuated ; some were in flames. The roads leading north-east and east from Nablus to Beisan and the Jordan Valley were congested with transport and troops. Small parties of troops were moving east along the numerous wadis. The disorganization which already existed was increased by the repeated attacks of the Royal Air Force ; in particular, on the closely packed column of transport moving north from Balata to Kh. Ferweh, where a road branches off, along the Wadi Farah, to Jisr ed Damieh. Some of the transport continued along the road to Beisan, where it fell into the hands of the 4th Cavalry Division. The greater part made for the Jordan along the Wadi Farah. Nine miles from Kh. Ferweh, at Ain Shibleh, a road branches off to the north to Beisan. A mile beyond this point the Wadi Farah passes through a gorge. The head of the column was heavily bombed at this point. The drivers left their vehicles in panic, wagons were overturned, and in a short time the road was completely blocked. Still attacked by the Royal Air Force, the remainder of the column turned off at Ain Shibleh and headed for Beisan.

The VIIth Turkish Army was by this time thoroughly disorganized, and was scattered in the area between the Kh. Ferweh-Beisan road and the Jordan. These parties had now to be collected.

At 01.30 on 22nd September the New Zealand Mounted Rifles Brigade and the British West Indies Battalions of Chaytor's Force seized the bridge at Jisr ed Damieh. All hope of escape for the enemy in that direction had vanished.

In the early hours of the morning parties of Turks, of strengths varying from 50 to 300, began to approach Beisan, preceded by white flags.

At 08.00 a column, with transport and guns, 10 miles long, was reported by the Royal Air Force to be moving north along the Ain Shibleh-Beisan road, its head being 9 miles south of Beisan. The 4th Cavalry Division was ordered to send detachments towards it, and also to patrol the road, which follows the Jordan on its east bank, to secure any parties which might escape across the Jordan.

At the same time the Worcester Yeomanry of the 20th Corps, supported by infantry, was ordered to advance northwards from Ain Shibleh, and the infantry of the 10th Division along the Tubas-Beisan road, to collect stragglers, and to drive any formed bodies into the hands of the 4th Cavalry Division.

Two Turkish Armies cease to Exist.

The Royal Air Force had proceeded to attack the Turkish column, which broke up and abandoned its guns and transport. The task of clearing the enemy between the Kh. Ferweh-Beisan road and the Jordan was continued during 23rd September. On this day the 20th Cavalry Corps met with occasional opposition, and its advance was hampered considerably by the large numbers of Turks who surrendered. Great quantities of transport and numerous guns were found abandoned by the roadsides. On one stretch of road, under five miles in length, 87 guns, 55 motor lorries, and 842 vehicles were found.

Numerous bodies of Turks surrendered to the 4th Cavalry Division. One column attempted to escape across the Jordan at Makhadet Abu Naj, 5 miles south-east of Beisan, but was intercepted by the 11th Cavalry Brigade. Part of the column had already crossed to the east bank. It was charged by the 36th (Jacob's) Horse, and broken up, few escaping. On the west bank the remainder of the column was charged by the 29th Lancers and Middlesex Yeomanry, who killed many and captured the remainder, together with 25 machine guns.

On 24th September the 11th Cavalry Brigade attacked and dispersed another column in the Wadi el Maleh. The last remnants of the VIIth and VIIIth Turkish Armies had been collected. As Armies they had ceased to exist, and but few had escaped.

19. Whilst the 4th Cavalry and the Australian Mounted Divisions were collecting the remnants of the VIIth and VIIIth Turkish Armies, I ordered the Desert Mounted Corps to occupy Acre and Haifa. The roads leading to Haifa from

Tul Keram are only country tracks, which, in the event of rain, might become impassable for motor lorries at any time. Any force advancing northwards from Haifa along the coast would have to depend on supplies landed at that port. It was necessary, therefore, to occupy the town without delay, in order that the harbour could be swept for mines, and the landing of stores taken in hand. The 13th Cavalry Brigade of the 5th Cavalry Division, which had entered Nazareth on 20th September, and had then marched to El Afule, returned to Nazareth the following day.

Haifa and Acre captured.

Part of the garrison of Haifa, which was attempting to reach Tiberias, was intercepted by this brigade on the morning of 22nd September. At 01.30 this column approached the outposts of the 13th Cavalry Brigade. It was attacked in the moonlight by the 18th Lancers, who killed a large number of Turks and captured over 300.

That afternoon Haifa was reconnoitred by a battery of armoured cars. It was still held by the enemy. The road was barricaded, and the armoured cars were shelled from the slopes of Mount Carmel.

On 23rd September the 5th Cavalry Division, less the 13th Cavalry Brigade, marched from El Afule to capture the town. The 13th Cavalry Brigade marched direct from Nazareth on Acre.

The road from El Afule to Haifa skirts the north-eastern edge of the Mount Carmel range. Some two miles before Haifa is reached the road is confined between a spur of Mount Carmel on the left and the marshy banks of the River Kishon and its tributaries on the right. When the 5th Cavalry Division reached this point on 23rd September it was shelled from the slopes of Mount Carmel, and found the road and the river crossings defended by numerous machine guns.

Whilst the Mysore Lancers were clearing the rocky slopes of Mount Carmel the Jodhpur Lancers charged through the

defile, and, riding over the enemy's machine guns, galloped into
the town, where a number of Turks were speared in the streets.
Colonel Thakur Dalput Singh, M.C., fell gallantly leading this
charge.

In this operation 1,350 prisoners and 17 guns were taken.

At Acre the 13th Cavalry Brigade met with little opposition. The small garrison, consisting of 150 men and two
guns, attempted to escape to the north, but was overtaken
and captured.

East Jordan Operations.

20. Interest now turned to the fate of the IVth Turkish
Army east of the Jordan. Up till 22nd September this army
showed no signs of moving from its positions on the east bank.
On the west bank the New Zealand Mounted Rifles Brigade
and the 1st and 2nd Battalions British West Indies Regiment
had advanced northwards on 21st September, west of the
Jericho-Beisan road, and had reached Khurbet Fusail, four
miles in advance of our defences at El Musalabeh. The enemy,
however, still held the bridgeheads on the west bank, covering
the crossings at Umm es Shert, Red Hill, Mafid Jozeleh, and
Jisr ed Damieh. Early in the morning of 22nd September
the 38th Battalion Royal Fusiliers captured the bridgehead
at Umm es Shert. The New Zealand Mounted Rifles placed
themselves astride the road which follows the Wadi Farah
from Nablus to Jisr ed Damieh, thus closing the last loophole
of escape to the Turkish forces west of the Jordan. The
crossing at Jisr ed Damieh was captured a few hours later.
The bridge was intact. Five hundred and fourteen prisoners
were taken.

Thus the west bank of the Jordan had been cleared. As
a result of the defeat of the VIIth and VIIIth Armies, the
position of the IVth Army east of the Jordan was no longer
tenable, and by the morning of 23rd September this army
was in full retreat on Es Salt and Amman, pursued by the
Australian and New Zealand Mounted Division, and bombed
by the Royal Air Force. At 16.30 the New Zealanders cap-

tured Es Salt, taking 380 prisoners and three guns. The pursuit was continued on a broad front, in face of stout opposition from the enemy's rearguards. On 25th September Amman was attacked and captured.

The enemy retreated northwards along the Hejaz railway and the Pilgrim route in a disorganized state, harassed by the Royal Air Force and the Arabs. He was pursued by the Australian and New Zealand Mounted Divisions, and left over 5,000 prisoners and 28 guns in their hands.

I ordered Chaytor's Force to remain at Amman to intercept the troops of the 2nd Turkish Army Corps, who were retreating from the Hejaz. Maan had been evacuated on 23rd September, and had been occupied by the Arab Army, which then advanced to Jordan, harassing the rear of the retreating garrison.

On 28th September these troops came into contact with the patrols of Chaytor's Force at Leban Station, 10 miles south of Amman. The Turkish commander, seeing that escape was impossible, surrendered on the following day with 5,000 men.

Advance on Damascus.

21. In addition to bringing about the retreat of the IVth Turkish Army, the total defeat of the VIIth and VIIIth Armies had removed any serious obstacle to an advance on Damascus. On 25th September I ordered the Desert Mounted Corps to carry out this operation, occupy the city, and intercept the retreat of the remnants of the IVth Turkish Army.

22. The Desert Mounted Corps was to advance on Damascus in two columns ; one column by the south end of the Sea of Galilee, *via* Irbid and Deraa, the other round the north end of the sea, *via* El Kuneitra.

On 24th September Semakh, at the south end of the Sea of Galilee, was captured by the 4th Australian Light Horse Brigade, after fierce hand-to-hand fighting, in which 350 Turks and Germans and a gun were captured. Tiberias was occupied on the following afternoon.

Thus on 26th September the Australian Mounted Division was concentrating round Tiberias, and the 5th Cavalry Division was marching from Haifa and Acre to Nazareth. The 4th Cavalry Division was concentrated round Beisan.

23. The 4th Cavalry Division started on its 120-mile march that afternoon. The Australian and 5th Cavalry Divisions started the following day, the distance they had to traverse being 30 miles less. Both columns met with opposition. The Australian Mounted Division experienced considerable difficulty in crossing the Jordan on 27th September. The bridge at Jisr Benat Yakub had been damaged, and Turkish rearguards commanded the crossings. After some delay, the 5th Australian Brigade succeeded in crossing the river a mile south of the bridge ; and, working round the enemy's flank, forced him to retire. Opposition was again met with on the eastern side of the Jordan plateau, at El Kuneitra, and the column was continually fired on by the Circassians who dwell on the plateau. Passing through El Kuneitra, the column entered first a plateau covered by boulders and then undulating pasture land, intersected by the numerous streams which rise in Mount Hermon. Fighting took place at Sasa, but the enemy's rearguards were driven back, and by 10.00 on 30th September, Katana, 12 miles south-west of Damascus, had been reached by the Australian Mounted Division, which was here checked for a time.

At this hour the 14th Cavalry Brigade, on the right of the Australian Mounted Division, was approaching Sahnaya on the old French railway. Farther south the 4th Cavalry Division, with the Arab Army on its right, was approaching Kiswe.

The route followed by the 4th Cavalry Division across the Jordan plateau had proved difficult, and considerable opposition had been encountered at Irbid, and again at Er Remte, where, after driving the enemy northwards towards Mezerib, the Cavalry gained touch with the Arab Army.

After its raids on the enemy's railways round Deraa be-

tween 16th and 18th September, the Arab Army had moved
into the Hauran. It issued thence to attack the IVth
Turkish Army, as the latter passed Mafrak in its retreat northwards, forcing the Turks to abandon guns and transport.
Moving rapidly northwards, the Arabs then captured the
stations of Ezra and Ghazale, between Damascus and Deraa.
On 27th September they entrenched themselves at Sheikh
Saad, 17 miles north of Deraa, across the Turkish line of
retreat. Sharp fighting took place all day, in which heavy
casualties were inflicted on the retreating Turks and Germans,
and in which numerous prisoners were taken. After breaking
up the retreating columns of the IVth Army, the Arabs
captured Deraa, and, on 28th September, joined hands with
the 4th Cavalry Division near Er Remte.

The Cavalry then advanced northwards through Mezerib
and along the old French railway, with the Arabs on its right
flank, collecting stragglers, and pressing on the heels of the
remnants of the IVth Turkish Army.

In this way a column of Turks some 1,500 strong was
driven at noon on 30th September into the arms of the 14th
Cavalry Brigade at Sahnaya.

Shortly after midday on 30th September the Australian
Mounted Division overcame the enemy's resistance at Katana.
By the evening it had closed the exits from Damascus to the
north and north-west, while the 5th Cavalry Division had
reached the southern outskirts of the town.

At 06.00 on 1st October the Desert Mounted Corps and
the Arab Army entered Damascus amidst scenes of great
enthusiasm. After the German and Turkish troops in the
town had been collected and guards had been posted, our
troops were withdrawn. In the meantime the 3rd Australian
Light Horse Brigade had proceeded northwards, in pursuit
of bodies of the enemy, which had succeeded in leaving the
town on the previous day, or had avoided it, and the cordon
round it, by making a detour to the east. On 2nd October
a column was overtaken at Kubbeth I Asafir, 17 miles north-

east of Damascus. This column was dispersed, 1,500 prisoners and three guns being taken.

Desert Corps' Fine Achievement.

24. The advance to Damascus, following on the operations in the Plain of Esdraelon and the Valley of Jezreel, had thrown a considerable strain on the Desert Mounted Corps. Great results were, however, achieved.

On 26th September, when the advance began, some 45,000 Turks and Germans were still in Damascus or were retreating on it. It is true that all units were in a state of disorganization, but, given time, the enemy could have formed a force capable of delaying my advance.

The destruction of the remnants of the IVth Army and the capture of an additional 20,000 prisoners prevented any possibility of this. The remnants of the Turkish Armies in Palestine and Syria, numbering some 17,000 men, of whom only 4,000 were effective rifles, fled northwards, a mass of individuals, without organization, without transport, and without any of the accessories required to enable it to act even on the defensive.

25. I determined to exploit this success and to advance to the line Rayak-Beirut. The occupation of Beirut would give me a port, with a road and a railway leading inland to Rayak and Damascus. An alternative and shorter line of supply would thus be obtained.

The Desert Mounted Corps, leaving the Australian Mounted Division at Damascus, moved on Rayak and Zahle on 5th October. No opposition was encountered, and both places were occupied on the following day.

At Rayak, the junction of the broad gauge railway from the north and the metre gauge lines to Beirut and to Damascus and the Hejaz, were found on the aerodrome the remains of thirty aeroplanes which had been burnt by the enemy before he retired. Large quantities of stores and rolling stock were captured, most of the latter in a damaged condition.

Beirut occupied.

In the meantime, the 7th (Meerut) Division had marched from Haifa to Beirut. Leaving Haifa on 3rd October, it marched along the coast. Crossing the Ladder of Tyre, it was received by the populace of Tyre and Sidon with enthusiasm. On 8th October it reached Beirut, where it was warmly welcomed, the inhabitants handing over 660 Turks, including 60 officers, who had surrendered to them. Ships of the French Navy had already entered the harbour.

26. On 9th October I ordered the Desert Mounted Corps to continue its advance and occupy Homs, leaving one division at Damascus. At the same time I ordered the 21st Corps to continue its march along the coast to Tripoli. Armoured cars occupied Baalbek on 9th October, taking over 500 Turks who had surrendered to the inhabitants. The 5th Cavalry Division, which led the advance, reached Baalbek on 11th October, and, crossing the watershed between the Nahr Litani on the south and the Orontes on the north, followed the valley of the latter river, past Lebwe, and reached Homs on 15th October, having marched over eighty miles since leaving Rayak.

The station buildings at Homs had been burnt by the enemy before he evacuated the town on 12th October.

On the coast, Tripoli was occupied by the 21st Corps Cavalry Regiment and armoured cars on 13th October. No opposition was encountered. The Corps Cavalry Regiment was followed by a brigade of the 7th (Meerut) Division. The occupation of Tripoli provided a shorter route by which the cavalry at Homs could be supplied.

From Homs to Aleppo.

27. Having secured Homs and Tripoli, I determined to seize Aleppo with the least possible delay. The 5th Cavalry Division and the Armoured Car Batteries were alone available. The Australian Mounted Division at Damascus was over 100

miles distant from Homs, and could not be brought up in time. The 4th Cavalry Division at Baalbek was much reduced in strength by sickness, and needed a rest to reorganize. Time was of importance, and I judged that the 5th Cavalry Division would be strong enough for the purpose. The information available indicated the presence of some 20,000 Turks and Germans at Aleppo. Of these, only some 8,000 were combatants, and they were demoralized. Moreover, reports from all sources showed that considerable numbers of the enemy were leaving the town daily by rail for the north.

The armoured cars had reached Hama without opposition on 20th October. On the following day the 5th Cavalry Division commenced its advance. On 22nd October the armoured cars reached Khan Sebit, halfway between Homs and Aleppo, as the enemy's rearguard left the village in lorries. A German armoured car, a lorry, and some prisoners were captured. The enemy were not encountered again till 24th October, when a body of cavalry were dispersed at Khan Tuman, 10 miles south of Aleppo. Five miles farther on the armoured cars were checked by strong Turkish rearguards and had to remain in observation till the cavalry came up.

On the afternoon of 25th October the armoured cars were joined by the 15th (Imperial Service) Cavalry Brigade. That evening a detachment of the Arab Army reached the eastern outskirts of Aleppo, and during the night forced their way in, inflicting heavy casualties on the enemy.

Early on the morning of 26th October the armoured cars and the 15th Cavalry Brigade, moving round the west side of the town, followed the enemy along the Aleppo-Katma road and gained touch with him south-east of Haritan. The Turkish rearguard consisted of some 2,500 infantry, 150 cavalry, and eight guns. The Mysore Lancers and two squadrons of the Jodhpur Lancers attacked the enemy's left, covered by the fire of the armoured cars, the Machine Gun Squadron, and two dismounted squadrons of the Jodhpur Lancers. The Mysore and Jodhpur Lancers charged most gallantly. A number of Turks were speared, and many threw down their arms, only to pick them up again when the cavalry had passed through, and their weakness had become apparent. The squadrons were not strong enough to complete the victory, and were withdrawn till a larger force could be assembled.

That night the Turkish rearguard withdrew to position near Deir el Jemel, twenty miles north-west of Aleppo. The 5th Cavalry Division remained in observation, astride the roads leading from Aleppo to Killis and Katma, and occupied Muslimie Junction.

It was too weak to continue the advance to Alexandretta till the arrival of the Australian Mounted Division, which had already left Damascus to join it.

Before the latter could arrive the armistice between the Allies and Turkey had been concluded, and came into force at noon on 31st October.

The 5th Cavalry Division captured fifty prisoners and eighteen guns in Aleppo. The Turks had carried out demolitions on the railway at Aleppo and Muslimie Junction before retiring, but had left eight engines and over 100 trucks, which, though damaged, are not beyond repair.

A 300 *Miles Advance.*

Aleppo is over 300 miles from our former front line. The 5th Cavalry Division covered 500 miles between 19th September and 26th October, and captured over 11,000 prisoners and fifty-two guns. During this period the 5th Cavalry Division lost only 21 per cent. of its horses.

28. Between 19th September and 26th October 75,000 prisoners have been captured. Of these over 200 officers and 3,500 other ranks are Germans or Austrians.

In addition, 360 guns have fallen into our hands, and the transport and equipment of three Turkish armies. It is not yet possible to give accurate figures, owing to the rapidity and the extent of the advance. In the first three phases of the operations material and equipment were hastily abandoned by the enemy in a mountainous area, extending over 2,500 square miles, while in the remaining phases a further advance of over 300 miles has been made. The captures, however, include over 800 machine guns, 210 motor lorries, 44 motor cars, some 3,500 animals, 89 railway engines, and 468 carriages and trucks. Of these many are unserviceable, but none have been included that are beyond repair.

Tributes to Staffs and Troops.

29. The plan of operations and the arrangements for the concentration were carefully prepared and well executed by Commanders and Staffs. During the subsequent days of fighting full advantage was taken of every opportunity offered.

The gallantry and determination of all ranks and of all arms has been most marked. Many units had already made their reputation in this and other theatres of the war. Some had yet to gain their first experience of modern warfare. British, French, and Indian troops, and those of the Dominions and Colonies, have all alike done magnificently.

The infantry, in a few hours, broke through the defences, which the enemy had spent months in strengthening, thus enabling the cavalry to accomplish its mission. The subsequent advance through the hills, over most difficult country, and in face of determined and organized resistance by the enemy's rearguards, tried the infantry severely. Nothing, however, stopped its progress, and the relentless pressure maintained on the enemy's rearguards allowed him no time to carry out an organized retreat, and drove him, in disorganized bodies, into the arms of the cavalry.

The Desert Mounted Corps took some 46,000 prisoners during the operations. The complete destruction of the VIIth and VIIIth Turkish Armies depended mainly on the rapidity with which their communications were reached, and on quick decision in dealing with the enemy's columns as they attempted to escape. The vigorous handling of the cavalry by its leaders, and the rapidity of its movements, overcame all attempts to delay its progress. The enemy's columns, after they had outdistanced the pursuing infantry, were given no time to reorganize and fight their way through.

In these brilliant achievements the regiment of French cavalry took its full share ; whilst east of the Jordan the Australian and New Zealand Mounted Division, by its untiring pursuit, threw the IVth Turkish Army into a state of disorganization, intercepted the garrison of Maan, and compelled it to surrender. Chaytor's Force took 10,000 prisoners in the valley of the Jordan and the hills of Moab.

The cavalry and infantry received every help from the Royal Artillery and the Royal Engineers, whilst the infantry, in its attack along the coast, was given valuable assistance by the Destroyers *Druid* and *Forester*, which Rear-Admiral T. Jackson, C.B., M.V.O., had detailed to assist me.

Of the fighting troops, all have taken their share, and have carried out what was required of them. I would bring to notice the good fighting qualities shown by the newer units. These include the Armenian troops of the Légion d'Orient, the Tirailleurs Algériens, the 1st Battalion Cape Corps, the 38th and 39th (Jewish) Battalions of the Royal Fusiliers, the 1st and 2nd Battalions of the British West Indies Regiment, and all the recently formed battalions of Indian Infantry.

Brilliant work has been done by the Palestine Brigade, Royal Air Force, and the Australian Flying Corps, not only during the actual operations, but in the preceding months. The process of wearing down the enemy's strength in the air had been continuous throughout the summer. Our ascendancy in the air became so marked towards the end of August that only a few of the enemy's aeroplanes were able to fly, with the result that my troops were immune from air attacks during the operations, and the whole strength of the Air Forces could be concentrated on the enemy in his retreat.

Besides taking an active part in the fighting, the Air Forces provided me with full and accurate information as to the enemy's movements.

Arab Army's Aid.

The Arab Army has rendered valuable assistance, both in cutting the enemy's communications before and during the operations, and in co-operating with my cavalry during the advance on Damascus. By throwing itself across the enemy's line of retreat north of Deraa it prevented the escape of portions of the IVth Turkish Army, and inflicted heavy casualties on the enemy.

The fighting troops have been loyally assisted by the administrative services and departments, who have carried a heavy burden on their shoulders, both in front of and behind railhead. The accumulation of ammunition and stores before operations commenced threw a great strain on the railway. The delivery of these stores to the troops during operations proved a difficult task. Supply columns have had long distances to cover, over bad roads, but all difficulties have been overcome.

My thanks are due to the Royal Navy for its assistance in arranging and securing the landing of supplies at the various harbours along my line of advance, and to the French Navy for valuable information gained in the reconnaissance of the northern ports.

The Italian detachment carried out to my entire satisfaction the task allotted to it, and throughout the operations gave valuable and loyal assistance.

From the first day of operations the Egyptian Labour Corps has followed the troops as they advanced, working hard and successfully to improve the roads. On 19th September companies were working on the roads in front of our original line while our guns were still firing.

The Camel Transport Corps has rendered valuable services, which have greatly aided in the victorious campaign.

The Signal Service, strained to its utmost, has maintained uninterrupted communication with units of the Army as far east as Amman and as far north as Aleppo.

The rapid advance has rendered difficult the task of evacuating the sick and wounded. The difficulty was increased by the large number of prisoners who, after marching for days, with little food or water, surrendered in a state of extreme weakness, unable to march another day. The care and evacuation of these men has heavily taxed the Medical Services, who have worked untiringly.

I have the honour to be,
Your Lordship's most obedient servant,
E. E. H. ALLENBY, General,
Commanding-in-Chief,
Egyptian Expeditionary Force.

THE ARMISTICE CONVENTION WITH TURKEY, SIGNED OCTOBER 30, 1918.

1. The opening of the Dardanelles and the Bosphorus, and secure access to the Black Sea. Allied occupation of the Dardanelles and the Bosphorus forts.

2. The positions of all minefields, torpedo-tubes, and other obstructions in Turkish waters to be indicated, and assistance to be given to sweep or remove them as may be required.

3. All available information as to mines in the Black Sea to be communicated.

4. All Allied prisoners of war and Armenian interned persons and prisoners to be collected in Constantinople and handed over unconditionally to the Allies.

5. The immediate demobilization of the Turkish army, except for such troops as are required for the surveillance of the frontiers and for the maintenance of internal order. The number of effectives and their disposition to be determined later by the Allies after consultation with the Turkish Government.

6. The surrender of all war vessels in Turkish waters or in waters occupied by Turkey ; these ships to be interned at such Turkish port or ports as may be directed, except such small vessels as are required for police or similar purposes in Turkish territorial waters.

7. The Allies to have the right to occupy any strategic points in the event of any situation arising which threatens the security of the Allies.

8. Free use by Allied ships of all ports and anchorages now in Turkish occupation and the denial of their use to the enemy. Similar conditions to apply to Turkish mercantile shipping in Turkish waters for purposes of trade and the demobilization of the army.

9. Use of all ship-repair facilities at all Turkish ports and arsenals.

10. Allied occupation of the Taurus tunnel system.

11. The immediate withdrawal of the Turkish troops from North-West Persia to behind the pre-war frontier has already been ordered and will be carried out. Part of Trans-Caucasia has already been ordered to be evacuated by Turkish troops ; the remainder is to be evacuated if required by the Allies after they have studied the situation there.

12. Wireless, telegraph, and cable stations to be controlled by the Allies, Turkish Government messages excepted.

13. Prohibition to destroy any naval, military, or commercial material.

14. Facilities to be given for the purchase of coal, oil-fuel, and naval material from Turkish sources, after the requirements of the country have been met. None of the above material to be exported.

15. Allied Control Officers to be placed on all railways, including such portions of the Trans-Caucasian Railways as are now under Turkish control, which must be placed at the free and complete disposal of the Allied authorities, due consideration being given to the needs of the population. This clause is to include Allied occupation of Batoum. Turkey will raise no objection to the occupation of Baku by the Allies.

16. The surrender of all garrisons in the Hedjaz, Assir, Yemen, Syria, and Mesopotamia to the nearest Allied Commander ; and the withdrawal of troops from Cicilia, except those necessary to maintain order, as will be determined under clause 5.

17. The surrender of all Turkish officers in Tripolitania and Cyrenaica to the nearest Italian garrison. Turkey guar-

antees to stop supplies and communication with these officers if they do not obey the order to surrender.

18. The surrender of all ports occupied in Tripolitania and Cyrenaica, including Misurata, to the nearest Allied garrison.

19. All Germans and Austrians, naval, military, and civilian, to be evacuated within one month from the Turkish dominions : those in remote districts to be evacuated as soon after as may be possible.

20. The compliance with such orders as may be conveyed for the disposal of the equipment, arms, and ammunition, including transport, of that portion of the Turkish army which is demobilized under clause 5.

21. An Allied representative to be attached to the Turkish Ministry of Supplies in order to safeguard Allied interests. This representative is to be furnished with all that may be necessary for this purpose.

22. Turkish prisoners to be kept at the disposal of the Allied Powers. The release of Turkish civilian prisoners over military age to be considered.

23. Obligation on the part of Turkey to cease all relations with the Central Powers.

24. In case of disorder in the six Armenian vilayets, the Allies reserve to themselves the right to occupy any part of them.

25. Hostilities between the Allies and Turkey shall cease from noon, local time, on Thursday, the 31st October, 1918.

PRINTED IN GREAT BRITAIN AT
THE PRESS OF THE PUBLISHERS.